Play Google's Game

Greg Bright

Shadow Jacks Publishing
945 McKinney St
STE 560
Houston, TX 77002

www.shadowjacks.com
info@shadowjacks.com

Ordering Information:

Available at amazon.com – For quantity sales: Special discounts are available on quantity purchases by corporations, associations, and others. For details, contact the publisher at the address above.

Orders by U.S. trade bookstores and wholesalers. Please contact the publisher.

Printed in the United States of America

ISBN: 1517486246
ISBN-13: 978-1517486242

DEDICATION

I dedicated my first Google book to my father in 2008. He was the ultimate retailer and while growing up in the family Ace Hardware stores, Dad taught me way more than my college education ever could have about brick and mortar retail. Dad - you are truly missed.

However, it was my mother who introduced us to the digital age. I'll never forget traveling to Ace headquarters in Chicago in 1985 to get trained on that first $10,000 "IBM compatible" PC we bought so Mom would not have to use a paper ledger to keep the books anymore! We were so proud of the half meg hard drive!

I fondly remember our first point of sale computer system in 1989, also my Mom's brain child. We were ground breakers. It took an entire year for Dad to learn how to ring up a customer!

Mom, you continue to inspire me with your thirst for knowledge and embracement of technology. Thanks for pushing me into the technology era at an early age. I love you and I dedicate this book to you.

CONTENTS

Disclaimer and Other Legal Stuff

This book, nor its author is in any way associated with Google Inc.

This book was written to provide readers with a general overview of Search Engine Optimization & Basic Internet Marketing, shared by the experiences and opinions of the author.

Given the vagaries of the subject and frequent changes among the search engines' and other platforms' terms of service, there is always certain risk involved in implementing changes. The reader agrees to consult the terms of service of each platform before making any changes that might impact their website or business.

This book in no way guarantees results of any kind. Neither the publisher nor the author assume any liability of any kind for any losses that may be sustained as a result of inaccuracies or applications of the methods and opinions suggested in this book, and any such liability is hereby expressly disclaimed. The only guarantee we can make is that there will be change – so please keep yourself updated on the latest changes.

In addition, the author recommends that readers consult with a specialist if they are not fully comfortable in making changes to their websites or business practices.

The author also highly recommends that readers make backup copies of their entire website prior to making any changes, and also during the continual updating of their website. These copies should be stored on removable media (like a DVD) – OFF PREMISES.

Play Google's Game

Preface

My first book written in 2008, *Get Top Ranking On Google….,* was born from notes to friends and colleagues—sharing simple tips and techniques that I had learned from the SEO School of Hard Knocks—while bootstrapping my patented products on a very tight budget.

By tight budget - I mean free. Unfortunately I had spent all of my money setting up manufacturing and had nothing left for marketing. Big mistake! However, it taught me how to use these free internet platforms, like Google Search, to grow my business. Everything I talk about in this book is Free!

While there are many new concepts in this book, all of the tips in my first book are still valid – even surviving all of the latest changes Google has made to their rules. In fact, if people would have followed the advice in my first book, they would not have been penalized by Google's latest updates.

How is that possible? Because I don't chase the latest fads. I stick to the fundamentals.

Google has not changed their fundamental mission to provide the best quality websites to their searchers. The only thing that has changed is how they identify which websites are quality and which ones are not.

The book you have in your hand today draws from 25 years of business consulting; learning from my successes and challenges – from my business, students, clients, readers, partners, friends, and colleagues.

Through them, I continually gather intelligence for my own businesses and for you. I'm happy to share these secrets with you in this book and on the www.PlayGooglesGame.com blog.

There are quite a number of books written on this subject by techies and programmers - for other techies and programmers. My objective is to bring simple, easy to understand tips to the average business leader, using layman's terms versus technical jargon.

Most importantly, I saw a need to explain internet marketing from a business perspective – using real world examples.

My goal is not to turn my readers or students into website designers. We all have businesses to run, right? The goal is to give you enough information so that you can find a good website designer and internet marketer.

Once you find a good website designer, you will be able to have a meaningful two-way conversation with them, so you can participate in building a website that is suitable for growing your business.

How could anyone design a good website for you without your active participation? No one knows your business like you do.

Will you be a spectator or a participant in this single most important aspect of growing your business?

I have seen far too many times where the business owner did not participate and ended up with a "cookie cutter" website that had little to do with their business growth plans – after all, you are the expert in your field, right?

Once your website is set up properly, you or your staff will be able to continue to create the new and interesting content that Google rewards.

My wish is for you is that you gain enough knowledge from this book to enable you to hire the best website designer or internet marketer your budget will allow, and to give you the skills to boost your online business growth. Most good internet marketing companies and website designers appreciate an educated client. After all, you know your business best, and they would want to see you succeed.

Enjoy! I wish you fun and prosperity online!

Greg

ACKNOWLEDGMENTS

A heartfelt thank you to all that contributed to this book. From bouncing crazy ideas for book covers and titles off colleagues and friends – to all of my Facebook friends as we participated in this social media revolution – to the hundreds of students' questions and answers – to my clients. I am honored to grow and learn from you all.

A special heartfelt thanks to my wife. Baby, your brilliance never ceases to amaze me. I am in awe of your business acumen and ability to communicate, with the shortest number of words possible. One day I hope to attain 1/10th of your compassion, knowledge, and communication skills.

Especially thank you for your patience, input, and falling asleep in my arms while I type the night away. I love you baby!

Introduction

You Can Be Found

Everyone Has Equal Opportunity – It's Not Rocket Science

Are you ready to get found on Google, Facebook, Mobile Phones, and more? These are exciting times to be marketing and growing our businesses on the internet and we're going to show you how to win by Playing Google's Game!

We know you can do this—it's not rocket science. We see it every day with our students, readers, and clients. Every business owner has the same opportunity to grow their business online.

You can do it yourself, or use this book to arm yourself with enough information to find the best website designer for your business. The knowledge you gain here will allow you to join conversations and participate with the professionals that you hire to support your internet marketing strategy.

Every day my manufacturing business is realizing more efficiency, productivity, and sales through our internet marketing efforts. I am able to cast a much larger net, with far less expense than ever before. Your internet opportunities are increasing in importance every day as new generations of buyers and sellers enter the economy. Young buyers don't remember life before the internet and seasoned buyers are changing their habits (seniors are the fastest growing segment on the internet—thank you Facebook!).

Do you sell mainly to other business? Forrester research shows that the number of fortune 100 business buying over half their purchases online today will jump almost 60% in the next couple of years!

Your results might not happen overnight. However, with systematic and regular application of Google's rules, we see success every single time. These success stories come from business owners in all industries and at all levels of technical know-how. We will teach you how, using real world examples from our own businesses, speaking in non-technical, layman's terms—one business owner to another.

This book was intentionally written to help anyone, at any level of technical knowledge, whether you are just preparing to organize your start-up business or your tired old website needs a little refreshing. You can decide what level of participation that you are comfortable with and what makes sense for your business.

Entrepreneurs have a special kindred spirit. We're passionate about helping the little guy or gal compete on the same playing field as the big boys. In fact, there has never been a better time in history than right now for the small business owner to compete at the same level as the corporate giants. Indeed, the internet levels the playing field!

Written in practical easy to understand language, this book reveals our twelve most important SEO strategies to attract new customers online. Using case studies from our clients and feedback from our university classes, as well as real world strategies from our own businesses, we'll show you how easy it is to be found on Google and other free internet platforms like Facebook, YouTube, Yahoo, and Google Images. Did we mention that all of these internet platforms are free?

Findability, whether on a computer or mobile phone, is not limited to the search engines. Being found also involves engaging customers on platforms like Facebook, Twitter, Blogs and YouTube. Marketing is about finding new customers and building long term relationships with those customers. These new platforms allow our customers to participate in ways never dreamed of just a few years ago. We'll show you how easy it is to use the two way customer interaction available on the internet today.

The Internet Is Your Best Marketing Tool

Like it or not, good or bad, the internet has turned the advertising and marketing world on its ear. Traditional advertising media are struggling with this paradigm shift. For the first time in history, companies are spending more in online advertising than broadcast TV. Print publications are in trouble, both AT&T and Verizon have dumped their Yellow Page divisions, Tivo killed the TV commercial, and Pandora/Satellite radio changed the way we access music.

In the advertising and marketing world, it's all about *Usage Numbers*. The number of users that our customers engaged with the internet are unprecedented. That's why major companies are spending their advertising dollars here—because it works. Below are seven reasons why you should be investing in your online marketing efforts.

1. **Customers Are Looking For YOU:** First and foremost, the internet is the only medium that customers are actively searching for your products and services. Most advertising is intrusive, meaning that the ads interrupt us while reading an article, listening to music, or watching a show. With the internet, customers want our information and they want it fast—will they find you?... or will they find your competitor?

2. **Cost Effective:** Most businesses have limited resources. This book does not go into *Pay Per Click* or sponsored advertising (*Google Adwords*). We are not going to elaborate on banner ads or any other form of paid advertising. We'll only focus on the free stuff. While we have seen an ROI for paid internet advertising in our own businesses, we see a better *ROI* from the free platforms available to you.

   For us, there is nothing more satisfying than making a big sale from someone who found our products or services on a free search listing off Google. OK… we take that back, it is equally satisfying to hear from a student or reader who has just made their first sale, or increased sales as a result of the techniques we teach.

3. **Surrounded By The Internet:** First it was laptop computers, now it's smartphones and tablets providing continuous access to our businesses 24-7.

   Microsoft founder Bill Gates has given numerous keynotes at the annual Consumer Electronics Shows in Las Vegas over the years. He predicted that in the near future we will be "surrounded" by the internet. He said it would be in our clothes, in our cars and in our walls.

   While some of these predictions are still futuristic, one thing is for sure; most everyone has the internet in their pocket these days in the form of a smart phone or tablet providing continual access to the internet. * **Note:** Now days, more searches are done on smartphones than computers. Furthermore, double digit growth is forecasted for smartphones in the future, fostering one more step toward a more social, mobile and inter-connected internet.

4. **The Masses Are Using The Internet:** The rest of the world has finally found the internet - and it came in the form of Facebook. Sure, Facebook is great for marketing our businesses (as detailed in Chapter 10). However, what really excites us about Facebook are the billion + members, all getting comfortable with the internet. Young children and even their grandparents are embracing the internet through Facebook – forming groups, uploading images, and connecting to your products! Some even predict that Facebook could be the next killer search engine to beat Google! Have you noticed that little search box on the top of every Facebook page?

5. **More Big Growth in Ecommerce:** Ecommerce has been growing at a double digit pace for a decade now. All research firms predict the future to be equally as impressive.

6. **Customers are Pre-Shopping You:** Just because you do not sell products directly on the internet (ecommerce) does not mean that your customers are not going to the internet to

check you out and compare you to your competition before they pick up the phone or walk into your "brick and mortar" location.

7. **Visitors Come From Search Engines:** The vast majority of your new internet customers are going to come from an internet search versus a business card or ad.

8. **Forrester Buying Behavior Survey Results:** A survey of 161 buyers from major corporations, including many fortune 100 companies, showed consistent growth in internet based purchases. In 2014, 30% made half or more of their work purchases online. In 2017, 56% expect to make half or more of their work purchases online. And 74% research half or more of their work purchases online before they buy.

> *Quick Fact: Another First – Spending on online advertising is surpassing print advertising.*

Stick With The Fundamentals

The fundamentals never change - even as every new Google algorithm comes out, their message about SEO has been consistent over the years:

> *Offer interesting content that visitors will like well enough to share with their friends and want to come back for more.*

"First and foremost we care about trying to get the stuff that people really will like, the good, the compelling content in front of them." (quote by Matt Cutts, Google's voice on SEO)

We know that everything Google does focuses on the end user – the searcher. Google even employs this philosophy with their money-making advertising division *Google Adwords*, where the end user (not the advertiser) is priority number one. This is proven by how Google ranks the order of the ads as they appear along the top or side bar; it's just as much about how many searchers clicked on the ads, as it is how much advertisers are willing to pay for the ads. Simply paying more does not guarantee a higher rank in Google Adwords. They instill this "end user" philosophy into every single employee.

> *Define: Compelling Content – Consists of the Text, Video, and Images on our websites that arouse interest, attention, or admiration from our visitors in a powerfully irresistible way. "Google's mission is to organize the world's*

information and make it universally accessible and useful."

The image below is from Google's About page – It says it all.

Play Google's Game – Focus on the Big Picture

Participate in every platform they own and by default you will have good content. By the way—it's all free.

- YouTube (a search engine of videos)
- Google Image Search (a search engine of images)
- Google+
- Google My Business (the map listings)

Internet marketing activities are intimately interconnected, and therefore should be approached holistically. Google (and other search engines) have many ways to "connect the dots." One dot might be at one of their own enterprises like YouTube (yes, Google owns YouTube), or maybe your dot is on a backlink from another website that they monitor. You have the opportunity to participate in many Google-owned enterprises. For example, the map that shows up on the search results in Google (Google Places is discussed in chapter 9). Just be sure to play Google's game and complete as much of the information as you can. By working through these strategies one by one, you will start showing up on Google's radar screen.

SEO is not just one single thing you can do. There is no silver bullet—it's the many things you do, all working together; a holistic approach. Focus on the Big Picture!

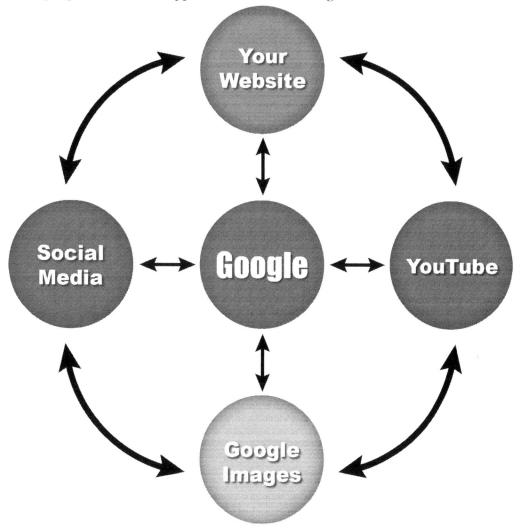

In order to determine how "interesting" or "compelling" our content is to their customers (the searching public), Google watches what we do and how engaged we are with the entire internet—both on our website and off our website. Google watches us on Social Media and Blogs. They look at our on-page and off-page Videos and Images. "Play Google's Game."

What Google Says

Google's message has been simple and consistent over the years: "Present original content that visitors will enjoy. Do not offer content simply for the benefit of the search engines and update it often." Content can take the form of text, images, and video. This is a simple but powerful statement. If you keep this one simple goal in mind, you will win!

Visitors can spot content that is written simply for high ranking a mile away. Content stuffed with keywords is not only painful for visitors to read, Google will penalize you for it.

Our techniques are not only effective, they are perfectly acceptable (it's called *White Hat SEO*) and even encouraged by the search engines. Google wants you to help them categorize, (*index*) your business properly.

Google's Philosophy

Below is an expert from Google's About page under Philosophy. We thought we would share the #1 item they started off with.

> **Focus on the user and all else will follow.** *Since the beginning, we've focused on providing the best user experience possible Whether we're designing a new Internet browser or a new tweak to the look of the homepage, we take great care to ensure that they will ultimately serve you, rather than our own internal goal or bottom line Our homepage interface is clear and simple, and pages load instantly* <u>*Placement in search results is never sold to anyone, and advertising is not only clearly marked as such, it offers relevant content and is not distracting*</u>*. And when we build new tools and applications, we believe they should work so well you don't have to consider how they might have been designed differently.*

Here's another Google quote:

> *"...When Google correctly identifies these pages and is able to extract the relevant information from them, it is more likely to surface that information to searchers looking for the business."*

Focus On What You Can Win At

You will hear us talk a lot about focusing on the things you can win at throughout this book.

The same business strategies apply to internet marketing as they do to any other "real world" business strategy you might have. For example, most business find it easier to "win" if they focus on a specialty, or niche. What is it that makes you special and helps you stand out?

Use your business's unique personality and attitude to establish your authority and leadership. Your online community will start to recognize this and follow you. Sure there are businesses that are successful competing against Walmart, but do you really want to work that hard? Work smarter and focus your internet marketing efforts on strategies you can win at. We'll give numerous example of this through the book.

> ***Real World Example:*** *After one of Greg's classes an attorney came up and announced that he wanted to be #1 for the search term "Attorney Austin." Well... good luck with that. Greg asked him what his area of specialty was He was a real estate attorney Bingo—Focus on 'Austin Real Estate Attorney."*

- Win local business by focusing on your city, your suburb or an area of town. It's better to be a big fish in a small pond than to try and compete with the entire world.
- Win by focusing your keyword strategy on a niche or specialty.
- Win with Google Images. It's much easier to get high ranking for your keywords on a Google Image search (versus a regular Google search), because most of your customers are not optimizing their images for this search engine.
- Win with YouTube – it's also easier to rank higher here (versus a regular Google search) by optimizing your YouTube videos for your keywords. Plus, being active on YouTube will help your regular Google search ranking for those same keywords.
- Win with Blogs – Google loves blogs on our websites. In fact, they favor websites with blogs. It's also our best opportunity for great "fresh" content.

Black Hat is Dead

If you're looking for some trickery or quick tips to cheat Google's system, you're in the wrong place. Google hates cheaters and so does everyone else. No one likes spammy websites and we can all smell them a mile away.

We only teach White Hat SEO—the kind of SEO that Google actually asks us to use to help them rank our websites properly for their users (our potential customers). This is exactly the reason that everything that we wrote about in our first book (way back in 2008) still stands true today.

Anyway, the days of cheating Google are long gone. You're going to lose at that game— big time. Google has been hiring the best and brightest PhDs for years. There is no way you, or I, or the spammy website designer claiming to get your website number one on Google is going to outsmart Google.

> *"Optimizing our websites for the search engines isn't about cheating the system… it's about building a better website."*

Google's business model has always revolved around one simple mantra: *relevance*. They built their search engine based on the fact that if they could return that perfect website result to a searcher, they would win—and win they did!

Google and all the other search engines are relying on us to be ethical, honest, and fair, providing the information they need to rank us properly for the searchers keywords. Helping searchers find the best web pages for their search queries relates back to their golden rule of relevancy. Google wants searchers to find the highest quality answers, as quickly as possible.

Spammy Text

Textual content must be written for the benefit and enjoyment of your visitors. Text should not be written simply to influence the search engines. Google has very sophisticated programs that can sniff out spammy text that is only written to influence search engines. Google will reward you for writing content that your users enjoy, interact with, share with their friends, and come back for more.

Who Needs This Book?

You do, if you like free advertising. Free advertising is addictive: once you make your first sale as a result of being on page one of the Google results, or maybe after your blog post gets featured on a popular website for your product review—or perhaps someone sees your company on Facebook, LinkedIn, or Twitter and makes a purchase—you will hunger for more!

Our simple strategies are equally applicable to businesses, charitable organizations, and individuals interested in personal branding. The best news… Everything we talk about is free other than the time it takes to implement.

> **Tip:** *Private corporate Intranets rely on documents, images, and web pages to be searchable within their organization. Some even use the Google Site Search box to implement this feature. Many of the concepts in this book apply to a private Intranet, allowing employees to easily search and retrieve information.*

Before You Hire a Website Designer

Professional website designers and internet marketers can be worth their weight in gold. There are many competent web designers around; many are our friends and colleagues, and many come to our classes and presentations in order to sharpen their skills.

Unfortunately, accredited website design certifications and internet marketing certifications do not exist. Therefore, anyone can promote themselves as a website designer or internet marketer.

Consequently, there are a good number of these businesses that are giving our industry a black eye. Our readers and students have shared some real horror stories with us. Almost every week we hear of a business owner that lost all of their content because their old website designer either left town, went out of business, or just plain refused to hand it over, because they owned the copyright to all of the content!

Every day we all get the same calls and emails… "We'll get you #1 on Google." You're probably thinking, "Everyone can't possibly be #1 on Google" …and you would be right.

First of all, realize that 100% of those calls and emails are scams. Even if they are successful at getting you #1, they do it by *Black Hat SEO* techniques. Usually their game is to get you high ranking for some obscure keyword phrase that might include one of your keywords, but is something no one would ever actually search for. They use trickery to do it; you might get ranking for a little while, then Google will catch you and spank you.

Even reputable SEO and internet marketing firms play a game. They buy you website traffic by using your money to buy Google Ads (*Google Adwords*). It's a lot easier to just buy the Google Ads— especially when they are using your money!

It takes hard work to get you natural ranking; better yet, you get more "qualified" traffic coming from a click on a *Natural Search Result*. Marketers have another incentive to buy you those Google ads: they make a commission from Google.

Our techniques will teach you how to get high ranking with the free *Natural Search Results*. We'll show you how to "win" by focusing on a niche, not some obscure keyword phrase. We'll teach you how to target keywords that you can expect to rank well for and bring you *Qualified Traffic* so you can close more sales.

It takes many skill sets to build a great website and internet marketing program. Website design, graphic arts, computer programming, and internet marketing are all different disciplines. Just because someone can program a website for you, does not mean that they can employ sound internet marketing principles to grow your business. Don't get us wrong, geeks are cool and all, we're just not sure that they should be 100% in charge of your business growth strategies.

Many website designers are fantastic graphic artists and can dazzle business owners with amazing and beautiful graphic design. However, do you really want a beautiful billboard in the middle of the desert? Unfortunately, *Findability* on the search engines is an afterthought of some web designers.

As mentioned above, this book gives you enough information to get involved in the process of your web design. It also enables you to distinguish a good website designer from one that is not.

> ***Caution:*** *As will be discussed in Chapter 2, three things are needed to launch a website: **1.** Register your URL—www.(your domain name).com; **2.** Use a website design program to place all images, layout, and text properly; **3.** Host that program on a server, so the world can view it. **It's a good idea to establish up front who owns all three of these—you or your website designer.***

> *It's also a good idea to retain all the user names and passwords to access all three services. Companies like GoDaddy and Host Gator will do any combination of the above services for you. See* <u>*www.PlayGooglesGame.com/godaddy*</u> *for a link to registration and/or hosting.*

The Website Designer's Business Model

To be fair to website designers, most business owners do not value the work of a true internet marketer or SEO consultant. This is exactly the reason that you have so much opportunity to grow your business by being proactive with the techniques we'll show you in this book—most of your competition does not value it.

Most business owners expect to pay several thousand dollars or less for a website. There is absolutely no way that you are going to get ongoing help, continual updates, nor a self-maintaining SEO website for this kind of money. SEO is never a "set it and forget it" one time solution to marketing. You have to be there for the engagement with your customers. Heck, even Greg set out in the beginning to offer SEO consulting services and found out that there is no money in it! If they only knew that he was winning million dollar annual contracts in his own business by practicing what he preaches…

The truth is that all of these efforts take time. While everything we talk about is free, it does take a time commitment from you or your staff. Most business owners are not willing to pay a website designer or internet marketing consultant for this time.

If you will learn the techniques that we teach in this book, you will get a head start by having a website built right in the first place, and one that you can easily maintain your SEO and internet marketing efforts on yourself.

How to Use this Book

We recommend reading this book while having the www.PlayGooglesGame.com website open. You can easily click on Real World Examples, expanded How To's, White Papers with step by step, easy to follow screenshots, and Instructional Videos. You can find out about attending our latest workshop, class, or presentation and even share your own stories.

Bonus for Our Print Readers

Hard copy purchasers qualify for a **free download of our PDF eBook**. The value of the eBook is that many important areas and terms are hyperlinked to the book website.

The eBook also provides live links to the various **Real World Examples** on the book website. Visit www.PlayGooglesGame.com/members-seo-ebook for all the details (psssst—you'll need a secret pass code emailed to you upon registration).

Use it like a Workbook

We purposely left the margins wide so you could use the book as a workbook and make notes in the margins.

At the end of each chapter, you will see bullet points of the main topics, with blank lines to make your notes. Use this as your blueprint with your website designer. Many website designers come to our classes and also find the workbook format useful in working with their clients.

After you complete the workbooks, you can show off your skills by taking our online test. Visit www.PlayGooglesGame.com/seo-test.html. We'll send you a certificate of completion, good for **20% off** the admission price of our ***Play Google's Game - SEO Boot Camp***, **Workshops**, **Video Training** and other services. (Discounts do not apply to our University of Texas classes.)

Define:

We use the same process that Google uses to find the definition of a word. Try typing **define: (the word you want defined)** without the brackets, into the Google search box whenever you want to find the definition of a word.

Throughout the book you will see **Define:** where we define important terminology.

We Replaced Text Boxes with Indented and Italic Callouts

Our first book had text boxes. We found out that text boxes don't play well with Kindle and other e-book formats. Throughout the book you will see various indented and italicized sections of text, beginning with one of the topics below in bold. These call out important information. The callouts come in 12 styles:

1. Tip
2. Note
3. Caution
4. Off Page SEO
5. Bright Idea
6. Learn More

7. How To
8. Quick Fact
9. Real World Example
10. Black Hat Warning
11. SEO Juice Alert
12. Define

Most of these callouts include links to free White Papers on our website and are for those of you who want to dive in a little deeper into the technical aspects. For the rest of us, we promise to keep the technical jargon to a minimum!

You will also see common internet marketing terms *Italicized*. This indicates that they are defined in the glossary in the back of the book.

At the back of the book, you will find a **Tools** section with valuable links, resources.

Screen Shot Imagery

Screen shots from the web are problematic. First off, most website images are 72 dpi. Print media requires 300 dpi for clarity. That's off by a factor of four!

Second, most websites shrink images down to their lowest size resolution so that the page loads faster (which is good and bad; see Chapter 3).

For these reasons, we almost decided not to include them. However, they are so informative that in the end, we did. We apologize in advance for their lower quality. We even tried sprucing them up as best we could in Photoshop—so just know that we did the best with what we had.

Where Do You Start?

When you are new to internet marketing and website design it all seems very overwhelming. Trust us, we've all been there.

By start we mean: What is the very first action you are going to take? Are you going to do a Google search to find a website designer to build your very first website? Are you going to join Facebook and set up a business page? Are you going to call your existing website designer and ask them to update your images so they show up on the Google Image Search Engine? These are just a few of many examples we will teach you to grow your business using various internet platforms—as well as your website.

You just need to start with one small thing. There are a couple of exceptions but, for the most part, it really doesn't matter where you start, just get started with something. It will all start to build on itself.

Throughout this book and your entire internet marketing journey, you're going to see things that you're not going to understand right away. Then you are going to see things that all of a sudden that light bulb goes off and you have that aha moment. Do those things first. Just pick something you are comfortable with and go for it.

Obviously, you need to start by educating yourself. If this book is your first effort at gaining a basic understanding of internet marketing, then we are honored to help you begin your journey. We think it's a great place to start! After all we wrote this book with you in mind—beginners.

How you read this book and implement the action plans at the end of each chapter are generally up to you, and what you are comfortable with. We do recommend that you read all the front matter first (the sections before the first chapter, like this one) and absolutely start with the first two chapters. After that, you can go in pretty much any order you want.

Just remember, it's not just one thing that will grow your business online and it's not going to happen overnight; it's many things working together as a whole. Google is watching all things that happen on the internet. They don't care in what order you do these things, they just want to observe that you are doing something; of course the more things that you do, the more Google will take notice and the more chances you have to sell something!

First Step

1. Read ALL sections that appear before Chapter 1 (the front matter)
2. Read Chapter 1 and 2
3. Start with any other chapter—read it. If you are comfortable and ready to take action, then complete the action plan; if not, see the Last Step below.

Last Step

Decide whether to hire (or fire) a Website Designer, or Do It Yourself only after you have read this entire book.

Folks, this is the whole goal of this book, to educate business owners so they can have the knowledge to hire the best website designer or internet marketer for their business. Of course many of our students and readers over the years have used our books to launch their own journey into website design and internet marketing. However, we are not trying to turn our readers into website designers. We all have businesses to run right?

As discussed earlier about website designers, as with any profession they're not all created equal. Of course there are many reputable and effective individuals and firms, but how do you find the right ones?

Unfortunately, there is no accredited certification or license to become a website designer or internet marketer. Anyone who might have a little technical expertise or basic graphic design skills can hang a shingle out that advertises their services.

Probably even more alarming than incompetent website designers are all of the scams going on in our industry. You can read more about the seedy Black Hat marketers in this front matter area of the book.

Therefore, we recommend that you read the entire book before you hire someone for the first time, or start re-working your website with your current website designer. Just remember to line out the expectations. If you are only paying for certain services, you can't expect to get others for free— they have a business to run too. A lot of the responsibility falls on you to educate yourself, work with your team and grow your business online.

You Can Do This - Take One Step At A Time

Over 101 tips can seem overwhelming, and our main goal is not to overwhelm you with too much information or too much technical jargon. The whole reason we teach our classes and write about this is to bring it down to the layperson's level and not talk over anyone's head. So here's some advice: Start with any tip in the book. The good news is that it does not matter where you start. Pick something that you are comfortable with; if you see something that you don't understand, just move on to something that you do understand and start there. You will start seeing results as you work your way through various techniques.

What to Expect – No Silver Bullet

If you are looking for a silver bullet that will magically propel you to the top, you're in luck—here it is:

> *"Write amazing content that engages your visitors, compels them to share it with their friends, and come back for more."*

Seriously though, the twelve strategies we'll teach you are probably not going to bring overnight results. However, we have seen this many times, especially if you focus on a niche or you are in a low competition business category. Most of the strategies are meant to be part of a long term plan, and if you systematically and regularly implement them you will see results.

If you are in an extremely competitive industry, for example an attorney in a major metropolitan city, you probably should not expect to be number one for the search term "Attorney Houston" any time soon. However, if you focus on a niche or specialty like "Houston Real Estate Attorney" (we'll talk about the importance of the order of the words in Chapter 2), you should expect faster results.

You should expect to be ranked high for basic keyword searches like your business name and maybe your product or service, along with the name of your city. You should also expect visitors to stick around for a little while once they get to your website, and maybe even buy something! We'll talk about how to do this with good customer service and good usability in Chapter 12.

How Long Before I'm # 1 on Google?

There is no silver Bullet, which means that there is not one single shortcut or secret tip that will propel you to the top of Google, Facebook, or any other platform. Top ranking involves many things working together that get Google's attention. We know that Google watches all things that happen everywhere on the internet. They determine how those things relate back to our websites. It's all connected!

That does not mean you have to do all the things we recommend in this book tomorrow. Just start whittling them down one by one and you will see results. Over time Google will start to connect the dots.

Caution: *SEO is not a "set it and forget it" strategy. Even after you implement* *one strategy, you must continually tweak it, enhance it, and change it. In fact, Google will penalize you if you never make any changes. Ongoing maintenance is paramount. Google rewards fresh websites that are updated often!*

Get Our #1 Tip Right Now

There are over 101 tips and techniques in this book. We'll entice you to go to www.PlayGooglesGame.com by giving you the #1 easiest to implement, single most important tip that is working for us today. Sign up for our monthly tip and get your #1 tip today: www.PlayGooglesGame.com/best-seo-tip-today.

On the website you can also view our **Top Ten List** of the 10 best strategies that are working right now. Things change rapidly on the internet. Therefore, you will see many links throughout this book, taking you to our latest findings and current blog posts at www.PlayGooglesGame.com.

Top 10 Resources You Need to Know

1. **Matt Cutts – Google SEO & Quality Guy – YouTube Channel**
   www.PlayGooglesGame.com/matt-cutts-youtube-channel
   He also has many, many videos on Google's Channel.
   www.PlayGooglesGame.com/google-youtube-channel

2. **How Google & SEO Works**
   www.PlayGooglesGame.com/how-search-engines-work

3. **Google Search Console Help**
   www.PlayGooglesGame.com/google-search-console-help

4. **Google Search Console "Dashboard"**
   www.PlayGooglesGame.com/google-search-console

5. **Google's Quality Guidelines**
   www.PlayGooglesGame.com/google-quality-guidelines

6. **Top 5 SEO Tips Working Right Now**
   www.PlayGooglesGame.com/best-seo-tip-today

7. **Official Google SEO Guide:**
   www.PlayGooglesGame.com/official-google-seo-guide
8. **SEO MOZ**
   www.PlayGooglesGame.com/seo-moz

9. **Search Engine Land**
   www.PlayGooglesGame.com/search-engine-land

10. **Get Updates Right From Google**
    www.PlayGooglesGame.com/google-seo-blog

Play Google's Game

Chapter 1

Be Found on Google

Nobody sees a beautiful billboard in the middle of the desert

✓ SEO = Search Engine Optimization
✓ Do it Yourself? Hire a Pro?
✓ Everything We Teach is Free
✓ Google's Secret Code - The Rules

Everything starts with being found in the first place. Of course, the best place to be found is where people are looking and your customers are looking for you on Google and the other search engines. Will you be found?

Highlights

Very Important:

- Learn to use Google's SEO Learning Tool – Search Console

Important:

- The value of in-house SEO
- Understand the various components of the Search Results Page

Helpful:

- Understand what differentiates good content from content that's meant to influence search engines
- Relevance - Google's Golden Rule

What is SEO?

People Are Searching – They Are Not Typing In Your Web Address

First and foremost, you must understand how people are searching for you.

Whether it's a new or an old customer, people are not going to take the time to physically type in your website address as seen on your business card or other advertisements. New customers simply Google a product or service and old customers expect that they can just Google your business name and be able to find you in two seconds.

We are amazed at how common it is to run across a business that does not show up on the Google results when you type in their business name! Those businesses are losing both new sales and frustrating their existing customers.

Equally important is to be found, on page one, when people search for your products and services. Throughout this book, we'll use practical tips used in our own businesses to show you easy ways to be found.

This first chapter defines *SEO (Search Engine Optimization)*. *SEO* is the field of study dedicated to getting website pages found on search engines. It's pretty simple; the higher you are ranked on page one of Google—the search engine's results page (*SERP*)—the more visitors you will get to your website.

Unfortunately, many websites are only designed to look pretty and *findability* is an afterthought—please review the introduction for a word on website designers. We like to say "It's more about the SEO and less about the show." Many website designers get this backwards. Of course we want beautiful, functional websites, but what good is a beautiful billboard in the middle of the desert, where no one sees it?

The good news is that every technique we teach throughout this book affects your findability on the search engines—everything connects to Google in one way or another!

Do it Yourself? Hire a Pro?

Keep something in mind as you read through these chapters… First of all, we are not trying to turn business owners into website designers. This book is designed to teach you what you need to know so you can find a great website designer. We also want you to be able to communicate with your website designer, speaking in their language. Without that two way communication, you'll end up with a templated website that might not have a lot to do with your business goals.

Let's be clear. There is a huge difference between website design and SEO. Just because a website designer can code a beautiful website, does not necessarily mean that they can optimize it for SEO. Worse yet, can they set it up for easy, ongoing SEO maintenance by the business owner?

Conversely, you do not have to know how to code a website to perform SEO. In fact many of the techniques that we teach can be accomplished if you know bare boned basics of how to use the Windows or Mac operating system and know how to type!

Remember, SEO is not a "set it and forget it" process. In fact, if your website designer states that "SEO is included" in your website design package—Run! At least get clarification, because most times that statement means that they think it's a one-time event. If they do not take the time to show you how you can go about continually maintain your website for SEO, then they are doing you a disservice.

We'll also teach you how to become a good internet marketer. We'll show you how to find a website designer that understands the importance of integrating SEO, internet marketing, functionality, and beauty.

Alternatively, many of our readers and students have told us that this book and our courses have been a springboard for them to learn how to take charge of 100% of their website and online growth goals.

By the nature of what we talk about, we will touch on some basic website design topics. However, this is not a book on website design. A common misconception is to use the term website designer and internet marketer interchangeably. These are two separate disciplines. This book is on SEO, which is just one piece of your *internet marketing* puzzle. We think it's the most important piece!

Ultimately, your website has to be set up (designed) right in the first place in order to reap the benefits of the SEO activities that we teach. This places a lot of responsibility on the initial website designer. We'll get a little more into the structure of a website and how it works in the next chapter and also in Chapter 8 on blogs. Just know that a website designer uses a website design program to set up the structure, layout, images, video, and textual content of your website.

Google Wants You to Do This Yourself

However you approach your website design and internet marketing, it's now clear that Google wants the business to maintain the majority of SEO in-house. By majority we mean the content management and customer interactions, which is all Google cares about. Google knows that the best way that a website can provide interesting and compelling content is for the business owner or management to create it. They know that their customers want a real world experience.

At the very least, we recommend that simple updates be done in-house by you or your staff. These updates might include a newsworthy event posted to your home page (a blog post), a new YouTube video, a new image, a Facebook business page update, etc.

Sure, you can hire this out and contract with online marketing companies to perform monthly maintenance. However, if your website is set up properly, it can empower you to make small updates and changes very easily. Maybe it's your recent news event, an updated picture of your latest and greatest product, or simply updating some text on your *About Us* website page. We'll show you how easy it is with WordPress in Chapter 8 "Google Loves Blogs"

Throughout this book, we'll show you how simple these tasks can be. So simple, even the local high school kid on your staff can perform them, as long as your website designer has set it up properly. Of course, management would want to oversee and guide their employees. After all, you know your business best!

Tip: We realize that for some business owners, creating content is kind of a

daunting task, especially in the beginning. Maybe you're not that comfortable writing copy, communicating on social media platforms like Twitter or Facebook, taking pictures, or creating video. For our favorite resources to help you create awesome content or least give you a head start click here:
www.PlayGooglesGame.com/website-content-creating-services

Google Provides an SEO Tool & Learning Center – Search Console

Google re-branded *Webmaster Tools* into *Search Console* in 2015. Their intent was loud and clear. They took a platform from super geeky down to the layperson's level overnight. They made it intuitive, easy to navigate, and fully searchable. They are now offering clear answers to SEO questions, which were vague (to say the least) prior to the Search Console.

This is Google's main SEO tool and learning center. They re-branded it by purposely de-emphasizing the geeky word "Webmaster" so that they could attract the business owner to use it.

In fact, their home screen says it all: "We want to help you have a Google friendly site."

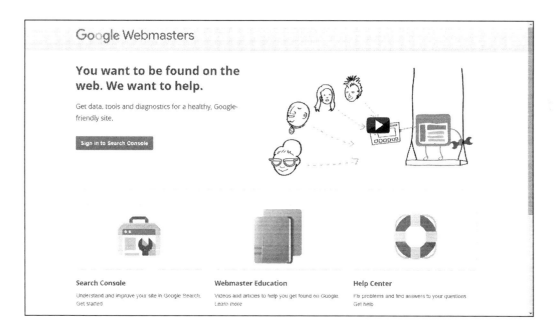

How To: *There are actually two tools offered here: Google Search Console* <u>*Help*</u> *and Google Search Console* <u>*Dashboard*</u>*.*
You can access Google Search Console Help without having a Google account at <u>*www.PlayGooglesGame.com/google-search-console-help*</u>

www.PlayGooglesGame.com/google-search-console-dashboard

For Accessing your Google Search Console Dashboard, you must be logged into your Google account.

The Search Console tool is free, and at the present time you only need to have a Google account to log in. If Google decides to go the same route it did with their Keyword Tool, then we expect that you will eventually need an AdWords account to access the Search Console too.

You'll learn more about the Google Keyword tool (renamed Keyword Planner) in the next chapter. To use the Keyword Planner, they make you sign up for an AdWords account. You don't have to actually buy anything— for now anyway…

How to Set Up the Google Search Console

Set up your Search Console account:

- Sign in to Search Console with your Google account. If you don't have a Google account, you'll need to create one.
- Once you sign in, click on Add a Site.

Verify that you're the owner of the site by doing one of the following (your web designer can easily help you with this, if you don't know how):

- Upload a file to your server
- Add a meta tag to your website's HTML
- Add a new DNS record
- Use your Google Analytics or Google Tag Manager account
- Easy GoDaddy verification—if GoDaddy is your host

Folks, you need to start playing around with Google's SEO tool. This is the best way to learn about what Google wants to see from your SEO efforts and to see the results of your efforts by getting feedback straight from Google itself. Google is also tracking to see how often you log on and they are noting your changes.

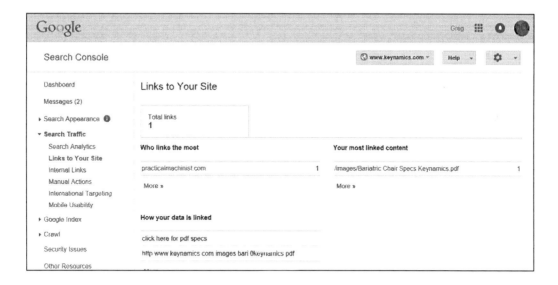

Active Search Console users are being rewarded with higher ranking! Google refers to this as having an *agile SEO cycle* or conversely, slow iteration. Google can also tell if the Search Console is being accessed by the business or by your marketing firm. Again, they prefer that the business owner access this more often than someone else.

The SERP Listings Are Free

In this chapter we'll be talking about optimizing and tweaking our websites so that search engines will love them. If done honestly, correctly and continuously, you will be rewarded with a free link to your website on page #1 on Google's *search engine results page,* or *SERP* for short. There are *paid SERP listings* and *free SERP listings.* We only talk about the free stuff in this book.

> **Note:** *Everything we talk about in this entire book is free, versus paid online advertising. Let's be clear: YOU CAN NOT BUY YOUR WAY TO THE TOP OF THE NATURAL SEARCH RESULTS!*

These free listings are also known as the *natural search results* or *organic search* results and are depicted in the image below. A searcher gets to the SERP page by typing a keyword, or *keyword phrase* into the search box on the Google home page.

> **Define: SERP** – *From Wikipedia –* "*A search engine results page (SERP) is the listing of results returned by a search engine in response to a keyword query. The results normally include a list of items with titles, a reference to the full version, and a short description showing where the keywords have matched content within the page.* **A SERP may refer to a single page of links returned, or to the set of all links returned for a search query***."*

There are usually 10 free listings on the page and they are located in the main body of the SERP. You can recognize them by the first line called the *SERP Title.* This title line stands out with a larger, bold, blue font. Directly below this title line are a couple of smaller black lines referred to as the *SERP Description.* We'll discuss how you can change the SERP Title and the SERP Description so it stands out and gets chosen in Chapter 7. Hint: Getting chosen more helps ranking!

The free SERP listings are not to be confused with the paid advertisements, *Google Shopping, Blended Listings,* or *Map Listings* which are also located on the SERP. Ads and Google Shopping are part of the *Google Adwords* program. These sponsored links are located along the right hand side and the very top of the page, directly above the free listings.

The picture below shows a typical SERP, where we have arrows calling out the various types of listing appearing on a SERP. Obviously it does not show a map, because the search has nothing to do with local business. Also note that the first image in the *Blended Search* results is Greg's iPhone Stand. We'll show you how you can compete in highly competitive categories like this in Chapter 3 on Image Search.

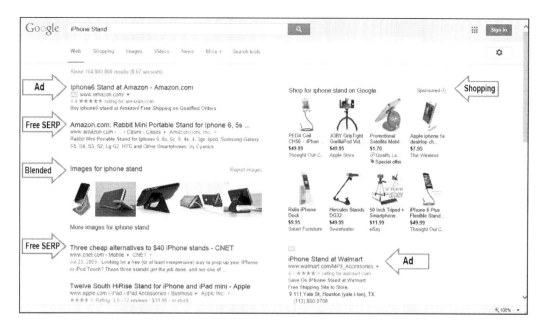

The SERP also contains other free listing opportunities besides the *natural search results*. SEO also involves making sure you get high ranking within these other areas. We'll talk more about these other free listing opportunities in later chapters. These include getting your images listed on *Google Image Search* and your videos listed on YouTube. Google will also frequently show a map with businesses located on the map that pertain to the keywords the searcher has typed into the search box. Beside the map are the corresponding business listings. This is called *Google Maps* or *local search*. Listings on the map are free. You will learn more about Google Maps in Chapter 9.

Sometimes you will see products listed on the SERP, and this is part of the *Google Shopping* program. Google charges businesses to have their products located on the *Google Shopping* results. This used to be free.

The entire goal of SEO is to get Google to reward us with a free listing on the SERP for the keyword or keyword phrase that we expect our customer will be searching for. We'll spend more time on keywords and keyword strategy in the next chapter.

The good news is that searchers pay much more attention to the free natural search results and not as much attention to the sponsored links. We have all been accustomed to "avoiding" advertisements whenever we read, listen to the radio, or watch TV. This avoidance has evolved us into the habit of ignoring the ads and is called *Ad Blindness*. That's how Tivo killed the TV commercial…

Caution: *Everything in moderation. Just like a good spice, a little can be delicious. Too much will ruin the entire meal. Overdoing any SEO technique in* *this book will get you penalized or banned from Google and the other search engines.*

It's painfully obvious that Google is aware of the Ad Blindness phenomenon. Look at the listings along the top, the ones just above the free natural search results. Notice how you can barely tell that the listing is a sponsored link. The background fill is ever so lightly shaded in pink so it blends in with the white background. Look at this area closely on your computer—this is camouflaged on purpose so that most people do not even realize that these are not part of the free natural search results. Even the words "Ads" at the top is in smaller lighter text. Of course advertising on Google Adwords is a great way to get traffic to your website. We've done it for years with much success. However, it's outside of the scope of this book —because it's not free.

Black Hat vs. White Hat

Throughout this book we will teach you legitimate, *White Hat* techniques to help you get high ranking among the search engines. This book is not about "cheating the system" or *Black Hat* trickery. Google hates cheaters.

White Hat techniques are encouraged by the search engines. After all, their goal is to return relevant websites as they pertain to the searcher's keywords. For example, Google would never show websites selling used cars when someone is searching for pizza. That's why we all love Google; they return what we need.

Let's help Google get your website ranked properly for the products and services you sell!

In the last chapter of the book, we'll share some *Black Hat* techniques that can actually get you banned from Google. You definitely want to stay on Google's good side!

Quick Fact: Google spiders first look to see if there are any changes on your website since they last crawled it. No change, means no fresh content and they just move on, dinging you a little in the process.

Google's Secret Code – The Rules

Google is very secretive about the *algorithms* they use to index and rank websites for any particular keyword. *Algorithms* are simply the rules that search engines use to rank webpages. Their algorithms are plugged into computer programs, also referred to as *spiders*. These are programs that take a snapshot of our websites, looking through all of our programming code for our keywords and deciding how to rank us for those keywords. They read every bit of programming code including the text, images, and video on our website. We'll spend more time in the remaining chapters talking about this, but here are a few points to keep in mind.

These spiders are not only searching for our individual keywords, they are also taking a holistic view of all of the elements on the webpage. They want to know the true meaning of our words. Therefore, they use *syntax* and *semantics* to look at the *context* and the sentence structure of the other words surrounding our keywords. Google is looking for the relationship and cohesion between our words, how they fit in with our keywords, images, and videos on the rest of the page. Simply put, is it grammatically correct, logical, and using words that one would expect to find on similar websites with the same topic? This is exactly why stuffing a bunch of keywords into your content does nothing but hurt you. We'll talk more about this in later chapters on Content and staying on Google's good side.

They also look for any changes since the last time they crawled our websites; change is good—it means the website has fresh content. They follow our hyperlinks to other websites on the internet and scan them as well to see how they relate and interact with our keywords. Ultimately they are trying to decide how to rank us for those keywords, based on the rules set out in the algorithms and the overall *relevance* our site has to those keywords. This all happens in a split second and with regular frequency. We notice that our websites seem to get crawled once a week or so.

Guess what—no one but Google has the secret algorithmic code. Their secrets are locked away tight in the Google vault!

However, Google has had one consistent message of the years: "Provide Good Content." Once you start using Google's Search Console above, you will notice that everything revolves around good content that pleases Google's users. We do know that the algorithms are designed around this basic concept.

Good Content - According to Google

We'll talk more about content in Chapter 6, but here are Google's guidelines. Just keep in mind that content consists of text, images, and videos.

1. People find it interesting enough to stick around for a while, tell their friends, and come back for more. Google tracks how fast visitors bounce right back to the search results. (The average *bounce rate* is 3 seconds; you have to get their attention quick!)

2. Relevant to your business. Therefore it revolves around your keywords and contains both incoming and outgoing hyperlinks to authoritative websites relevant to your industry.

3. Fresh & Original – it's created by you, the owner (or manager), not some sponsored content, paid guest blogging service, or worse, copied and pasted from another website. Create something, anything— a new image, some new text, or a video once a week. Just be sure whatever you create focuses on your keywords.

4. Your text copy is written for the enjoyment of people and not to influence the search engines.

- **Readable** – Is your content written for humans, or just to influence the search engines?

- **Compelling** – Do your visitors want to share it with their friends after visiting your website? Is your content arousing their interest, attention, and admiration in a powerful and captivating way?

- **Informative** – Is it interesting? Is it helpful? Does it answer any questions or concerns they might have?

Black Hat Warning: Never repeat or stuff a bunch of keywords anywhere, especially in your content elements. Google watches out for this. Your visitors can also tell when keywords have been crammed in because the text reads funny and Google can tell too. Remember, Google wants your content to be Readable, Compelling, and Informative!

Time Tested - Educated Guess

Professionals like us are constantly reviewing the Google Search Console, Google's Quality Guidelines, and other resources. We're observing what works and what doesn't and sharing those secrets among ourselves. When we see something working over a long period of time, we recommend it.

We never, ever chase the latest fad or trick. We spend time doing what Google wants us to do, and in our case we teach these techniques to our students and during our presentations. We feel this keeps us up to date on the latest and greatest technologies and techniques. Be warned though: Google changes can the rules at the drop of a hat and without warning.

You probably get as many phone calls and emails a day as we do, with promises to get us on page #1 of Google. These spammers pretend they know the secret code. It's really funny when we get the calls and the caller has not even taken the time to realize that we are in the business!

The internet marketing and SEO industries were created by professionals who make a living at this by trying to crack the code. Some use *white hat* techniques and some are *black hatters*. There are varied opinions as to what works and what does not work, and there are some hard and fast rules. Just remember, Google's information is proprietary and can change at any time, but they always stick to their basic rule: "Provide Good Content."

There are no guarantees that what works today is going to work tomorrow. Please become a member at www.PlayGooglesGame.com/members to stay on top of all the latest—basic membership is free.

A testament to the fundamental nature of what we'll teach you in this book and on our website is that all 101 tips from the first book, published in 2008, are still relevant today. These recommendations even survived the most notorious Google algorithm changes recently (Panda & Penguin). The reason our techniques stand the test of time is that we do not employ any *black hat* trickery or try to cheat the system —all of the cheats have now been exposed by the Panda and Penguin updates. Those who followed the advice of the first book were spared any penalties from Panda or Penguin.

> **Bright Idea:** *Before we make any change or add anything new to our websites, first and foremost, we think about how it will affect our ranking. We evaluate every single keystroke for SEO. It's also imperative that you save the previous version of your website on a regular basis, and especially before you make any changes. Save it to an external media (like a CD) to be held in safe keeping off site.*

Google's Golden Rule – Relevance

Try to put yourself in Google's shoes. What is Google's main philosophy, and why do most of us love using the Google search engine so much? Because they provide a good user experience by returning the results that are *relevant* to our search words. A good user experience is enhanced by good content that the visitor will enjoy, which would not be content written simply to trick or influence the search engines. Every single time that Google is asked about SEO, the standard response is, "Write Good Content."

The best news… Because these listings are free, Google does not return results based on what companies are willing to pay. Folks, that one fact alone levels the playing field between you and the corporate giants.

Google even ranks ads or *sponsored links* on their *Google AdWords* program by the relevance to the searcher's search words. In short, you can't even buy your way to the top of the sponsored links list. Pretty cool! Again, it levels the playing field.

One way Google measures the *relevance*, both on the *natural search results* and the *AdWords* program, is by how often a searcher clicks on any particular website result listing or ad in relation to other ads or website listing. They assume that if more people are clicking on your website that must mean it is more relevant to the keyword (or phrase) that the searcher typed into the Google search box. We will discuss some ways Google measures relevancy in Chapter 7, *Stand Out & Get Picked*.

> **Real World Example:** *A not so bright idea... In the early days, when Greg launched his patented laptop stands he was cash strapped and had to bootstrap himself using SEO to drive customers to his website. He knew that HP sold a ton of laptops. Therefore, he tried to rank high on searches for "HP laptops." He learned quickly how futile this was. A search for "HP laptops" is not very relevant to a search for "laptop stands" and Google would never rank him very high for those keywords—and they didn't.*

Goals of SEO

There are two goals in optimizing our websites for the search engines. **1.** Get top ranking on the search engines. **2.** Create a SERP listing that people actually follow through to our websites and stick around long enough to buy something, give us a call, walk in, or recommend to their friends. We'll show you how to do both.

The sad truth is that 95% of searchers do not look past the first page on the search results. Even if you are on page one, the higher you are ranked the more likely someone will click on your listing. Being in the top three search results improves your chances of being picked by 80%.

Want some really good news? The same techniques that we use to optimize our websites on Google also work on all the search engines. We focus on Google because they are the 10,000 pound elephant in the middle of the room.

Folks, this is not rocket science. Most of the techniques we talk about simply involve inserting your most important keywords in the proper places. This helps Google find you and rank you for those keywords. Throughout the rest of the book we'll talk about various internet marketing activities that can help your business grow. You will notice a common theme in all of these activities: Keywords. In one way or another, everything in our book revolves around using proper keywords. Many techniques will not involve Google directly, but rest assured, Google is watching and notices how and where you use those keywords. We'll share our secrets to getting your business found, as well as commonly known industry knowledge that very few of the pros are willing to share. We'll also steer you clear of the many deceptive tricks which can get you penalized or possibly banned from Google.

No Silver Bullet

A student emailed Greg after one of his classes, complaining that her brand new website was not on page one. Her website had been live for two weeks and she had implemented many of the suggestions from the class.

Folks, this takes time; sometimes, a lot of time, depending on how competitive your industry is. Remember to keep Google's golden rule in mind by writing original, good content that is relevant to your website. Then start applying the techniques in this book one by one, focusing on strategies that you can win at. After a while, Google will recognize that you are playing their game, and as long as you are playing fairly, you will be rewarded.

Best Practices - Action Plan

1. Start thinking about who will implement these strategies as you come across them in this book. Perhaps you have a person on staff that can write really well. Maybe another likes photography, and another likes Twitter.

_____

_____

_____

_____

2. Who will build and maintain your website? Does your website designer understand the importance of integrating SEO, internet marketing, and beauty, then enabling you to maintain it in their

absence?

_____

_____

_____

_____

3. Set up your Google Search Console. Add and verify your website. Search the help area for any SEO question that pops into your mind. Wasn't that fun? What websites are linking to you?

_____

_____

_____

_____

4. Find one or two good resources that you can follow to learn more about SEO. We provided a list in the front of the book.

_____

_____

_____

_____

Chapter 2

Keyword Strategy

*The three most important things in being found are
Keywords, Keywords, and Keywords*

✓ Keywords & Website Structure
✓ Keywords on the Internet
✓ Finding the Right Keywords
✓ Put Keywords in All the Right Places

Keywords form the foundation for everything related to being found on any internet platform. This chapter will teach you the fundamentals of not only using keywords properly on your website, but also other platforms on the internet.

We'll show you how keywords are critical in all of your internet marketing activities. You should know that on any website, service, application or platform that you participate in on the internet, you will have the opportunity to insert your keywords.

As far as Google goes, we are trying to make an educated guess at which words the common public is typing into the Google search box when they are looking for our products or services.

> ***Note:*** *We use Keyword and Keyword Phrase interchangeably. Just know that a keyword can be one word or several words in a phrase.*

First, you must understand how keywords fit into the basic building blocks of your website. Once you understand this, you will have the basic fundamentals to understand the rest of this book. For those brand new to all this, we're going to get a little geeky in the next section on website structure. Don't worry; we'll keep it as simple and basic as possible.

For the folks that might already know this, please bear with us as we describe some of these fundamentals; this might be a good refresher for you.

Please remember that you can start with any tip in this book. Some techniques will seem more daunting than others. Therefore, we recommend that you read this chapter without getting too hung up on every little detail.

After your first pass of the entire chapter, you should have a holistic view of the various elements of a website and be able to see how your keywords can be applied to those elements. You might want to re-read the chapter again—it's that important.

If you can master this chapter, all of the others will be a breeze. You can do this! In addition to some fundamental basics in this chapter, other relevant terms used in the book are defined in the Glossary. Remember, any term in the glossary is italicized when it first appears in the book.

On our own websites, keywords are so important that before we make any change, before any keystroke, we think about how the change will maximize the findability of our keywords. This also includes any change or updates to our Blogs, Facebook pages, images, YouTube videos, Google Maps or other websites that link to us. Findability should not be an afterthought.

Highlights

Very Important:

- Understand how keywords fit into the website structure
- Title Tag is the most important place for keywords
- Google Keyword Planner
- Keywords in your internal website URLs

Important:

- Less is better
- Keywords in image file names
- Your City Name should go first and always be used for Local Search

Helpful:

- Increase your odds of winning by focusing on a niche
- Place Keywords on other platforms, like Facebook
- No Industry Jargon, unless the public is using it

***Black Hat Warning: Keyword Stuffing** is an old trick and Google watches this like a hawk. It's super easy for them to detect whenever someone does it and they will flag your entire website as a low quality site, or worse a spammy website, thus knocking you down in the rankings. Never, ever repeat a bunch of keywords ANYWHERE or in any strategy we teach. It will be obvious to you and others when you do this.*

However, Google does encourage us to help them by placing our relevant keywords in the appropriate places. Matt Cutts from Google actually gave a good example of the right and wrong way to place Keywords in Image ALT tags, which could also apply to any place we put our keywords:

***Right** - alt="Dalmatian puppy playing fetch"*

***Wrong** – alt="puppy dog baby dog pup pups puppies doggies pups litter puppies dog retriever labrador wolfhound setter pointer puppy jack russell terrier puppies dog food cheap dogfood puppy food"*

Mr. Cutts goes on to say "Filling alt attributes with keywords ("keyword stuffing") results in a negative user experience, and may cause your site to be perceived as spam."

Keywords & Website Structure

Getting some basic knowledge about how a website is structured will give us a better understanding of where to place the keywords within it.

You should know these basics even if you hire a website designer versus doing it yourself. The following provides a very simplistic overview of the various components of a website.

A website is nothing more than a bunch of computer files organized within folders and structured in a format that is visible and usable by humans. These files contain the various content (text, code, images, animation, tables, audio, and videos) and instructions for the layout, text, and color scheme of the website.

Three Things Needed for a Website to Exist:

1. **Website Address** – Register your *Domain Name* (ie. www.PlayGooglesGame.com) with an internet *Domain Registrar* like *GoDaddy* or *HostGator*.
2. **Website Design Program** – You build the website using a *Web Development Program*, also known as a *Website Design Program* or *Content Management System*. *Dreamweaver* and *WordPress* are examples. This program manages all of the content and presents it in human readable format.
3. **Hosting** – Stores the website design program on a *Server* (hard drive) with a *Web Hosting* company like GoDaddy and HostGator.

Website Address

In much the same way as your business has a street address, every website needs a unique web address on the internet so that people can access it. There are three common terms regarding website addresses that are sometimes used interchangeably: Domain Name, IP Address, and URL.

Your entire website address is called the *URL*, which stands for *Universal Resource Locator*; your *Domain Name* is only the portion included with the ".com" and looks something like this: www.PlayGooglesGame.com

*Caution: We can't give legal advice. However, when you register a domain name, you don't actually "own" it; you are simply paying for the exclusive right to use it for a specified period of time. For legal issues involving your rights, you should consult an attorney. We do recommend that you own the rights to use it, versus having your web designer register it in their name and them owning these rights. This is a common occurrence. *Be sure they register it in your name and give you all of the user names and passwords to access the account, in case you need it in their absence!*

The URL address of the home page is simply your main web address (domain name): http://www.PlayGooglesGame.com. The URLs of your other *Internal Web Pages* are designated by anything between the "www." and after the .com/ (forward slash), as in http://www.PlayGooglesGame.com/contact. In this example, the forward slash indicates that all of the content for the internal webpage for "Contact Us" is located within a folder (also known as a *Directory*) named "contact". These other internal web pages are navigated to from the home page by an internal *hyperlink*. In this example the hyperlink displays the Contact page from the Contact page's folder. Another example of an internal webpage might be the "About Us" page and the URL might look like: http://www.PlayGooglesGame.com/about.

The *IP Address (Internet Protocol Address)* is simply the numerical equivalent to the domain name and URLs mentioned above. The IP Address is technically what the internet uses to locate a website and any page within the website. We don't want to get too geeky on you here and this is an overly simplistic explanation because it's really not that important for you to know. Just think about a domain name as the human readable version of the IP Address. Memorizing a string of numbers for every webpage we wanted to visit would be a real pain.

For fun, type this IP Address into your *Internet Browser* address bar: http://74.125.224.72/ …this is currently one of Google's IP addresses and will take you directly to the Google home page.

Tip: When initially registering your new domain name with a registrar like GoDaddy, you will have the option to pay for one or more years. Most experts agree that registering and paying for multiple years (3 to 5) helps with SEO. Think about it. Does Google want to reward a business that does not plan to be around for more than one year, or one that has registered for 5 plus years? Google will not admit this, but we think it's true.

Quick Fact: Characters allowed in the URL & Domain Name: The domain is between the "www" and the ".com" and only Letters, Numbers, and Hyphens (dashes) are allowed. For the rest of the URL (after the ".com/") there are many *characters "allowed." However, the following are considered safe: Letters, Numbers, Hyphens, and Underscores. *Note: Many times a blank space is used somewhere after the ".com/" to separate words. While this is allowable, it's a really bad idea—it shows up as "%20" and spaces are generally bad when it comes to computers.*

Correct: http://laptop-stand.com/contact-us/
Incorrect: www.laptop_stand.com/contact us *(underscore not allowed before the ".com" and a blank space between "contact" and "us" is bad).*

 Note: *The part before the ".com" in a URL is not case sensitive; the part after the .com" is. Therefore, keep all lettering lower case after the .com.*

Website Design Program

A website design program organizes the files and content into a visible and usable interface that we see as a website.

These design programs use programming code (examples are HTML & PHP) and allow website designers to design a website with little or no knowledge of the programming code itself.

This is similar to writing a letter using a word processor like Microsoft Word. Most of us are clueless about the programming code going on in the background that enables Word to function; it doesn't matter, we just compose our letter. The website design program uses various code elements to form the basic building blocks of the website.

Most website design programs use *WYSIWYG* functionality (What You See Is What You Get – pronounced "wizeewig"). Basically, you mock up and edit the webpage by inserting text and images into a predesigned template. What you see on the template closely resembles the final webpage. Therefore, you can see how it will look before you upload it to your host's server. A web design program is sometimes referred to as a *Web Content Management System.*

A couple of popular web design programs are WordPress and Dreamweaver. We'll discuss the value of WordPress in Chapter 8.

Learn More: *The programming code follows an overall basic structure and hierarchy, much the same as a letter you would write. It starts at the top and reads left to right. At the top there is a brief section called the Head, and then the Body* *is next. The head contains our very important Meta Tags and other overall instructions affecting the look and feel of the website. We'll discuss meta tags shortly. The body contains all the text, images, and layout of the website.*

It's important to know that the Google spiders read the code much like we read a letter. They start at the top; therefore, they value what's at the top more than what's at the bottom.

See an example of HTML code at: www.PlayGooglesGame.com/html-seo

Hosting

The website design program, including all of your content, is then uploaded and *Hosted* on a hard drive or *Server* which is connected to the internet. This content includes text, images, and video.

The hosting company's servers host your website, making it available for instant access from anyone who connects to it over the internet 24/7.

You can host your website on your own server, but renting out the space from a web hosting company like GoDaddy or HostGator is the best solution for most small businesses.

Who Owns What?

As noted in the introduction, you should own all of the above (the rights to use your URL, a copy of your Website Program, and your Hosting Account). You should also store backup copies of the website design program and all of the user names and passwords needed for ongoing maintenance of the website.

This seems like a simple and intuitive suggestion. However, you would not believe how many times we hear from a business owner that they lost everything because they did not own their content, domain name, artwork, images, or the programming code of their website. They have to start over from scratch!

While we can't give legal advice, a good practice is to establish **in writing**—and at the very beginning—who owns what. Some web designers feel that they wrote the code, content, and designed the artwork as their original work, so they own the copyright to it. This actually could be their rightful ownership if no one establishes it one way or another. This is a grey area, and who wants to go to court over a grey area? You should consult an attorney for advice on this!

We know many good website designers out there. Many are our friends and colleagues. We always have a few in our classes and we commend them for honing their internet marketing skills. We all agree on this point: hire a web designer that allows you to own your content—the code, text, images, artwork, and the rights to use your URL—all of it.

Pages of a Website

The *Home Page* is usually the *Landing Page* that visitors land on when searching for your business or when directly typing in your domain name.

An *Internal Page* is any page within your website other than the home page. Examples include your *Contact Us* page, *About*, *Product Page*, and the *Blog* page.

The *Sitemap* is a page listing all of the pages, posts, content and meta data on your website. It keeps track of when your content was last modified and identifies the most important parts of the website.

A sitemap allows Google to easily and accurately *Index* or rank your website. This is how the search engines determine what your website is all about and how *Relevant* it is for a particular search term. Play Google's Game and include a sitemap page on your website!

> **Learn More:** *For an example of a great plugin for WordPress that automates your sitemap page, please see:* www.PlayGooglesGame.com/sitemap-seo

> **Tip:** *The searching public expects to find at least two "Internal Pages" within your website: the "Contact Us" and the "About" pages. These should have prominent links along the top from the home page. The vast majority of searchers will click on your "About" page within a few seconds of arriving at your home page. Google expects this too, since this is Relevant to the searchers' expectations. You'll see in Chapter 12 that you will get dinged for not having a "Contact Us" page.*

Keywords on the Internet

The Internet is a system of connected *Servers* allowing each of us to connect to websites with our devices. These devices might be our computers, cell phones, iPhones, iPads, or other tablets.

A server is much like your old desktop PC. It's a slim square enclosure; however, it contains numerous hard drives where all of the files and folders for websites are stored. These enclosures are stacked on top of each other in racks located in rooms all over the world. For the most part, all of the servers in the world are connected to each other by various wires, cables, phone lines, optical fibers, and even wirelessly. The devices we use to access the websites are connected to the internet in the same way. Everything connects to each other... hence the *World Wide Web.*

Our websites are stored on these servers, along with many other websites, assuming we have rented the space from a website hosting company like GoDaddy or Host Gator and not hosted our website on our own server. You can also get a *Dedicated Server* from these companies—it's just a lot more expensive than a *Shared Server.* A dedicated server only hosts your website on it.

The *Google Spiders* travel along the various connections between the servers and look inside website files and folders for keywords and rank them according to the Google rules—the *Algorithms.*

Finding the Right Keywords

Keyword Strategy should be an ever evolving journey for your business. It's definitely not a set it and forget it strategy!

We could spend weeks discussing keyword strategy. The bottom line is that you are going to have to discover what the common public is searching for in your industry and more importantly, your *Niche.* The following are a few things to consider during your journey. What we discover in our own journey always surprises us; the keywords that the common public is searching for are not what we expect them to be!

Less is Better

If you try to focus on too many keywords, you will dilute the effectiveness of your most important keywords, so try to narrow it down to two or three per website page. This strategy applies anywhere you place keywords: individual website pages, blogs, YouTube, etc.

Keyword strategy is usually a balancing act of getting our keywords worked in properly and having the text make sense to the humans that are reading it. More on website *Usability* in the final chapter of the book.

When coming up with keywords, think of what people might be searching for when they look for a business like yours. Ask your customers what they search for when looking up this information. Asking new customers how they found you is especially insightful. We value the less technical customers' feedback way more than others, because this is your typical customer base. The searching public is made up mainly of non-technical people. Their answers always surprise us!

> **Tip:** *Whenever you have a chance to talk to a new customer, strike while the iron is hot. These folks always seem eager to tell us how they found us, plus their search path to us is fresh on their minds.*

Research Your Competitors' Keywords

Most times we don't have to reinvent the wheel when trying to come up with keywords. Simply look at the programming code of your high ranking competitors' websites. It's really easy.

The ability to see the code is incorporated into any *website browser*. First open your competitor's website. Go to the webpage that has to do with your business and your keywords. On both the Google Chrome browser and Internet Explorer, just right click and select "View Source".

The most valuable information is in the top area which is known as the *head* area of the programming code.

To see what they think is most important, first look at their *title tag*. Then look at their *keyword meta tag* and *description meta tag*. These tags will be surrounded by <>. For example <title>.

Let's look at an example of the HTML code from Greg's business:

```
<head>
<title>Laptop Stand $19.99 Recycled Compact Lightweight FREE SHIPPING
OFFER</title>
<meta name="keywords" content="laptop stand, Notebook Stands, Tray">
<meta name="description" content="Laptop Stand - $19.99 | Order 2 Get
Free Shipping | Recycled Material | Folds Flat | Lightweight | Reduces
Heat | More Comfort, Less Hunch | PINK Donations">
```

It's clear that "Laptop Stand" is his most important keyword phrase.

We'll discuss more on why Greg chose some of the other "non-keywords" in his title and description in Chapter 7, "How to Get Chosen from the Search Results."

> **Caution:** *Most SEO experts will tell you that the keyword meta tag is no longer valued at all by Google, and this is true in the sense that Google has realized that most people abuse this and therefore they don't give you any SEO juice for it. However, we believe that Google looks at this as your first chance to prove your integrity and white hat SEO. If they see that you have stuffed a bunch of keywords here and repeated them many times, you will get spanked. Therefore, list your main keyword or keyword phrase once and that's it!*

Google Keyword Tool – Re-named Google Keyword Planner

The *Google Keyword Planner* is your best resource for finding the most popular keywords for your business. It's free and easy to use. Visit www.PlayGooglesGame.com/google-keyword-tool for the latest link. This tool is part of the *Google Adwords* program. Adwords is an advertising program for Google and can be seen with a few *Sponsored Ads* that show up at the top and on the right side of the *Search Results Page*. You will need to register for a Google AdWords account. However, you do not have to actually buy any ads to use the tool. By the way, we are a fan of the Google AdWords program—another topic for another book, because all we talk about is the free stuff in this book.

You can type in a keyword that you think is popular and Google will list the number of times people search on it by region. They also list the competitiveness of the keyword, which is based off the number of people advertising for that keyword on their Adwords program. One strategy would be to look for keywords that are highly searched, with low competition.

One of the best features we like about this tool is that it will suggest other keywords that might be related to our keyword based on people's searching habits. These suggestions always surprise us as to what the common public is searching for in our industry. We're sure they will surprise you too, which is exactly why we say, "Don't get hung up on your industry jargon, or even the technically correct word."

See an example of the Google Keyword Planner below.

Focus On a Niche

Folks, this is useful for any industry, but it's imperative if you are in a highly competitive industry. We often talk about focusing on what you can win at. It's much easier to win in a specialized niche than trying to compete for the main category. Use the Google Keyword Planner to help identify niche keywords with low to medium competition and also that have high search volume.

> **Tip:** *It's much easier to be a big fish in a small pond, than a small fish in a big pond.*

One example from Greg's office ergonomic business is on the page where he sells office chairs. The keyword phrase "Office Chairs" is extremely competitive. However, he has hit a sweet spot with searchers for "911 Emergency Call Center Chairs" and "24/7 Chairs". These customers are looking for heavy duty chairs designed to hold up for 24/7 use, and Greg happens to sell a line of chairs that are specifically made for this. 911 Emergency call centers all over the country frequently buy from him—and it all originates from a Google search.

Industry Jargon

Be aware of I*ndustry Jargon*, *street jargon*, and *politically correct jargon*. We all learned early on in marketing 101 of English class that it's always better to "speak the reader's language" when writing anything. The common public might not be searching for the keywords from your industry jargon. It does not matter if your words are technically correct. The terms that folks are using in real life, and therefore plugging into Google, is what matters.

Technical jargon examples include "HVAC repair" when folks are just searching for "heater repair" to get their broken heater fixed.

Politically correct examples might be "Visually Impaired" versus "Blind" or "Stewardess", versus "Flight Attendant"—you get the picture.

> ***Real World Example:*** *See some examples on using industry jargon from Greg's manufacturing business: "Laptop" computers versus "Notebook" computers and "Concrete" versus "Cement".*
> *www.PlayGooglesGame/industry-jargon-keywords*

Older Words Are Safer

Many websites want to appear hip and up with the times and use newfangled words or even made up words. The truth is that people use old and familiar words when they search. Old words are best because people know them instinctively. Familiar words will pop into their heads easily when they do a quick search.

Long Tail Keywords

Long tail keywords are exactly that: complete sentences revolving around keywords. Google is paying more and more attention to long tail keywords because of voice search. People are starting to speak their search queries and Google is even encouraging it by the little speaker icon located prominently near the search box.

You can incorporate long tail keywords into your context by thinking about how a searcher might ask a question to Google. "How to tie a tie?" might be a good example of a popular long tail search query. If you sell ties, you might start your text on your page with: "Stop by and learn how to tie a tie at Bubba's tie shop." In fact we like incorporating "How to…" into our YouTube video titles as well. We think Google favors this; just a hunch…

Misspelled Words

Common *Misspelled Keywords* should also be a part of your strategy. Use the Google Keyword tool to discover these.

Keywords for the Home Page

One of the most important aspects of keyword strategy is to decide what main keyword or keyword "phrase" you want for the home page of your website. This should be your overall most important keyword or phrase. This should be no more than 2 to 4 words. There are exceptions, but the point is not to water it down with too many. It's easier to win for just a few focused keywords.

Your other "internal" pages within your website should have their own unique keywords as well. However, the home page needs special attention.

Keywords in File Names

A website is just a bunch of files strung together, as described in the website structure section above. You will have many opportunities to create file names on your website. A file can refer to anything from an *Image File* to a file that holds one of your *Internal Web Pages*. We'll elaborate on this in the "Keywords in URLs" section below.

> ***Caution:*** *When naming any file on your website, if you have more than one keyword as in a keyword phrase, you <u>must</u> separate the keywords with hyphens (dashes). Don't run the words together and never use a blank space to separate the keywords. You can also separate the words with underscores. However, hyphens are preferred. Either way, it is extremely important to separate the words and no blank spaces. A blank space shows up as %20 on website addresses, plus computers don't like blank spaces. The search engine spiders can find and read keywords more easily if you separate the words with hyphens, versus all the words running together.*

> ***Caution:*** *The characters in the file name should not contain any capital letters. Stick with all lower case.*

Keywords in Folder Names

All website files are stored in folders, also known as directories. You can also name a folder with your keywords. An example of this is the folder that holds all the image files of your website: www.PlayGooglesGame.com/images.

The significance of both file names and folder names is that this is all that the Google spiders see. **Other than the common folders like Images, Contact, and About, every single file and folder should have your keywords in it—make it easy for the spiders to see your keywords!**

Keywords in the Meta Tags

Meta Tags consist of internal information, hidden within the programming code of the website. Usually this information is never seen by human eye, but the *Google Spider Programs (Spiders)* see it and pay extra special attention to it. There are three important Meta Tags: 1. *Title Tag*; 2. *Description Meta Tag*; and 3. *Keyword Meta Tag*. (The keyword meta tag is not very important anymore, but fill them out and NEVER repeat a keyword here; that is called *Keyword Stuffing.*)

Meta Tags serve two purposes. First, they tell the search engines what your website is all about. Second, they can show up in the search results and tell people what your site is about.

> ***Learn More:*** *We know, we promised not to get to geeky on you. However, we have to talk about these Meta Tags. You don't have to know exactly how they work from a programming standpoint, you just have to know they are there and they are very important.*
>
> *The good news is that they are super easy to insert. Any website design program will make it obvious where to insert these meta tags, or your website designer will now how. Learn more and see screenshot examples from two popular website design programs (WordPress and Dreamweaver) at:* *www.PlayGooglesGame.com/meta-tags.*

Keywords in the Title Tag

The *Title Tag* (sometimes referred to as a Title Meta Tag) appears in two places visible to the human eye, which technically makes it just a tag, not a meta tag. It appears on the very top tab of most website browsers like Internet Explorer, Google Chrome or Mozilla. It also appears as the first bold blue line on your listing on the *Search Engine Results Page* (SERP). We'll discuss more on the value of that in Chapter 7.

Drum roll please…… **The absolute #1 best place to put keywords is in the** *Title Tag* **of your webpage.** Your home page title tag is the most important. Additionally, each internal page within your website should have its own unique title tag.

If all you get out of this entire chapter is this one tip, you will be well on your way to high ranking for those keywords.

Most websites get this completely wrong! Nine times out of ten, they will put the business name in the title tag. This is commonly referred to as *Vanity Advertising.* On top of that mistake, many websites assign the same title tag to every internal web page instead of using a unique title tag for each page, focusing on the most important keywords for that page.

We know, as much as it hurts—new customers do not know our names. Therefore, they are not searching for our names. They are searching for our products and services. Don't waste this most valuable keyword opportunity on something that your potential customers are not searching for.

In the Chrome browser example below, the Title Tag is shown as "Laptop Stand - Comfort is Ergonomic".

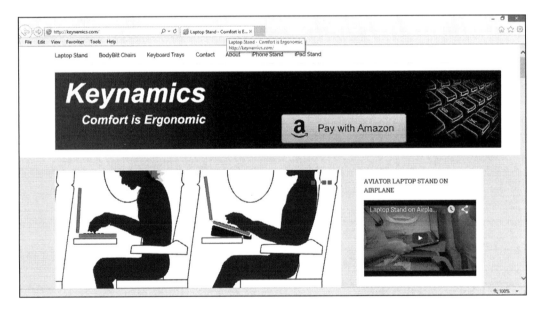

How To: *If you are absolutely bent on including your company name, then put it at the end of the keyword phrase and separate with a "pipe" symbol. For example, "Laptop Stand | Keynamics LLC" would be an OK title tag. However, we would never do this on our business websites, because if we are doing even the*

slightest things right in our SEO efforts, we will get high ranking for our business name without wasting this valuable real estate on it.

> **Tip:** *As with any keyword placement, your most important keyword must go first in the order of keywords in the Title Tag. For example, if you want local business, put your city name first; if Greg wanted local business from New York he would have used "New York Laptop Stand".*

An interesting side note is that the title tag appears very near the top of the HTML programming code, so it's the first thing that a spider sees. Spiders go from top to bottom when reading the programming code. An example of how the Title Tag looks in the HTML programming code:

```
<title>Laptop Stand $19.99 Recycled Compact Lightweight FREE SHIPPING OFFER</title>
```

More in Chapter 7 about why Greg chose these words for his home page Title.

Keywords in the Description Meta Tag

The *Description Meta Tag* serves two purposes and will be discussed in great detail in Chapter 7. First, it should include your keywords. Second, it should be worded with something catchy to get the attention of searchers and entice them with a *Call to Action*.

Plus, **now we are recommending that you include your phone number near the beginning of the description meta tag**, because many times people never open the link to your website, especially if they are searching from a mobile phone. Because they already have their phone in their hand, they simply call you directly from your phone number listed in Search Results on Google.

> **Quick Fact:** *If you don't specify a Description Meta Tag in your HTML code, Google will arbitrarily pick something out of your text and insert it there. That's a bad idea—you should pick the text you want!*

Keyword Meta Tag

Most experts agree that the *Keyword Meta Tag* is pretty much useless for SEO Juice because so many people abused it and stuffed it with keywords in the early days of SEO *Keyword Stuffing*.

We believe that Google uses the keyword tag as a test. If you stuff a bunch of keywords in it or repeat keywords, you have failed the test and Google will penalize you as being spammy or a black hat.

Therefore, list your focus keywords here, separate them with a comma and DO NOT REPEAT THEM!

Keywords in URLs

Drum roll again please...... Keywords in your URL are the second most important place to put keywords.

If you look at the structure and purpose of a URL, it can exist in one of three situations:

1. The Main Domain Name, as in PlayGooglesGame.com
2. A folder or directory (PlayGooglesGame.com/images)
3. An internal page or file name (PlayGooglesGame.com/keywords-in-url.html)

We're going to talk about two of these: *Internal Page* URLs and *Domain Name* URLs.

Domain Name Keywords: Let's start at the very beginning when you're first setting up your website and registering your *Domain Name*. You will jumpstart your findability for any keyword listed as your main domain name if you register it as your *Main URL*. If you have a keyword phrase, it is better to separate the keywords with hyphens (dashes).

Most businesses like to register their business name as their main domain name, and that's fine. One strategy to consider is to start off by registering a website with the keywords as the domain name.

> ***Real World Examples:***
> *www.Laptop-Stand.com*
> *www.Laptop-Ergonomics.com*
> *www.ancient-art-concrete-countertops.com*

You are probably thinking, "Boy, that's a lot of typing for folks to have to do." And you would be right, except for one thing. The vast majority (if not 100%) of people trying to get to your website are not going to be typing in your web address off your business card, or other forms of print advertisement; they are simply going to Google you.

> **Caution:** *If you have already established a history with your main domain name, DO NOT take it down for the sake of registering a new Domain with keywords in it. Your history has valuable SEO Juice!*

> **Note:** *We often debate the value of having keywords separated with dashes in the domain name with our peers. Most SEO professionals do not think this adds any SEO Juice. Some wrongly think that the Penguin update killed this. We always win the debate. The main reason for this is that it will automatically place your keywords in your anchor text when other websites link to you. You will learn more in Chapter 5 on Backlinks.*

Keywords in Anchor Text

Anchor text is the visible characters and words that appear in the hyperlink as it displays on the page, which is usually in blue and underlined. Anchor text should always contain your important keywords, whether you are linking to an internal page on your own website or when it comes from a *Backlink* from someone else's website. The value of anchor text in Backlinks is discussed in Chapter 5.

> **Quick Fact:** *Textual Hyperlinks can appear on a page as the actual URL web address or they can be coded to show only the Anchor Text. This is usually indicated by any words underlined and in blue.*

Keywords in the Internal Web Page URLs

You should decide what keywords are important for every page "within" your website—the *Internal Link Structure*—and not just your homepage.

For Example, on Greg's Keynamics website, he manufactures and sells iPhone Stands. On that page, "iPhone Stand" is the most important keyword phrase on that particular page. www.keynamics.com/laptop-stand.html

An *Internal Link* is a link to the other "internal pages" within your website. These links are how your visitors navigate to the various pages of your website. As seen in the example above, it appears after the ".com/". It is imperative that you list your most important keywords (separated by dashes) in the link structure. In our preceding Real World Example, "iPhone-Stand" is the keyword phrase appearing after the ".com/".

Please note that you should never use blank spaces to separate your keywords in these internal links and you should never run the words together. Hyphens (dashes) and underlines are allowed; dashes are the preferred method. This helps the spiders see your keywords.

In the Chrome example below the page link is www.keynamics.com/laptop-stand.html.

Note About Text Links & Internal Pages

There are two ways you can create a *Hyperlink* within your website: with real text or by using an image. This is the point of this heading and how it applies to your tabs or links along the top of your website to get to the various internal pages.

There are also two methods to put text on a website so that humans can read it. Text can be Textual (real text - actual typed letters, numbers, and symbols), or it can be Non-Textual (an image of the text).

A *JPEG* image of a logo with your company name spelled out on it is a perfect example of non-textual text. Your company name might consist of letters superimposed on the image, but it's not real text; it's just a picture of text.

Be aware that the computer programs that rank websites cannot read text that is simply an image; all it sees is one image (a JPEG image file) and no text. Therefore, you get zero *SEO Juice* for any text that might be on an image. It doesn't hurt and many times it's necessary to have images with text on them; just know that you don't get any value from it in ranking those keywords. A good rule of thumb is that if you can highlight the letters with your mouse, then it's "Real Text."

As far as our tabs along the top of our website linking to other internal pages go, using an image as a link is very common and is usually done with Buttons or Tabs. Buttons and Tabs are a more visually appealing way to link and navigate to all of the web pages within your website. These buttons are usually located along the top of any webpage and make it easy and intuitive to navigate throughout your website.

Using an image as a hyperlink to the other pages within your website is fine. However, you must repeat that link by using an actual *Textual Link* along the very bottom of your website in the footer. The Google spiders can follow text links much easier to navigate and discover all the pages within your website.

Keywords in Our Images

Being found on *Google Image Search* is such a huge opportunity and so underutilized that we decided to devote the entire next chapter to it. See Chapter 3, "Be Found on Image Search". This simple technique gets us so much business, it's just crazy that more people don't use it!

This basically involves renaming your image file with keywords. "dsc5267.jpg" straight out of the camera renames as "laptop-stand.jpg". Pay special attention to the next chapter on image search—you can win big time!

Keywords in Your Content

Chapter 6 will be devoted to *Content*. There are a few things to remember though.

First and foremost, Google will want to see those same keywords that we are placing in the other important areas, like the *Title Tag*, repeated in your text on your human readable webpage. If they do not see any of those keywords repeated in the textual content, you will get zero value for those keywords.

Keep your content keyword rich without overdoing it—no *Keyword Stuffing*! It's a balance between keyword rich and user friendly for the humans.

Your content should have your keywords sprinkled throughout. The challenge is to make it appear user friendly and logical to the humans that are reading it, while at the same time working in lots of keywords, so the Google spiders will also see it.

>**Note:** *It's very important to place your keywords in the very first sentence and in the last sentence on the human readable page.*

Remember, content consists of text, images and videos. Therefore, an image with the proper keywords needs to be surrounded with text with those same keywords in near proximity.

>**Learn More:** *You want the first sentence of text to appear as close to the top of the HTML code as possible. Therefore, look at your HTML code. Make sure your first sentence of text (hopefully with your keywords in it) appears as close to the Body Tag as possible. The Google spiders start at the top of the code and read down – just like humans do. The body tag appears up top right under the Head information. Hit those spiders right up front! Find out more at: www.PlayGooglesGame.com/keywords-near-top-of-code*

Keywords for Local Business

For those of us that want local business, be absolutely sure to include the name of your city, or the area/suburb of your city, as the central theme for your keyword strategy. Furthermore, it should be the first word in any keyword phrase.

It's much easier to rank high for a keyword along with your city name than trying to outrank the entire world for that keyword!

>**Note:** *Be sure and register your local business address in as many places as you can. Directories are a great place to register. For example, on Google Maps, Yelp, YellowPages, Yahoo Local, Bing, BBB.org, Angies List, Superpages, Citysearch. For a complete list visit www.PlayGooglesGame.com/local-seo.*

For off-page SEO, links from these sites are very important. Equally important are what's called citations. Citations are just mentions from these other websites of your business.

We'll discuss more about acquiring local business in Chapter 9, "Google Map Listings".

Keywords in the Footer

The footer refers to the bottom area of your visible website. If you want local business, then the best use of keywords in the footer is to include your physical address, which obviously includes your city name. Repeat this on the footer of every page.

Begin with and End with Keywords

Every webpage will have textual content. You must use your keywords in this content.

As mentioned above, the order of the keywords is important. This applies to just about any place you insert keywords. It also applies to the first appearance of visible text on any particular web page.

Visible text *(Textual Text)* is the text that humans can see. The text starts at the Body of the HTML code. We recommend that you work in your keywords into the very first sentence of visible text on each webpage. We are also finding that including those same keywords in the last paragraph helps too. Wrap the content on each page with keywords at the very beginning and the very end.

We'll talk more about content in Chapter 6, "Good Content – It's All Google Cares About".

Keywords in H1 Headings

The HTML programming code uses six levels of *Heading Tags* to help define the hierarchy and structure of a webpage. Just like a newspaper, all of your individual webpages need a good headline, and this is accomplished on a webpage with the highest level heading tag called the H1 tag.

Each level corresponds to a particular size of font. The highest level is H1 and equates to the largest font.

Not only does H1 indicate the largest font, it also signals the most important heading. Essentially, it creates the headline for your page. Place your important keywords in the H1 tag.

You can use the same keywords as your Title Tag. However, because it is actually viewed by humans, change it up a little so it reads like an attention grabbing and meaningful headline.

Focus on one H1 Heading per page and limit it to your most important keyword or keyword phrase; don't dilute it.

Just like the Meta Tags mentioned earlier, the H1 heading tag is easy to add in your website design program. See the WordPress page editor below.

Keywords in External Links

Anytime we link to another website, versus linking to a page within our own website, it's called an *External Link*. Using our keywords as anchor text in the hyperlink helps our SEO ranking.

Keywords in Other Websites

The single most important place to put your keywords *Off Page* is in the anchor text of a *Backlink*. The anchor text is the visible text that users click on to activate the link. We'll discuss this more in Chapter 5, "Get Backlinks – It's a Popularity Contest".

In Chapter 10, "Facebook – Google is Watching", we'll talk about the importance of proper keyword placement in naming your Facebook business page and coming up with a *Facebook User Name* which allows you to customize your Facebook business page URL.

Just keep one thing in mind when on other websites. Anytime you have a chance to participate in another internet platform or website, choose your keywords wisely and don't just put your company name in there.

Keywords in Schema.org

Schema.org is beyond the scope of this book because it involves programming code. However, we thought it was important to mention because it is a joint effort between the world's largest search engines: Bing, Google, Yahoo!, and Yandex.

These major search engines want to improve the web by creating a standard way to supplement the programming code of a website with additional *metadata* that helps search engines understand the true meaning and information on web pages.

Most webmasters are familiar with HTML tags on their pages. Usually, HTML tags tell the browser how to display the information included in the tag. However, the HTML tag doesn't give any information about the meaning of the text in the code, and this can make it more difficult for search engines to intelligently display relevant content to a user. Schema.org is a way for search engine spiders to make sense of content in your HTML.

The idea is to make it easier on webmasters by streamlining and standardizing this process, because currently, there are many standards and schemas for marking up different types of information on web pages.

Let's keep an eye on Schema.org because it is a work in progress. If you use WordPress to design your website, there are plugins and themes that automate the Schema markup for you. If not, talk to your website designer about including the Schema.org markup in your website.

Finding Keywords is Both Challenging & Ongoing

Coming up with keywords can be a challenge. You should allot a good amount of time and effort for your keyword strategy. Just like any business process, your keyword strategy should be in writing and defined as a business process.

Don't just rely on your own insight. Sometimes we can't see the forest through the trees. In order to get a good sampling of all web searchers, ask your customers, your employees, and friends how they would search for items you sell; especially new customers and "low tech" customers. Ask people with little or no experience in web search, not just the folks with online experience.

Try to figure out what words the lay person is using, not just the latest jargon from your industry. For example, the technically correct term for a portable computer is "notebook computer." However, they are most commonly referred to as "laptops." Greg decided early on that it was more important to feature "Laptop Stand" than the more technically correct term "Notebook Stand" for his invention.

> **Note:** *Throughout this book we will discuss many places that you can insert keywords (Websites – Title Tags – Content – Links - YouTube – Images – Facebook – Google Places - Blogs). The more places you insert them, the more Google can Connect The Dots— Play Google's Game.*

> **Bright Idea:** *Use YouTube for keyword research. First search YouTube for the keywords that you think are relevant. Note the descriptions people are putting in their videos. Also note the keywords in the comments people are typing. You should discover many new ideas this way!*

Best Practices – Action Plan

1. What Keyword (or keyword phrase) is the most important to your unique business qualities/services/products? More importantly, what keywords are your customers using to search for your unique qualities/services/products? These keywords should be emphasized everywhere on your home page, without overusing them. Go through this exercise for each individual webpage within your website. Do you want local business? Put your city name first in all of your keyword phrases.

_____

_____

_____

_____

2. Right click on your image files. What are they named? If they are composed of several keywords, are they separated by hyphens or underscores?

_____

_____

_____

_____

3. Are your links to all of the pages within your website "text" links with your most important keywords in them?

_____

_____

_____

_____

4. Right click on your competitors' images. Also, look at their meta tags (right click → view source) for good keyword ideas.

_____

_____

_____

_____

5. Sign up for an AdWords account and start using the Keyword Planner tool. Search for the keywords you think are relevant. What other keywords does it display? Are they getting lots of searches on them?

_____

_____

_____

_____

6. Are keywords (separated by underscores) used in the naming of your various "internal" web pages (the part after the ".com/")?

_____

Play Google's Game

Chapter 3

Be Found on Image Search

It's much easier to win on the Google Image search engine...

✓ Google is Asking for Our Help
✓ Get Good Images
✓ 5 Steps for Getting Images Found

This is such a huge opportunity that we decided to devote an entire chapter to Image Search. More and more people are using image search as a way to find products and services. Plus, most of your competitors have not figured this out. Optimizing your images for your keywords so that Google can rank them makes it easier to win with competitive industries or products. The fact that Google has dedicated an entire search engine to this should be an indication of its importance!

Highlights

Very Important:

- Google has a dedicated search engine just for images.
- Google wants us to help them rank our images.
- Google says: "Great image content is an excellent way to build traffic to your site."
- Images are easier to get top rank in competitive categories and industries
- Rename *all* image files with keywords.
- Give each image an ALT tag.
- Images on your webpage must be closely surrounded by text with the same keywords.
- Dedicate a space, equipment, and a program for capturing images.

Important:

- Blended search results boost the importance of image search.
- Google recommends that we optimize all of our images.
- Google prefers good quality, larger sized images.
- Put hyphens between keywords in the file name.
- Give images captions when inserting onto your website if your website design program supports it.
- Optimize PDFs for high ranking.

Helpful:

- Store all images in a folder (directory) called "images" on the server.
- Image searchers behave different than regular searchers.

Why is Google Image Search so Important?

Google Images is a very popular search engine service from Google. Optimizing your images to be found on *Google Image Search* is completely overlooked and underutilized by most businesses and web designers. Yahoo and Bing have their own *Image Search* versions as well.

It's so simple, we can't believe how many prominent websites do not optimize their images to be found. This is your opportunity folks!

Compounding the problem (or opportunity) is that some web designers don't believe in the value and importance of Google Image Search. They must not realize that Google and all the other search engines have an entire search engine devoted to ranking images.

We know that <u>all</u> Google cares about is good content. Content that their customers and our customers enjoy seeing. This content is in the form of Text, Images, and Video. Images really are worth 1,000 words and Google loves them so much, they created an entire search engine for them.

Google Dedicates a Separate Search Engine Just for Images

Prior to 2001, Google Search results were limited to simple pages of text with links. Interestingly enough, the most popular search query at the time was "Jennifer Lopez's green dress" (we can't make this stuff up). Google realized that an image search was required to answer this question. As a result of this, Google Image Search was born.

By 2001 over 250 million images were indexed. By 2005 this grew to 1,000,000,000 and by 2010, the index reached 10,000,000,000—that's ten billion images. By 2010, the service was receiving over one billion views a day.

Image Searchers Behave Differently

Another reason it's easier to win with Google Images is that the Google image searcher searches differently as compared to regular searchers—and it's not all about being in the first position on the first page, as it is with regular Google searches.

Google Images users tend to go very deep looking for the images they like, versus regular web searchers usually not going past the first page. This is actually one of the things we like about using Google Image Search ourselves in our personal searches. You can quickly scan a series of images and click on the one that grabs your attention. Therefore, there is a lot of "next paging" because users can consume results very quickly with the scan of the page.

Google also tells us that the filter bar at the top of Google image search gets used a lot. People filter by size, faces, etc. This behavior indicates that image searchers are digging deeper into the search results.

Blended Search Results

This is a more compelling reason for getting your images on Google Image Search. Have you have noticed that Google has been showing image search results right along with the regular *Universal Search* results on the main Google page? It's called *Blended Search Results.*

In the examples below, notice the top left "Web" underscored? That means that we are on the regular Google search engine (not image search). The first image is a picture of Greg's iPhone stand. iPhone stands are hyper competitive, but Greg can win with a #1 spot on Google image search.

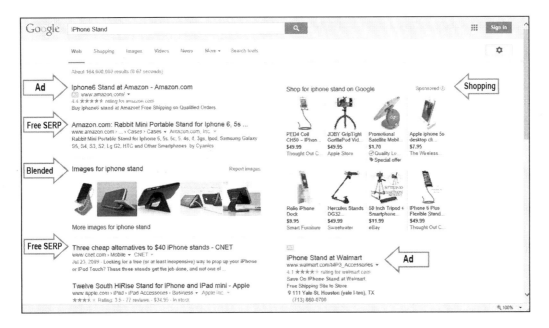

Play Google's Game with Images

Most importantly, it's all part of *Playing Google's Game.* Google *connects the dots* when you have images on your website, optimized for the same keywords that are located elsewhere in your website and in any of Google's other services (YouTube).

The good news is that not only do your images show up on Google Image Search, there is also a link from the image going directly to your website. If you have an interesting image of what they are looking for, it will increase your chances of getting them to click onto your website to "see more."

What we are talking about is the "Images" link/tab located in the top area of the main page when you open Google. In addition to its main search engine for searching webpages, which is also referred to as *Universal Search*, Google also provides many specialized search tools and services. Think of these as little miniature search engines within Google. By the way, if you are not using these additional search engines for your own personal searching activities, you are only getting about half of the value of Google. Examples are Books, Blogs, Shopping, etc.

Try the *Google Shopping* link the next time you want to buy something online—it will save you money! You can also study your competition's pricing on Google Shopping.

> **Tip:** *If you really want to go crazy on using Google Image Search, try their Advanced Google Image Search feature. Click here to see how:*
> *http://www.google.com/advanced_image_search*

With all of the fantastic features of Google Image Search, it's no wonder that this has become a very popular way to search and gather information on the internet. Will they find your images, or your competitor's?

Five Steps for Getting Your Images Found

While you can't directly upload your images into Google's Image Search engine, searchable images posted on most any website can show up in the search results after the Google spiders crawl that website. Simply by posting the image on your website, you'll make it possible for Google to find your image and add it to the Images index.

However, Google has asked us to help them rank our images. Their algorithms have gotten better at determining if an image contains people, animals and other basic elements. However, they can't tell the meaning behind the picture—the back story. After the Google spiders crawl your website, they try to classify your image and then rank it.

> **Caution:** *As part of the classifying and ranking process, Google tries to eliminate any duplications of images. They do not want to display the same images numerous times on the search results page! Therefore, we recommend that you use unique images that are created by you, versus copying images from other websites.*

Google ranks images using five factors: **1.** The file name of the image; **2.** The Alt Tag of the image; **3.** The Title Tag of the image; **4.** The link text pointing to the image; **5.** The text in the immediate proximity surrounding the image at the location it is on the website.

> **Learn more:** *Click here for a great video from Google on properly optimizing images.* www.PlayGooglesGame.com/optimize-images-google-search

> **SEO Juice Alert:** *Whether it's on your website or linking to your image from another website, use anchor text in links that point to the image or the page with the image.*

Step 1 - Image File Names

Google asks us to give our images detailed, informative filenames. The filename can give Google clues about the subject matter and back story of the image. It's also worthwhile to note that if Google can't find suitable text in the page on which we found the image, they'll use the filename as the image's snippet in the search results.

> **Caution:** *A descriptive file name is not the same as a bunch of keywords stuffed and repeated in the file name—Google watches for this and spanks you.*

As mentioned in the Chapter 2 section on Website structure, a website is nothing more than a bunch of files stung together. One of these file types is an *image file*.

"Every picture (or image) on your website should have a unique file name related to your keyword strategy."

The good news is that most of us are already doing this, even though we might not realize it. If you own a digital camera and know how to get the pictures off the camera onto your computer, then you are well on your way to optimizing your images to be found on Google.

You simply give an image a file name when you first save it out of the camera.

> ***How To:*** *Visit* www.PlayGooglesGame.com/saving-camera-images-to-your-computer *for a simple method of getting pictures from your camera to your hard drive. We use Windows functionality and it's much easier than using that bloated software (spyware) program that came out of the box from your camera manufacturer.*

> ***Quick Fact:*** *Google can index the following image file types: BMP – GIF – JPEG – PNG – WebP – SVG*

There are two common challenges with renaming image files to reflect your keyword strategy. First, the images come out of your camera with an arbitrary and meaningless file name like DCM8734. Second, your website designer is probably not going to manage all of the image file names for you. Even if they do, they are probably going to charge you for this, as it's not usually part of their service offerings.

Renaming Images from Your Camera

The first challenge is super easy. The image begins its life on the memory card in the digital camera where it's assigned an arbitrary name like DCM1234. During the transfer stage of getting the image from your camera to the hard drive of your computer is when you have the opportunity to rename it with a keyword or keyword phrase. You can also always change the file name (rename it) at a later date; just do it before you upload it to your website.

> ***Tip:*** *Two ways to rename an image:*
> ***1.*** *Open the image and click "File --> Save As" and type over the original file name which is usually highlighted in blue on the bottom of the open window;*

> ***2.*** *Windows: right click on the file, click "rename" in the new open window (the old name will be highlighted in blue), then type over it with your new file name.* ***Note:*** *Be careful not to change the file extension at the end (usually .jpg). We are only changing the part that comes before the ".jpg". You might have to un-highlight the blue over the .jpg.*
> *(On Macs: Click on the file to select it, then return on your keyboard. This*

will put the file/folder into rename mode, then you simply press return when you're done.)

At first you will probably transfer it from your camera to your "My Pictures" folder stored under your "My Documents" folder. We recommend that you set up a new file folder, just for your website pictures, within your "My Pictures" folder. You might want to name it "Website Pictures".

> **How To:** *Visit www.PlayGooglesGame.com/renaming-computer-images for a How-To White Paper with screen shots.*

Once saved on your hard drive, it remains there waiting to be emailed to your web designer, moved to your image file folder on your *website design program*, or uploaded directly to your website host server via a web based program like WordPress or an *FTP (File Transfer Protocol)* program.

> **Tip:** *Though it will not be absolutely necessary, we think it makes it easier on the Google Spiders to find all of your images if they are stored in a folder (directory) called "images". On the other hand, if you use WordPress, Google has also indicated that a good practice is to create a standalone landing page just for your images, with the ability to allow visitor comments.*

> **Tip:** *If you are using WordPress, visit this link to see a workaround for creating a special "images" file folder on your server that you can store your images in: www.PlayGooglesGame.com/wordpress-image-file-folder*

The JPEG file name ends up becoming part of the URL web address. Once it's placed within your website it might look something like:
http://www.keynamics.com/images/laptop-stand.jpg

Working backwards, you can see the JPEG image file name, which is stored in your images file folder, within your main domain (.com) directory on your host server. Think of each forward slash as a division up to the next file folder level of storage on the host server.

> **FYI:** *When naming any file on your website, if you have more than one keyword as in a keyword phrase, you <u>must</u> separate the keywords with hyphens (dashes). Don't run the words together and never use a blank space to separate the keywords. You can also separate the words with underscores. However, hyphens are preferred. Either way, it is extremely important to separate the words and no blank spaces. A blank space shows up as %20 on website addresses, plus*

computers don't like blank spaces. The search engine spiders can find and read keywords more easily if you separate the words with hyphens, versus all the words running together.

An example on naming files:
Right: *http://www.keynamics.com/ergonomic_office_chairs_bodybilt.htm*
Wrong: *http://www.keynamics.com/ergonomicofficechairsbodybilt.htm*

All Images are Internal Links

We discussed the value of keywords in the internal links of a website in the previous chapter. Every image on your website is an internal link that actually can open its own page, where just the image shows.

Try it yourself. Right click on any image on any website. From "Properties" copy and paste the link usually ending with .jpg into your browser address bar.

Therefore, every time you name your file name with keywords (the part attached to the .jpg), you are placing more keywords into internal links.

Helping Your Web Designer Helps You

Overcoming the second image challenge is easy. Most of the time we are supplying our web designers with images, whether it be our company logo or a picture of our latest product or service. Simply rename the image using the instructions above and forward it to your web designer, asking them not to change the file name. (You'll also want to give them similar instructions on assigning an *ALT Tag* and *Image Title* to each individual image as well, as discussed below.)

> ***Tip:*** *Create a simple Excel spreadsheet to help you keep track of all your image files. This helps you and your website designer. We create a separate worksheet for each page within our website. One column for the image file name, another for the location of the image on the page, another for the ALT Tag and another for the Image Title.*

Real World Example:
Correct file name: *"laptop-stand.jpg" or "laptop_stand.jpg" (without quotes)*
Incorrect: *"laptopstand.jpg" ... "laptop stand .jpg" ... "headerimagepage2.jpg"*

Step 2 – Alt Tags

The ALT attribute is used to describe the contents of an image file. It's important for several reasons.

It provides Google with useful information about the subject matter of the image. We use this information to help determine the best image to return for a user's query.

Many people—for example, users with visual impairments, or people using screen readers or who have low-bandwidth connections—may not be able to see images on web pages. Descriptive ALT text provides these users with important information.

Most website design programs make it super easy to assign an ALT Tag to your images when you first insert them into the website. It's as simple as filling in the blanks.

An ALT Tag serves a couple of functions in website design. It will display the text of the ALT Tag if the image can't display, and in some browsers it is the little yellow box that shows up when you hover your cursor over an image. The ALT tag is used for the visually impaired and will play the words of the text through their speakers.

The problem is that you can upload the image just fine with the ALT Tag option blank, and it is quicker and easier to do it this way, which is why most people do not take the extra two seconds it takes to fill in the blanks.

Step 3 – Image Title

The steps for assigning an image a title in your website design program are basically the same as they are for the image *ALT Tag* as described above. A few extra seconds of effort are well worth it.

On some browsers the *Image Title* is displayed as a short wide yellow box popup when a visitor hovers their mouse over an image (without clicking). Whereas the *ALT Tag* is for helping search engines rank your image AND visually impaired humans, the image title is more for people that can see.

So what's the difference? Just know that you should fill out both; worst case, just make sure you have an ALT Tag. Since the *Image Title* pops up when hovered over, it can be used as a "Call to

Action." As with any title, it should be relevant, catchy, concise and compelling. It's just sloppy SEO to leave either blank—especially the ALT Tag!

> ***Learn More: SEO Screen Reader Project*** *– Screen readers are mainly used by blind people. Instead of displaying web content visually in a Graphical User Interface on a monitor, screen readers convert the visual website text and the ALT Tags of visual images into synthesized speech (sounds like a robot) so that blind users can "hear our content." Our SEO Screen Reader Project uses one of the popular screen reading programs as a tool to review our websites. We think that if a site is totally accessible and friendly to a blind person, that's not only pretty cool, Google will also love it!*
> *www.PlayGooglesGame.com/seo-screen-reader*

Step 4 – Image Link Text

Image Link Text is also known as the *Anchor Text*. Basically it's the human visible text that is seen and highlighted as the hyperlink to the image on a website. Be sure and place keywords in this anchor text versus just showing the URL. Instead of www.keynamics.com/laptop-stand, consider "Laptop Stand Image". You can control how the link is displayed with a very simple command in the programming code, so just ask your website designer to always include anchor text on any text links to images.

Step 5 – Proximity Text

Provide good context for your image. The page the image is on, and the content around the image (including any captions or image titles), provide search engines with important information about the subject matter of your image. For example, if you have a picture of a polar bear on a page about home-grown tomatoes, you'll be sending a confusing message to the search engines about the subject matter of polarbear.jpg.

Wherever possible, it's a good idea to make sure that images are placed near the relevant text. In addition, we recommend providing good, descriptive titles and captions for your images.

Google also looks at the words that are located in the immediate vicinity of an image (*Proximity Text*). This is intuitive if you think about it. They figure the image must have something to do with the words that surround it on the webpage. Make sure your same keywords that you are optimizing the image for are in the text that is near the image.

Tip: *Right click on any of your competitors' website images, then click on "properties" to display the image's file name. It's a quick test to find out if they know this technique—plus you can find out their keyword strategy as well. For fun, do this on their company logo. Nine times out of ten, it's named something lame like homepagelogo.jpg. *Note: You might want to pay particular attention to those competitors with high ranking—do what they do. ;)*

Tip: *There is some debate about whether the characters in the file name should contain any capital letters. To be safe, I just stick to all lower case in my file naming scheme.*

SEO Juice Alert: *If your website design software allows you to put a caption with an image, that's also of great help to Google.*

Below is an example from Greg's concrete countertop business. WordPress allows him to insert captions on images. This example shows the source code. Notice "Caption" in the code?

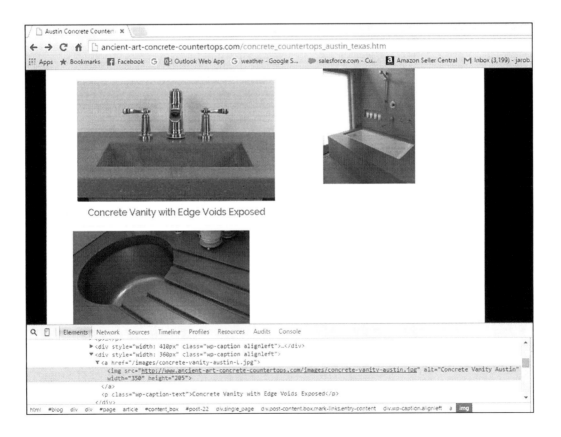

Caution: *Never remove or replace an image on your website without first checking to see if, by chance, it has high ranking. You never know, it could be number one, and if you remove it, it's lost.*

Learn More: *Click here for the latest image search guidelines from Google: www.PlayGooglesGame.com/google-image-search-guidelines*

SEO Juice Alert: *When uploading images to your website, specify a width and height for them. A web browser can begin to display a page even before images are downloaded, provided that it knows the dimensions. Specifying these dimensions can speed up page loading and improve the user experience, all of which Google loves! Without image dimensions, when the browser runs into an image, the browser has to pause loading the page, load the image, then continue loading the page. To learn more click: www.PlayGooglesGame.com/image-dimensions-seo*

Finding the Right Keywords

Naming files can be a little trickier than it would seem. For example, Greg has lot of image files on his www.keynamics.com website with "laptop-stand" in the file name.

You have to get creative to work in the same keyword rich name (laptop stand) while also keeping it organized by name for your own clarity. It does not matter what's after the keyword in the file name as long as you place a hyphen (or underscore) after the last letter of the keyword. (But make sure the keywords come first.) One file name could be **laptop-stand-black.jpg** and another **black-laptop-stand.jpg**. Notice how both image file names include the words "laptop stand". Note that the one with "laptop stand" at the beginning will probably rank higher because the order and the first words are important. Therefore, we would name our more important image that way.

There is a limit as to how many characters you can have in a file name, and your website design program will truncate it after you have reached the limit, so get creative with the keywords used in file names.

With hundreds of images, your keyword strategy can get complicated to keep track of. That's another good reason to create a spreadsheet for your image files, as mentioned in the tip box a couple of pages back, under "Helping Your Web Designer Helps You."

Capturing Good Images

The most common problem we see with business owners is that they do not have any good images, nor a dedicated program to capture ongoing images. Just like any business strategy, you need an ongoing policy to routinely capture images related to your business. You should incorporate your image program with your YouTube video program. More on YouTube in the next chapter.

Folks, the bottom line is that the searching public wants to see interesting images, and they need to be good quality images. That's the reason most of us love to search on the internet—images make websites look great—especially with the newer high definition screens. The iPad, for example, renders amazing images from webpages. Fresh images, continually updated, also get rewarded by Google as *fresh content*. The searching public wants to see videos for the same reasons, as discussed in the next chapter.

Dedicate a Space

A major obstacle we see with almost every business owner is that they do not have a dedicated space for their photography equipment. Establishing a space allows for quick access to your equipment, and it becomes a place where you can actually create photo shoots.

If you don't make it super easy to capture that special image, chances are that you will not bother with it.

Equipment Needed

You don't have to spend a lot of money and you don't have to be a photography expert to get quality images. Since you will be incorporating your image program with your YouTube video program, it uses the same equipment. If you don't want to capture videos (read the next chapter before you decide), then $150 buys you an awesome digital camera these days; you can get a set of photography lights by doing a "Google Shopping" search for less than $50, a tripod for $30, a white and black bed sheet (for backdrops) for $5 each, and many photo editing programs are free. You must have all of the above!

It is not that expensive to get set up, and once you start taking pictures and get comfortable with the process, it will not take up too much of your time, especially when you consider that your one time and effort to create the perfect image will also be creating a permanent 24/7 sales machine for your product or service. We recommend:

1. Table for placing product
2. Video Camera / Still Camera combo – $200 to $500
3. Tripod – $50
4. Three Photography Lights and stands (daylight, color balanced CFL Lights) – $150
5. Diffusion equipment and material for the lights – $50
6. Seamless Photo Paper Background and stand – $100
7. Colored Sheets – at least one black and one white $5 each
8. 3/16" Smooth plywood 48" x 48" for backdrops – two pieces – one painted flat black and the other painted flat white – $10 each

Taking great pictures is easy as well. Just remember the three most important things in photography: Lighting, Lighting, and Lighting. Poor lighting will make the most expensive camera in the world take a crappy picture and great lighting will make a cheap camera take awesome pictures.

Photography can be more art (or luck) than science. You might get one great shot for every ten pictures you take. This is why an ongoing policy to capture lots of images is best. The more you take, the better chance you will have of getting that great shot. Therefore, keep everything set up and ready to go in a designated area: camera on tripod, lighting and everything ready to capture that great moment.

Caution - What makes an annoying image?

1. Slow loading huge file sized images
2. Lack of pre-planning
3. Lack of proper editing (cropping, light balance, etc.)
4. Poor lighting
5. Small poor quality images (blurry, unclear images)
6. Buried way below the fold on the image landing page so they have to scroll all the way down to see it

Quick Fact: Google recommends large (dimensional size not file size), high quality images. This does not mean the image has to take up the entire page, and surely you don't want to slow down load times with an image that's large in file size. You can strike a balance with good photo editing software.

Framing the Shot

Your goal is to direct your audience's attention to the thing you want to focus on: the person, the product, the scenery, etc. You do not want anything in the frame area to be a distraction from what you want to focus on. Before you start, ask yourself, "Will this add to or take away from the video?" and think about the various positions of the objects in your frame—the composition.

> **Define: Framing** – *The presentation of visual elements in a video or still image, especially the placement of the subject in relation to other objects. Framing can make an image more aesthetically pleasing and keep the viewer's focus on the framed object. It can also be used to direct attention back into the scene. It can add depth to an image, and can add interest to the picture when the frame is thematically related to the object being framed.*

With framing, you can compose your shot to:

1. Give the image context (informing of the place/space you are in)
2. Give the image a sense of depth and layers
3. Lead the viewer's eye towards your main focal point

The goal is often to focus the viewer's attention upon the subject; this is accomplished by manipulating the viewpoint of the image, rather than the object(s) within. Framing is primarily concerned with the position and perspective of the viewer. The position of the observer has a lot of impact on their perception of the main subject, both in terms of aesthetics and in their interpretation of its meaning.

For example, if the viewer was placed very far away from a lone subject in an image, the viewer would gather more information about the environment and surroundings of the subject, but remain too far away to see his emotions.

In our businesses, many times we are taking a picture of a person. If you are, be sure to position them in the proper area of the frame. Their head should not be too close to the top, or the bottom. You should have enough distance between the camera and their face, but not too far. Consider placing their eyes at one of the four points in the frames using the Rule of Thirds.

> **Tip:** *Rule of Thirds – Divide the screen into three equally spaced, imaginary horizontal and vertical divisions. You'll end up with 6 equally spaced intersecting*

lines. The four points where the horizontal and vertical lines intersect offer four options to place your points of interest—the person's face, the interesting object, etc.

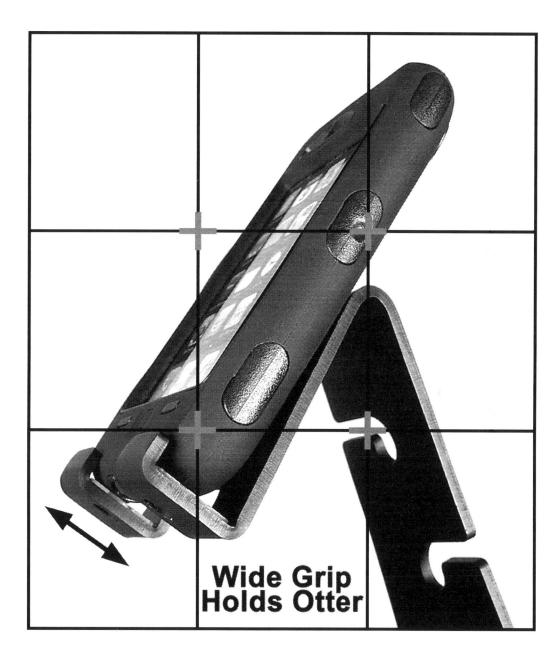

Lighting

Lighting is going to be your biggest challenge. Poor lighting can make an expensive camera look bad, and great lighting can make a cheap camera look fantastic. It's all about the lighting and you have to think ahead and plan for it: the time of day, the weather, etc.

> ***Learn More:*** *Lighting*
> *www.PlayGooglesGame.com/photography-lighting*

The goal of lighting is to create flat, diffused light and eliminate shadows. We're trying to mimic a bright overcast day, which are the best circumstances to take pictures. To do this indoors, use two lights, pointing towards the subject from a height just above the person's eye line. A good rule of thumb is to place the lights about three feet away from the subject. The lights should be located on either side of the camera, right in front of the lens.

Soften the light with diffusion material in front of the light source, or bouncing the light off another surface suitable for diffusing and reflecting it back on the subject.

> ***Tip:*** *A technique photographers use is to bounce the flash off a wall or ceiling. Conditions have to be right, but this works more often than not.*

Keep the subject off the background (wall) at least four feet to create separation between the subject and the background and eliminate shadows. A good trick is to bring in a third light and place it right behind the subject, low and pointing up to the back wall.

Background

Always think about and plan for your background. You never want a background to distract from your image. Your goal is to keep viewers focused on your message. Busy backgrounds and unorganized backgrounds usually deter viewers. There are several basic categories of backgrounds.

Never allow these things to clutter your background: messy paper stacks, cluttered bookshelves, dirty laundry, dirty walls, cluttered rooms, or cramped office space. Does the setting promote credibility, authority, and professionalism?

- **Natural Backgrounds** include any natural setting like the inside of your store, office, or maybe a product display. Natural backgrounds imply authenticity and are great for more personal impression—giving the viewer a peek at the "real world."
- **Solid Backdrops** are achieved with rolls of photography paper or some other sheet material as a backdrop. White backgrounds are effective for good contrast and adding text or other images in your photo editing software. See below for a great tip on giving the solid background a nice gradient affect.

- **Outdoor Backgrounds** are best shot on overcast days or in early morning or late afternoon hours; they call this the magic light. Shooting in bright sun, especially when the sun is directly overhead creates horrible shadows.

Best Practices for Backgrounds

1. For uninteresting or distracting backgrounds use a fast lens (50mm) to blur out the background and only have the subject in focus. This will keep the focus on the person and away from the background. This is called the Bokeh effect.
2. Indoor, natural backgrounds are best shot on cloudy days when the ambient light is diffused. Harsh sunlight coming in the windows at various times of the day make for distracting backgrounds.
3. For solid backgrounds, use seamless photo paper and create a nice gradient effect by shining a single light up from the floor, onto the backdrop, directly behind the person.
4. Remove any distracting things like paper on the floor, fake plants, etc.
5. Usually bright background colors like Yellow, Orange, or Red cause color reflection and can be unflattering to your subject. Stick with muted tones like grey and dark blue.

Learn More: Blurring the background (Bokeh) is a great way to bring focus to the subject, especially when the background is ugly or distracting. There are several techniques to do this. Learn more at:
www.PlayGooglesGame.com/blur-image-backgrounds

Editing Images

Sometimes we get lucky and can use the picture right out of the camera. Often times though an image will need a little editing to make it pop.

We use Photoshop, and with their new monthly cloud based fee program, it's not that expensive. There are many lower cost and free alternatives. With photo editing software you can:

- Crop the image
- Adjust the physical dimensions of the image
- Adjust the file size of the image (smaller = faster load time)
- Adjust the resolution of the image
- Adjust the brightness, contrast, exposure, and color balance

- Add effects

   How To: See www.PlayGooglesGame.com/editing-images for a few simple tips on taking great pictures, editing them, and the latest recommendations for photo editing software.

   Caution: We can't give legal advice. However, you should know that if you take a picture of a person, whether it be a family member, employee, or customer, you should get their permission to use their picture "likeness" on your website (or anywhere for that matter). Attorneys call this a <u>Model Release</u> and this should be in writing (ask your attorney; other legal issues might apply).

   Tip: Do you need some high quality, copyright free images? Check out Wikimedia Commons for over 12 million freely usable, high quality images: www.PlayGooglesGame.com/copyright-free-images

Image File Size – For Fast Loading

Google recommends fast loading websites and users like them as well. Therefore, there is a balance between creating a larger (dimensional sized) image, and a slow loading, humongous file sized image. We know Google recommends larger sized, beautiful images, appearing above the fold. With a good photo editing program, you can reduce the file size without reducing the apparent quality to the naked eye.

Optimizing PDFs to Be Found on Google

Optimizing PDF documents is another one of the most overlooked SEO strategies around. While technically a PDF is not an image per se, and it is not part of Google Image Search, we thought the best place to put PDF SEO Optimization was here in our Image Search Chapter. Plus, Google has announced that it has the ability to find and display images within PDFs in the Google Image Search results. We'll show you how below.

Google treats a PDF file as a standalone webpage. This means that when a user clicks on a link to a PDF file, Google displays the whole PDF as if it were an entire webpage. If you think about it, that means that Google must think PDFs are very important!

Further proof that Google likes PDFs is that you can go to "Advanced Search" on Google and

search by file type, as seen below:
http://www.google.com/advanced_search

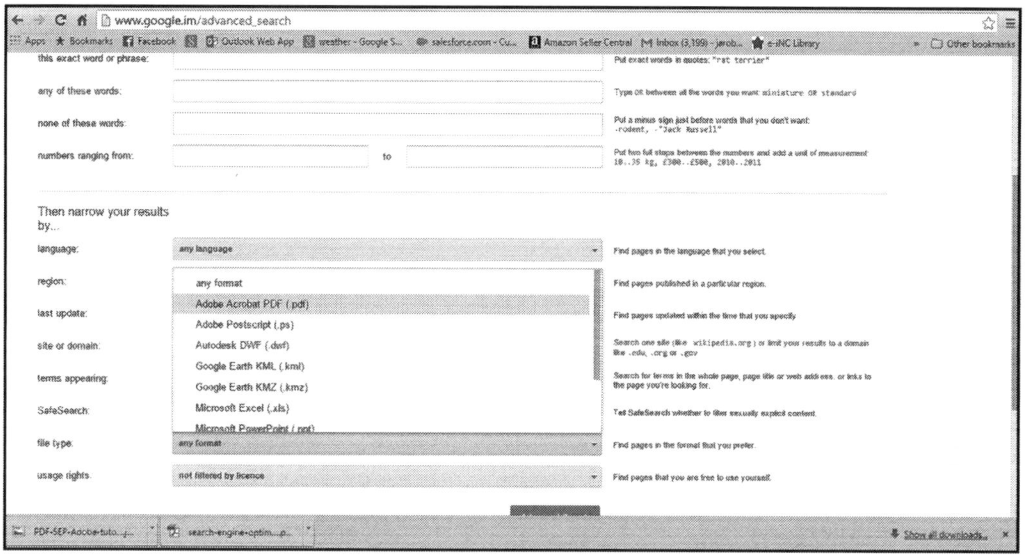

Quick Fact: *You can recognize a PDF webpage because it will have .PDF at the end of the URL.*

You will hear some SEO consultants discourage the use of PDFs as an SEO strategy. We wholeheartedly disagree! Sure, there are exceptions and sure, if it's so important that it should be incorporated as content in an actual page of your website, then it should be converted to a standalone webpage using standard HTML coding.

The fact is that is that Google loves content, and a properly optimized PDF is a treasure trove of content of which Google can recognize the text, images and links inside of the PDF. One of the first points we'll go over is that the text, links and images contained within the PDF must all be editable text, versus just a picture of text. Oftentimes you will get a picture of text whenever you scan a document and save as a PDF. In this sense the entire PDF is just one big image and Google can't index it properly. This is NOT what we are going after. WE want Google to be able to understand what the PDF is all about and rank it for us.

All the text, images, tags, and links within a PDF can be crawled as long as security has not been set on the PDF to disallow this.

Beware of using large PDF files. If your PDF files are many pages of text, images, and links, this might impact end-user satisfaction and water down the keywords, just as we have discussed in your keyword strategy. You want to focus on just a few keywords, so it's better to create smaller PDF files, and if you do have a large one, break it up and interlink them if necessary.

How Google Displays PDFs in the Search Results

A PDF is a very popular image and text file format from Adobe. Whenever you click to download a PDF document, you must have a program installed on your computer to open and see the image called *Adobe Reader* (formerly *Acrobat Reader*). This is a free program from Adobe. You have to download it and install it on your computer, and because it's so popular, most of us have already done this.

Usually a PDF has its own separate URL web page that comes up when you click to download it from any website. This is normally a separate page, or window that opens. In fact, Google views the PDF as just another web page and indexes it just like a normal web page along with all the search results.

Google will display your PDF right along with the other search results and note it with a [PDF] in the beginning.

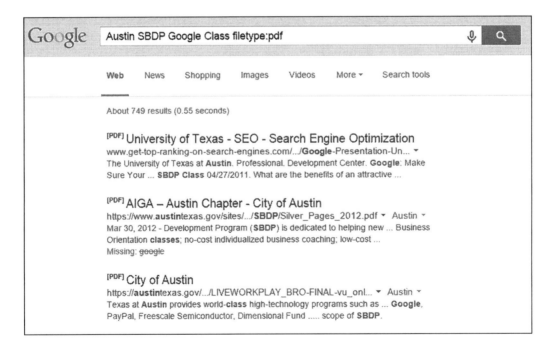

Eight Factors for PDF SEO

Google ranks PDFs according to eight factors. Does it contain: **1.** Real "editable" text; **2.** A keyword rich file name; **3.** Meta Data; **4.** A keyword rich title; **5.** Keyword rich textual content (just like a web page); **6.** Reduced file size; **7.** Links back to your own website within the PDF document; **8.** Keyword text used in your PDF links.

1. **Does it contain real "editable" text (no images of text):** Be sure that your PDF document contains plain text and not words in the form of pictures. PDF files can be an image only PDF or they can contain real text. When PDFs are scanned it usually creates this "image" problem. If your PDF document was scanned, you can use Optical Character Recognition (OCR) tools to convert it to text. Adobe Acrobat offers these tools. A good test to see if a PDF document is real text or just one big image is to open it in Abode Reader or Adobe Acrobat, select some of the text and to try to copy it. If you can select it, then it's editable! For the above reason, whenever creating PDFs from scratch, start with a text editor like Word or PowerPoint; never use an image editor like Photoshop.

2. **Set the SEO-friendly URL / file name:** The file name that you save the PDF document as becomes the last part of the URL. The most important thing you can do in PDF SEO is to give the document a short file name, which would contain the keywords. Be sure to separate the keywords with hyphens, or it will show up as %20, and we know that computers hate blank spaces.

3. **Meta Data:** Title, image ALT Tags, and Heading markup: Google crawls and indexes this meta data within the PDF.

4. **A keyword rich title:** In Adobe Acrobat follow these instructions: **File → Properties → Description**

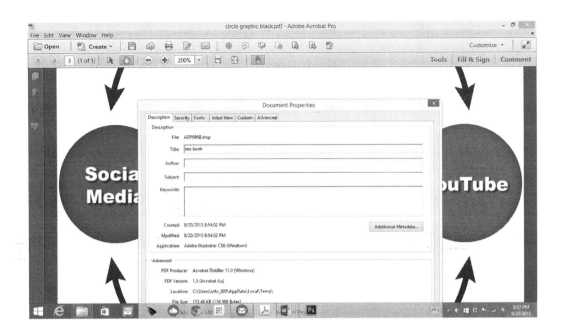

5. **Keyword rich textual content:** Just like a web page.
6. **Reduced file size:** Smaller is better. Try to keep it under 2.5 megabytes. Adobe Acrobat allows you to reduce the file size when you save it.
7. **Insert links back to your own website within the PDF document:** It's important to know that when a user opens a PDF from the search results, the entire PDF is displayed as a standalone "landing page." As far as usability goes, the user is not really on a page of your website, thus they will not have an easy way to use the typical navigation tabs along the top to get to your Home Page, the Contact Us page, or any other page for that matter. This is important because you really do want the visitor to "stick around" and explore more about your business. One way around this is to always include those links at the top of your PDF, along with your Logo for branding. At the very least, include a link to your home page prominently near the top. You could make a template for this in Adobe Acrobat, and use it to pop in your other content.

8. **Use keyword text in your PDF links:** The PDF's Link Text is also known as the *Anchor Text*. Basically it's the human visible text that is seen and highlighted as the hyperlink to the PDF on a website. Be sure and place keywords in this anchor text versus just showing the URL. Instead of www.keynamics.com/laptop-stand-instructions.pdf, consider "Laptop Stand Instructions". You can control how the link is displayed with a very simple command in the programming code, so just ask your website designer to always include anchor text on any text links to PDFs.

Place Keywords in the ALT Tags for Images within a PDF Document

Yes, you can even add image ALT tags to images within the PDF. This is just as important as including the ALT tag in regular image search, as mentioned earlier in this chapter. In Adobe Acrobat Pro follow these instructions:

View → Tools → Accessibility → Set Alternative Text

This opens a dialog box; just follow the screen prompts. Below is an example of Greg's PDF document of instructions for hosting a WordPress website on GoDaddy.

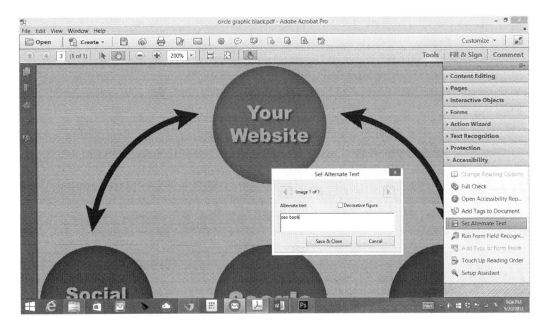

Tip: *Do not save the file to the latest Acrobat version. Instead save PDF files in an older version of Acrobat. Select maybe 2 versions back. Many users may not have the latest version of the Adobe Acrobat Reader.*

Quick Fact: *While <u>Adobe Reader</u> (formerly Acrobat Reader) is free, it only allows you to view and print the PDF file. If you want to create, edit, or change the meta data within a PDF (including the PDF Title), you will need to buy the full version of Adobe Acrobat Pro. This is a wise investment and will be beneficial in other areas of your business.*

Tip: *Personal Search Tip – If you want to search only for PDFs, add "**filetype:pdf**" to the end of the search term in the Google search box—this works on Yahoo and Bing as well.*

Best Practices – Action Plan

1. Research your competitors by right clicking on their images and looking at properties. What ideas can you get from studying your competition?

_____

_____

2. How will you dedicate a space, equipment, and a program for capturing images? How will you communicate this to all employees?

_____

_____

_____

_____

3. Start a spreadsheet with column headings: Image Location | Description | File Name | ALT Tag. Then go through every page on your website and fill in the blanks. WARNING: DO NOT CHANGE ANYTHING ON AN IMAGE THAT ALREADY HAS HIGH RANKING!

_____

_____

_____

_____

Chapter 4

Be Found on YouTube

Because Google owns it

✓ YouTube is the #2 Search Engine
✓ Easier to Win in Competitive Industries
✓ Improves Google Rankings

Folks, we are at a critical juncture in history when it comes to the internet and video. We already know that Google loves video; after all, they do own YouTube, the second largest search engine in the world (second to Google, of course).

Uploading videos to YouTube is another easy marketing strategy that you can win at by simply playing Google's game. This is a fantastic opportunity folks. We are finding that most businesses (your competitors) are not taking advantage of the power of YouTube to grow their business online. This can be game changer. Get in now—It's Free!

The statics are fantastic, with over a billion users, and the fact that eight out of the top ten celebrities among teens are not movie stars or famous singers, but YouTube creators, just like you. This speaks volumes about the tsunami that is upon us. Just over the past few years, the increases in mobile viewers watching video have been astonishing. In 2015 mobile video surpassed all video internet traffic!

This trend will continue as wireless providers continue to relax their caps on data and offer even more opportunities to connect to WiFi. Furthermore, mobile device hardware manufacturers will continue to develop faster, larger, and less expensive smartphones and tablets.

We previously talked about the power of Google Image search. If the old cliché proves true, "A picture is worth a thousand words," then a video is worth a million! No other media has the power to influence like video, and with recent advancements in technology, the level of consumer interaction available with our videos has gone through the roof!

We know that <u>all</u> Google cares about is good content. Content in the form of Text, Images, and Video. Video is the ultimate form of content—that's why Google paid billions of dollars for YouTube in the first place. Google knows that YouTube is the best way we can connect to our customers. It's those connections that Google is watching in order to rank us, on YouTube and on the regular Google search engine.

Furthermore, Google wants to help you be a successful creator of videos. Google knows that YouTube is only successful if their creators are successful. You will find links in this chapter to instructions where you can learn directly from Google itself. For help: www.PlayGooglesGame.com/youtube-learning

Define: Creator – *The producer of the video = YOU*

Highlights

Very Important:

- YouTube is owned by Google
- YouTube is the #2 Search Engine in the world
- YouTube videos boost your website in the regular search results
- Blended Search Results – videos mixed in with regular search listings
- YouTube is a search engine for videos
- Google counts video as the highest form of "Good Content"
- It's easier to rank high on video searches in competitive industries
- Learn to properly optimize your videos for high ranking

Important:

- Video is the most powerful form of communication
- Gritty video is Great – Real world is Best
- No need for high dollar professional videos
- Buy video editing software
- Always think about ways to engage your viewers to act (click – comment – like – share – subscribe)
- Build traffic to your website through engagement
- Build trust by connecting you to your audience

Helpful:

- Set up a dedicated area with a video camera ready to go; same for taking still photos
- Increase your repeat business by keeping customers engaged
- Use your mobile phone to edit and upload on the fly

Why is YouTube So Important?

YouTube is the third most visited website in the world. Technically, YouTube is a search engine of videos. Therefore, YouTube ranks #2 as the most visited search engine in the world—right behind Google itself!

Even better… **Google owns YouTube**, which means that Google is paying extra special attention to businesses that have uploaded YouTube videos, optimized those videos with their keywords, linked those videos back to their own websites (from YouTube), and then embedded those YouTube videos into their websites.

Because YouTube is a search engine unto itself, and the fact that YouTube is owned by Google, should be a clue that Google is starting to place a high priority on websites that embed YouTube videos, especially when they are uploaded by you, linked to your website (from YouTube) and the "YouTube" videos are embedded within your website.

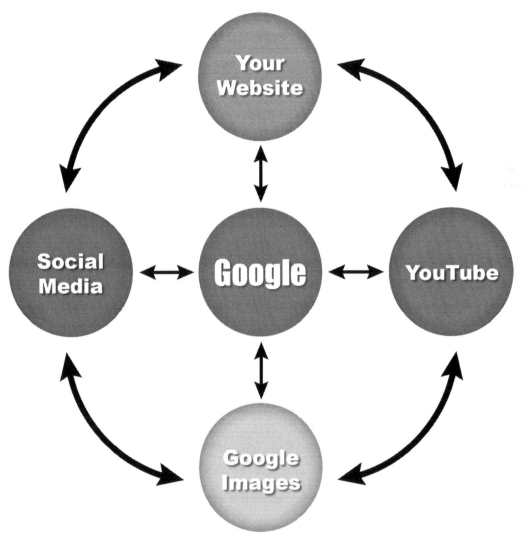

What we are talking about here is actually two separate search engines. Achieving high ranking on Google for competitive items is getting harder and harder. However, you can get higher ranking on YouTube simply because there are not as many websites incorporating videos.

The added benefit of having a video on your website is that it improves overall Google ranking because "Google Loves Content"—especially if that content is YouTube video content. Google figures that your website is more "relevant" and useful if you have a video; if not, they figure you are antiquated and not as useful.

Recent Consumer surveys reveal that three-quarters of shoppers are more likely to purchase a product or service if they can watch a video explaining it beforehand. Think about it; do you think a website with videos creates a better experience for the searching public?

> **Learn More:** *For the latest YouTube statistics, click* *www.PlayGooglesGame.com/youtube-statistics*

> **The Double Whammy:** *Optimized videos get high ranking on YouTube, plus they'll get your overall website higher ranking on regular Google searches. Google has this big umbrella over all of their enterprises (YouTube included) and they are connecting the dots between the YouTube and Google search engines. The reasoning behind all this is based on Google's golden rule: "relevance."*

Blended Search Results

Still not convinced? Maybe you have seen that Google is starting to "blend" YouTube Videos right at the top of the Google search results on page one. It's called *Blended Search Results*. Furthermore, the blended YouTube listing in the Google search result shows a little thumbnail of the video, which makes it stand out more and more likely that the searcher will click on it.

So even if you don't value YouTube searches (we don't know why you wouldn't), just know that Google is watching, and displaying thumbnails of our videos near the top of the search results. It's all connected!

In the example below, a regular Google search was conducted for "How To Install a Keyboard Tray". The very first listing above the regular search results is a YouTube video Greg did years ago. It's still there selling for him 24/7.

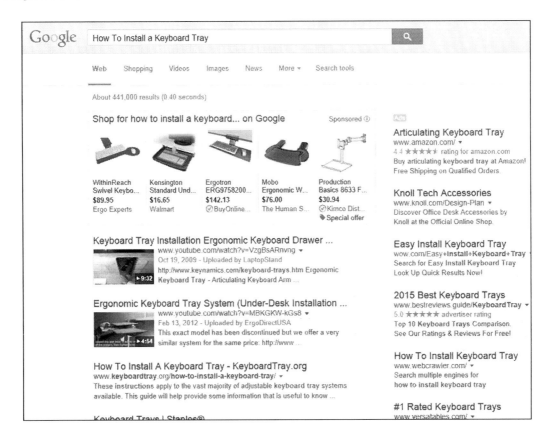

Furthermore, as we conduct informal surveys in every class, we ask how many of the business owners have ever uploaded a YouTube video at all. While the number has increased over the past few years, only about 10 to 15% of the students raise their hands. Even businesses that do take the time to upload videos are not optimizing those videos for their keywords correctly. This means that you have low competition in the #2 most visited search engine in the world. This is low hanging, easy picking fruit folks!

Video is the most engaging and effective form of marketing and communication.

Video is becoming more mobile and more social. Therefore, it is quickly becoming the most viable marketing opportunity for every business, from large corporations to local brick-and-mortar Mom and Pop businesses. Video provides your business with a chance to display your company's personality in living color.

Video has already become a primary focus for major advertisers and marketers. All other advertising formats will give way to video. The next big thing is already here!

Caution: *There is a rumor going around internet marketing circles that Google is* *penalizing websites without videos. In the near future, Google will probably soon ban websites that don't contain videos from the first page of the search results. Google knows videos are the ultimate form of content.*

The main point here is that achieving high ranking on a regular Google search for competitive items is getting harder and harder. However, you can get higher ranking on YouTube simply because there are not as many businesses uploading YouTube videos and optimizing them for your competitive keywords.

Benefits of YouTube Videos

1. Videos positively influence consumer buying decisions.
2. Videos leave a positive impression of your company.
3. Videos make the company look trustworthy.
4. Your perceived industry expertise goes up with a video of the business leader included on your website.
5. Increase stickiness, decrease bounce rates and increase conversion (sales) with a video on the landing page.
6. Blog or Facebook posts with videos attract three times as much interaction as plain text posts.
7. Consumers like product description/demonstration videos.
8. Everyone finds videos helpful when making a purchase decision.
9. Videos increase product knowledge.
10. YouTube is the #2 search engine in the world, beating out Yahoo and Bing.
11. YouTube is a social media site.
12. Most people will visit your website after viewing a video.
13. People are more likely to watch a video on your website than read text.
14. Google favors websites with videos in their ranking index.
15. More searchers will click on a video (blended) search result than a regular one.
16. Exponential growth is expected in the next few years.
17. Most of us are visual learners.

Tip: The ideal length of a video to inform a purchase decision is five minutes or less. However, there are circumstances where a longer video is fine too. For example, an instructional "How To" video.

Tip: Video Blog Posts – Any post that you have already published on your blog can be turned into a video. In fact, most blog posts can be turned into several videos. You can create a series of one to two minute videos that focus on a specific aspect of a topic. You just film yourself or another member of your team talking into the camera. You can answer a question, or you can just provide some useful information for your viewers. Most people prefer to watch instead of read—so take advantage.

Real World Example: *Gritty Video is great - You don't need to be a Hollywood director to make a great video. YouTubers want a "real world" experience; they want to see the owner, customers and employees interacting. Bottom line, you don't have to spend $20,000 on a professional video (RWE: 3M YouTube adhesive tutorials). See www.GrittyVideo.com*

Just Do It

OK, time out, take a breath… Hopefully we have convinced you that YouTube is the future of internet marketing and the ultimate form of content that Google is looking for. The rest of this chapter is devoted to helping you create interesting videos so you can please Google, build audiences, create loyal customers, and increase sales.

Basically there are four steps to making a video go live on YouTube:

1. Shoot it
2. Edit it
3. Upload it
4. Optimize it

Please, please don't let all of these details deter you from getting started right away. Just record something and upload it. You can always delete it later and you are going to need the practice! We promise, once you get used to doing this, you will gain the confidence that you need and it will become second nature. Folks, it needs to become second nature for you. If it isn't, you will either procrastinate or your lack of confidence will show through (or both), turning away potential customers.

After reading the next two sections about setting up your account & uploading, you should have a basic understanding of how to go live with your first video. Don't get hung up on all the details that follow in the next sections of editing and optimizing right now—Just Do It!

Setting Up a YouTube Account

A YouTube account is free and uploads are free. If you already have a Google account (Gmail or YouTube), simply log on. If you don't have an account, it takes less than a minute to create one. See tip below.

You need a Google Account to sign into YouTube. A Google Account works across all Google products (e.g. Gmail, Blogger, Maps, YouTube, and more).

> **Learn More:** *Setting up a YouTube account:* *www.PlayGooglesGame.com/youtube-account-setup*

If you've signed into any of these products before, you already have a Google Account. To sign in, enter the email address you entered on those products (if you use Gmail, it's your Gmail username). If you don't have a Google Account, you can create one on YouTube.

> **Note:** *Link to create a Google account: www.PlayGooglesGame.com/google-account-set-up*

A Google Account gives you access to Google products like Gmail, Google+, YouTube, and more with a single username and password. A Google Account comes with a Gmail address and a Google+ Profile. Once you create a Google Account, you can use that same username and password to sign in to any Google product.

Here are a few important things to remember about Google Accounts and YouTube:

1. You sign into YouTube with your Google Account. To sign in to YouTube, enter your Google Account email and password. After signing up for YouTube, if you sign in to your Google Account on another Google service, you'll be automatically signed in when you visit YouTube.
2. Deleting your Google Account will delete your YouTube data, including all videos, comments, and subscriptions. Before you can delete your Google Account, you will have to confirm that you understand that you're permanently deleting your data on all Google services, including YouTube.

With a Google Account, you can access many YouTube features, including Like, Subscribe, Watch Later, and Watch History. YouTube can also recommend videos based on what you've watched, liked, and subscribed to.

> ***Note***: *In order to upload videos, leave comments, or create playlists, you must create a channel on your account.*

Create and Optimize a Channel for Your Business

A YouTube channel is a central location for all your video content. Think of your YouTube channel as your home page on YouTube.

Just like we optimize videos for high ranking, we have the opportunity to optimize our channels as well. If they are optimized properly, YouTube will also show our channel itself listed high among the videos ranked in the YouTube Search Results.

> ***Learn More:*** *YouTube has a learning center called "Creator Academy":* <u>*www.PlayGooglesGame.com/youtube-learning*</u>

Just like a home page on your website, you can create a header with YouTube Channel Art, which is the banner image at the top. This should match your branding in your other marketing efforts.

Playlists are a feature in your channel that allows you to organize your videos into groupings based on topics. Begin grouping videos of a similar topic into playlists. Use keyword focused titles for your playlists. Write a keyword focused description for the playlist.

Playlists also help YouTube rank your videos, and the playlist's title and description are important in that process. Google and YouTube are even ranking playlists in the search results.

Steps to Create and Optimize Your Channel

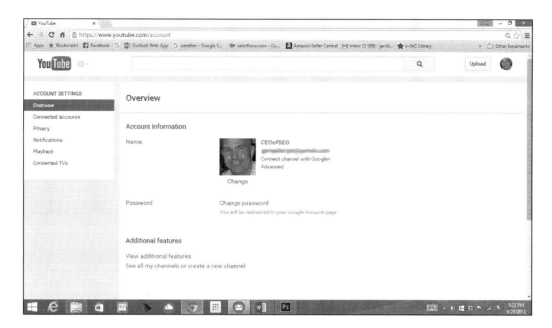

1. Make sure you're signed in to YouTube (or your Google/Gmail account).
2. From your account page, go to "See all my channels". If you want to make a YouTube channel for a Google+ page that you manage, you can choose it here. Otherwise, click Create a new channel.
3. Name your Channel Title with your company name and a couple of keywords.
4. Give it a description, which appears under the About tab. The first sentence is very important on the description because it shows up in the snippet on the search result listing.
5. Enter your channel keywords, starting off with your main ones first. The keywords use spaces to separate, so if you have a keyword phrase, surround it with quotations.
6. Create your Channel Header.
7. Create your Channel Icon.
8. Create your Channel Trailer.
9. Create Your Playlist. After you have uploaded a few videos, playlists are helpful for organizing and showcasing your different types of content.

Tip: Curate Sections in your playlist from other channels that might have interesting content for your viewers. Collecting and sharing videos from across YouTube on your channel will help you offer even more value to your fans.

Uploading & Optimizing Your Videos for YouTube & Google Search

Now that you have set up an account and optimized your channel properly it's time to start uploading some videos. The order of this might seem a little out of sorts, since technically you have to record the video first. However, we're saving that for the next section.

Optimizing our videos for YouTube uses the same concept as optimizing our website for the search engines and most of it is done during the uploading process. We're simply optimizing the video for our keywords that our customers are searching for on YouTube (and Google). Like regular search engine optimization, the goal is to get our videos to show up high in the YouTube search results— preferably in the top 10. This only takes a few seconds and it is done using the various metadata areas, which YouTube provides at the YouTube upload dashboard.

> ***Define: Metadata*** *– In this case YouTube refers to Metadata as any and all additional information provided on a video. This includes the title, description, tags, clickable annotations, and thumbnail image.*

YouTube uses ranking factors to determine which videos get shown at the top of each search results page (SERP). Google is looking at signals from things like your video's click through rate, number of views, the amount of time viewers spend watching it, the ratings, comments, sharing, and last but not least, the backlinks directly to the YouTube video URL. They're looking at the interactions of real people sharing and discussing your content.

> ***Learn More:*** *Learn how to "get discovered" by optimizing your YouTube videos on YouTube's Creator Academy.*
> *www.PlayGooglesGame.com/youtube-academy*

YouTube is also going to look at the total number of channel subscribers, how many times your video appears in a user's playlist, how often a viewer favorites it, and how many times it's been embedded on a website; see "embed code" a few chapters down.

> ***Black Hat Warning:*** *Please don't try and game the system; YouTube will catch you. Google says, "Please do not use these features to game or trick our search algorithms. All metadata should be representative of the content contained in your video. Among other things, metadata added in an attempt to game search algorithms will lead to the removal of your video and a strike against your account."*
> *www.PlayGooglesGame.com/youtube-quality-guidelines*

***Define: Click Through Rate** – Google tracks how often a video is clicked on as compared to other videos in the search results for those same keywords. If your video is clicked on more, then you are going to go up in the rankings.*

Uploading Your Video File to YouTube

YouTube supports just about any popular video recording file format and uploading is simple. First you have to save your video file into a folder on your computer. We find the process of uploading much easier on a PC or Mac, but it's also becoming easier and more intuitive with new mobile devices every day.

Log into your Google account, preferably on Google Chrome (if you are not already logged on). Click the YouTube icon near the top right part of the webpage, under "Apps". Once YouTube.com is loaded, you will see a big icon button at the top right that says "Upload".

***Learn More:** For the latest tips on uploading from various devices*
www.PlayGooglesGame.com/uploading-to-youtube

***Tip:** If you are going to be uploading a lot of videos, you should seriously consider a second or larger hard drive. Videos eat up a huge amount of space on your hard drive. Fortunately, large hard drives are dropping in price and storage is becoming cheap. We're a huge fan of solid state hard drives. They're super-fast!*

***Define: Uploading** – The step where you are transferring the video file from one of your devices (PC, smart phone, or tablet) to YouTube, via an internet connection.*

***Define: Publishing** – What you do after the video has been uploaded to YouTube in order to make it live. **Note:** Only publish after you have optimized your video for search!*

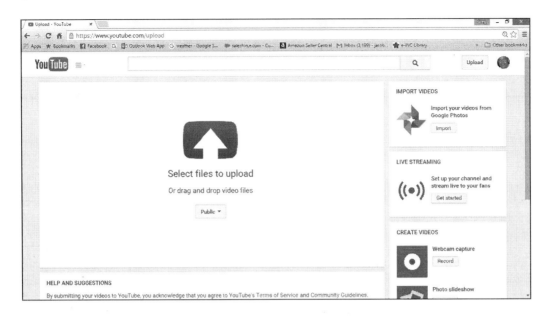

> **Learn More:** *For more advanced information on uploading:*
> *www.PlayGooglesGame.com/uploading-to-youtube*

Upload videos longer than 15 minutes: Currently you can upload videos that are up to 15 minutes long. To upload longer videos, verify your account with the following steps.

1. On a computer, visit the upload page.
2. Click Increase your limit at the bottom of the page, or visit:
   https://www.youtube.com/verify

Follow the steps to verify your account with a phone. You can choose between receiving the verification code through a text message (on a mobile phone) or an automated voice call. The maximum file size you'll be able to upload to YouTube is 128GB and the maximum duration is 11 hours.

> **SEO Juice:** *Before you upload your final edited version of your video, rename the file name (on your hard drive) with the same keywords you use in the Title of the video. For example, depending on your editing software and camera you might choose laptop-stand.avi or maybe laptop-stand.mov*

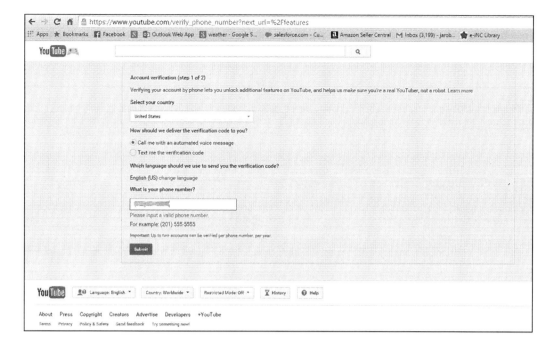

Title – The Most Important Place to Put Keywords!

When you upload a video, the first thing you are asked to do is give it a title. The title shows up in bold right below the video (like a headline). **Placing the proper keywords in the "Title" of the YouTube video is the most critical step in this entire chapter!**

> *Tip: If you want Local Business, put your city first! In any case, the order is important—first keywords rank higher—so put your most important keywords towards the beginning.*

Description – Optimize with Your Website Link, Keywords, and Phone Number

The description area appears directly under the video and is a place to add several lines of text. Only the first part is shown with a down arrow to "show more," so use an attention grabbing, keyword rich strategy (a good call to action would be nice too).

It's important to include all of the following in the description area:

- A live Backlink to your website up front, and you must use this format http://www., not just www.yourwebsite.com. *This is helpful on two fronts: **1.** Viewers can click on it to learn more about what you do on your website; **after all, we are trying to drive traffic back to our website**; **2.** It helps Google identify and rank your website on the regular Google search results for the keywords in the Title of the video.

- More Keywords in the description area—don't water it down with too many!
- Phone number in first sentence. This is especially important for local business—use your local area code, not a toll free number.

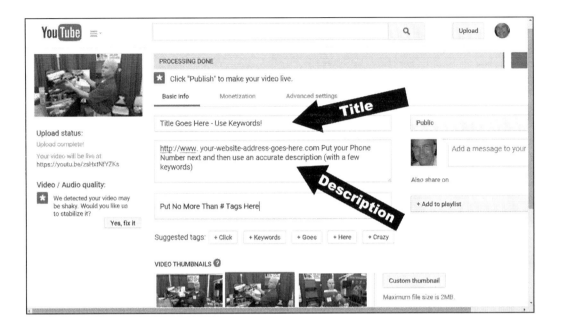

Embed Code – Copy & Paste to Play the Video on Your Website

This final step completes the circle and is super important. The next time the Google spiders scan your website, they will pick up this code indicating to them that you have embedded a video that has a title and description with your keywords. Conversely, when they scan YouTube itself, they will see in the description of the video that it is linked back to your website. Simply copy and paste the embed code into your website to play the video on your website. Note, this must be done in your website editing software and it's very similar to inserting an image onto your web page.

> ***Real World Example:*** *See how Greg got to number one for one of his clients in less than 7 hours for the highly competitive category "Used Cars Austin" www.PlayGooglesGame.com/youtube-ranking.*

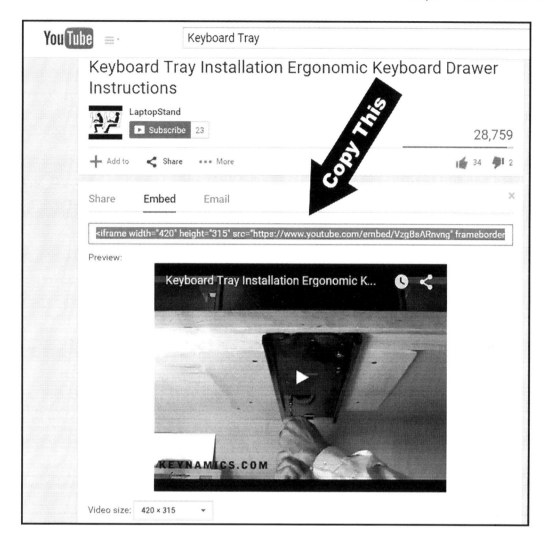

As seen in the previous image, simply select the size of the video frame you want to appear on your website from the little drop down menu, then copy the code that appears in the box above.

> *Note: As you will see in the Blog chapter, pasting this video embed code into your blog post takes about two seconds. What a fantastic way to create fresh video content!*

Now the really cool thing is that this creates a little window which acts like a "player" for the YouTube video to play on your website. You can select what size you want when you are copying the embed code from YouTube. It's a little drop down box. The above example shows a 420 x 315 Video size.

This player is actually playing the video from YouTube. The video file is actually hosted and plays from YouTube's servers, which means it will not suck any bandwidth from your website.

> **Learn More:** See www.PlayGooglesGame.com/embed-code-youtube for website video embedding screenshots for both the WordPress and the Dreamweaver web design programs.

> **Bright Idea:** YouTube allows channel owners to turn off embedding. On your own YouTube channel, you should allow embedding. Wouldn't it be great if lots of other websites embedded your video? Just be sure you properly fill out the description with your website information and phone number, and also embed text (website or phone number) in your video with either your video editing program or using YouTube's clickable annotations and captions; that way your branding stays with it wherever it goes.

Customize the Thumbnail Image

You can do this either during the upload or after the video is published. See the editing section at the end of the chapter for more details.

Tags

Select the most relevant tags and do not pick too many, as this will just water your efforts down, by spreading your keywords out across too many categories. Pick about five or less.

> **Note:** Be sure to save all the changes after the upload finishes.

Optimizing After Upload

Later in this chapter we'll show you how you can also enhance your video directly on YouTube after you upload it by adding Captions, Clickable Annotations, Cards, and even Subtitles. Many of these enhancements allowed on YouTube also optimize your video for search by placing your important keywords in them. This is more of an editing feature, so we will elaborate later in the chapter under the Editing Best Practices section.

Ask For Reviews

From Google: Businesses can strengthen their relationship with customers by directly engaging with reviewers on Google. To encourage reviews for your business simply remind your customers to leave feedback on Google. Reminding customers that it's quick and easy to leave feedback on Google on mobile or desktop can help your business stand out from sites with fewer reviews.

Conflict of interest: Reviews are most valuable when they are honest and unbiased. Google does not want you to review your own business, or if you're an employee don't review your employer. Don't offer or accept money, products, or services to write reviews for a business and don't write negative reviews about a competitor. Don't set up review stations or kiosks at your place of business just to ask for reviews written at your place of business. See the guidelines: *www.PlayGooglesGame.com/youtube-guidelines*

> ***Off Page SEO:*** *Asking people to subscribe to your channel and make comments on your video helps with off page SEO. Remember Google is watching the interactions on your videos to judge how to rank them. You can do this on your social media channels, when you're talking to them, in your advertisements, etc.*

How To: *YouTube Help Center:*
www.PlayGooglesGame.com/youtube-help

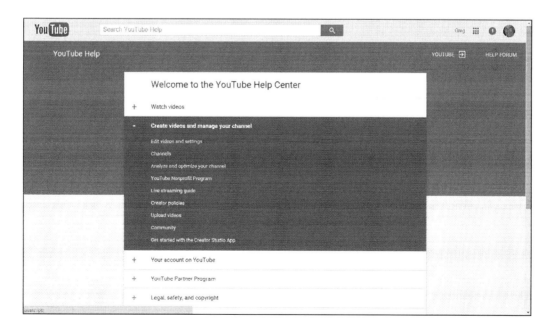

Recording Best Practices

We have already mentioned that there is no need to spend $20,000 hiring a professional videographer. Nothing against our videographer friends, but not only is this way out of the budget of most business owners, YouTube viewers expect more of a real world experience (see www.GrittyVideo.com). Plus, getting our message out is often time sensitive, and most video production companies are a long lead time.

This brief outline below is very much generalized for the typical business owner's use. You can actually get a PhD in media and film production—so we're obviously leaving a lot out—but this will give you a head start on shooting great videos.

We're going to touch on some very basic techniques that will help you produce enjoyable videos. We know, once you make a few videos and start seeing the results by your customer engagement, you'll get hooked, and you'll want to dig even deeper. You can learn much more by searching YouTube itself.

The bottom line is that you have got to figure this out. Ignoring the opportunities—or worse yet, fearing the process—only limits your ability to reach potential customers that are searching for your products or services on YouTube. Either pay big bucks for someone to do it for you or take a few hours to start learning it yourself.

Learn More: Creator Hub – YouTube's home for resources to help create better content, build fan bases, and turn your creativity into sales:
www.PlayGooglesGame.com/youtube-creator-hub
Creator Academy – www.PlayGooglesGame.com/youtube-creator-academy

Caution: DO NOT GET DISCOURAGED BY ALL THE DETAILS BELOW. Please, just begin by hitting the record button on your camera and uploading something—anything. Once you record and upload a few times, you'll start to get the hang of it, but you have to start somewhere. The information below will help you fine tune your videos for a better viewer experience.

Tip: To practice, make your video private on YouTube. That way only you can view it. This should make you a little more comfortable uploading your first few videos. It's free and good practice, so no harm can be done. :)

Dedicate a Space

A major obstacle we see with almost every business owner is that they do not have a dedicated space for their video production and equipment. Establishing a space allows for quick access to your equipment and is a place where you can actually record some talking head, product demos, and whiteboard videos utilizing backdrops.

If you don't make it super easy to capture that special moment, chances are that you will not bother with it. We'll elaborate on this below in the "Shooting the Video" section.

Dedicate a Process

Just like any business process or strategy, you should have a written policy or program for how you and your staff will create, upload, and optimize videos. You should incorporate this into your business playbook. If you don't have a playbook, we highly recommend that you read "The E Myth", our all-time favorite business book.

Basic Equipment Needed

If it's the equipment that's holding you back, there really is no excuse anymore. Equipment quality keeps going up while prices keep coming down. In fact, most good phones can record great quality video. There are even great apps for phones allowing you to create, edit and upload YouTube videos, all with one device!

> *Tip: There are great video editor apps available for your phone. We use and like iMovie and YouTube's Capture for iPhone and KineMaster for Android. Shoot video, edit and upload great videos right from your phone!*
> *www.PlayGooglesGame.com/youtube-capture*

However, if you want to get serious about this (and we know you will after reading this chapter) you really need to invest a little money. Heck, one of Greg's first videos pays for his equipment over and over again—month after month.

It is not that expensive to get set up, and once you have done several videos and get comfortable with the process, it will not take up too much of your time, especially when you consider that your one time and effort to create that video will also be creating a permanent 24/7 sales machine for your product or service.

1. Video Camera/Still Camera combo – $200 to $500
2. Tripod – $50
3. Three Photography Lights and stands (daylight, color balanced CFL Lights) – $150
4. Diffusion equipment and material for the lights – $50
5. Seamless Photo Paper Background and stand – $100

Learn More: *Visit our webpage for our latest recommendations on inexpensive equipment sources:*
www.PlayGooglesGame.com/youtube-video-equipment

Tip: *Set up two video cameras and film from two different angles. This works great for transitioning in different angles (segments) during editing. It makes a much more interesting video. Your mobile phone could also serve as a second camera; just get an adapter (clamp type setup) that will allow mounting it to a tripod.*

Gritty Video is Perfect

Searchers want a real world experience. They want to hear from the owners and employees. Professional videos are nice—if you can afford them. However, a real world video, with decent sound, and some basic editing is best.

Just because we are creating gritty, real world videos does not mean you want to create something that is annoying. This will drive people right back to the YouTube search results after watching your video for five seconds! Google tracks this bounce back rate and dings you if everyone is avoiding your videos.

Furthermore, as more and more people flock to YouTube, the bar will continue to be raised for better quality. Real world is one thing, but if your viewers are not engaged within the first few seconds, they are going to bounce right back to all of the other cool videos on YouTube.

Caution - What makes an annoying video?

1. Lack of pre-planning
2. Lack of proper editing (clipping into segments and reassembling)
3. Uploading one continuous video straight from the camera

4. Poor lighting
5. Poor sound
6. Lack of still images transitioned in your timeline
7. Lack of smooth Transitions between the segments

> ***Learn More:*** *For Great Video Production Ideas:*
> *www.PlayGooglesGame.com/youtube-video-production*

Pre-Planning

Pre-planning, also known as pre-production, is a crucial step to think about and write down before you start filming. Depending on your goals and the complexity of the video, this can be accomplished in a few minutes or a few days.

.

> ***Learn More:*** *Pre-Production:*
> *www.PlayGooglesGame.com/youtube-video-production*

Many times, when we're shooting video on the fly with a mobile phone, we'll scribble a few bullet points down on a scrap of paper of the points we want to discuss. The more you shoot video the easier this will become. For more complex videos, like product demonstrations or tutorials, this pre-planning step can take days.

> ***Learn More:*** *Creating Great Content:*
> *www.PlayGooglesGame.com/youtube-video-production*

> ***Real World Example:*** *Greg created an instructional video for installing his under-mount keyboard trays. He got the idea because customers kept calling in and asking questions about installation. The written instructions were long and detailed. Greg simply videoed himself from the unpackaging to the final screw and then later recorded a voiceover to match what he was doing during installation. Lots of pre-planning was needed to think about the layout, the angle of the video, hand tool and power tool placement, etc. However, very little pre-planning was needed for the script, because he was able to do it afterwards. One important thing he kept in mind was to do very slow deliberate moves, knowing he would have to explain each move in the audio overlay. This video has over 25,000 views. Not only can he reference the video on his website next to the product, it's also very helpful when customers have questions. Not to mention that the video is now*

Greg's silent salesman—working 24/7—selling hundreds of keyboard trays. www.PlayGooglesGame.com/keyboard-tray-installation

Note: Video Length *– In the past we were instructed to keep videos under 2 minutes in length, and today that is still a good practice. However, there are always exceptions. If you have really interesting content that you know your viewers will stay engaged with and keep watching until the end, then by all means make it longer. Greg's example of an instructional video above is a perfect example. That's not to say that a long rambling video is good; keep it just as long as it needs to be.*

Framing the Shot

Your goal is to direct your audience's attention to the thing you want to focus on: the person talking, an image, the scenery, etc. You do not want anything in the frame area to be a distraction from what you want to focus on. Before you start filing, ask yourself, "Will this add to or take away from the video?" and think about the various positions of the objects in your frame—the composition.

Define: Framing *– The presentation of visual elements in a video or still image, especially the placement of the subject in relation to other objects. Framing can make an image more aesthetically pleasing and keep the viewer's focus on the framed object. It can also be used to direct attention back into the scene. It can add depth to an image, and can add interest to the picture when the frame is thematically related to the object being framed.*

With framing, you can compose your shot to:

1. Give the video context (informing of the place/space you are in)
2. Give the video a sense of depth and layers
3. Lead the viewer's eye towards your main focal point

The goal is often to focus the viewer's attention upon the subject; this is accomplished by manipulating the viewpoint of the image, rather than the object(s) within. Framing is primarily concerned with the position and perspective of the viewer. The position of the observer has a lot of impact on their perception of the main subject, both in terms of aesthetics and in their interpretation of its meaning.

For example, if the viewer was placed very far away from a lone subject in a video, the viewer would gather more information about the environment and surroundings of the subject, but remain too far away to see his emotions.

In our businesses, many times we are filming someone talking. If you are, be sure to position them in the proper area of the frame. Their head should not be too close to the top, or the bottom. You should have enough distance between the camera and their face, but not too far. Consider placing their eyes at one of the four points in the frames using the Rule of Thirds.

> ***Tip:*** *Rule of Thirds (applies to still images too) – Divide the screen into three equally spaced, imaginary horizontal and vertical divisions. You'll end up with 6 equally spaced intersecting lines. The four points where the horizontal and vertical lines intersect offer four options to place your points of interest—the person's face, the interesting object, detail etc.*

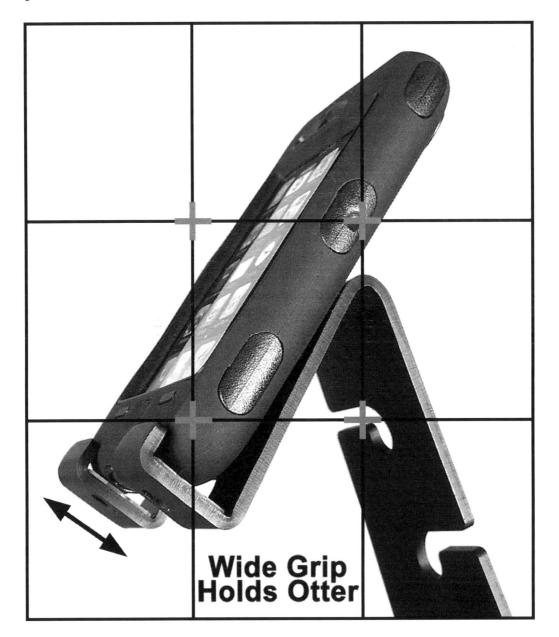

Wide Grip
Holds Otter

Lighting

As with still photography, lighting is going to be your biggest challenge. Poor lighting can make an expensive video camera look bad, and great lighting can make a cheap video camera look fantastic. It's all about the lighting and you have to think ahead and plan for it: the time of day, the weather, etc.

Learn More: *Lighting*
www.PlayGooglesGame.com/youtube-video-lighting

The goal of lighting is to create flat, diffused light and eliminate shadows. We're trying to mimic an overcast day, which are the best circumstances to shoot video or still photography. To do this indoors, use two lights, pointing towards the subject from a height just above the person's eye line. A good rule of thumb is to place the lights about three feet away from the subject. The lights should be located on either side of the camera, right in front of the lens.

Soften the light with diffusion material in front of the light source, or bouncing the light off another surface suitable for diffusing and reflecting it back on the subject.

> ***Tip:*** *A technique photographers use is to bounce the light off a wall or ceiling. Conditions have to be right, but this works more often than not.*

Keep the subject off the background (wall) at least four feet to create separation between the subject and the background and eliminate shadows. A good trick is to bring in a third light and place it right behind the subject, low and pointing up to the back wall.

Background

Always think about and plan for your background. You never want a background to distract from your video. Your goal is to keep viewers focused on your message. Busy backgrounds and unorganized backgrounds usually deter viewers. There are several basic categories of backgrounds.

Never allow these things to clutter your background: messy paper stacks, cluttered bookshelves, dirty laundry, dirty walls, cluttered rooms, or cramped office space. Does the setting promote credibility, authority, and professionalism? Never use your webcam on your computer!

- **Natural Backgrounds** include any natural setting like the inside of your store, office, or maybe a product display. Natural backgrounds imply authenticity and are great for more personal messages and testimonials— giving the viewer a peek at the "real world."
- **Solid Backdrops** are achieved with rolls of photography paper, or some other sheet material as a backdrop. This is also known as the talking head video and can be effective to convey and important message. White backgrounds are effective for good contrast and adding text or images on the screen while talking. See below for a great tip on giving the solid background a nice gradient affect.

- **Whiteboard Backgrounds** (real or animated) are very effective for hand drawing a sequence of events, drawing charts, writing out instructions, etc. They involve an animated use of images, shapes, characters, sounds and voice-overs to create a clip. You can use a real whiteboard as a background or a digital one. Khan Academy made these famous. Typically whiteboard videos are created by videoing a hand (or marking pen) drawing out concepts behind your video or voice, and might or might not include the actual person (hand) drawing it. Having a simple white background is an exceptional way to showcase the most important thing: your content.
- **Outdoor Backgrounds** are best shot on overcast days or in early morning or late afternoon hours—the magic light. Shooting when the sun is directly overhead creates horrible shadows.
- **Action Shot Backgrounds** have the background moving, like filming while driving or walking down the beach. Think GoPro.

Best Practices for Backgrounds

1. For uninteresting or distracting backgrounds use a fast lens (50mm) to blur out the background and only have the subject in focus. This will keep the focus on the person and away from the background.
2. Indoor, natural backgrounds are best shot on cloudy days when the ambient light is diffused. Harsh sunlight coming in the windows at various times of the day make for distracting backgrounds and often change with the angle of the sun, such as when one video segment is shot at a different time of the day.
3. For solid backgrounds, use seamless photo paper and create a nice gradient effect by shining a single light up from the floor, onto the backdrop, directly behind the person.
4. Remove any distracting things like paper on the floor, fake plants, etc.
5. Usually bright background colors like Yellow, Orange, or Red cause color reflection and can be unflattering to your subject. Stick with muted tones like grey and dark blue.
6. If you have more than one person in your video with natural backgrounds, shoot them in different locations within the same setting, with solid backgrounds, using the same color.

***Learn More:** Blurring the background (Bokeh) is a great way to bring focus to the subject, especially when the background is ugly or distracting. There are several techniques to do this. Learn more at www.PlayGooglesGame.com/blur-video-backgrounds*

Sound

Nothing will turn a viewer away faster than an annoying sound. Turn off sources of background noise: air conditioners, refrigerators, etc. Many times we don't like the sound captured during filming and just overlay YouTube's copyright free music. Another technique is to not worry about capturing the voice and later adding the audio as a voice over. This works great when you are not showing someone's face, as in a product demo.

> ***Learn more:*** *Sound*
> *www.PlayGooglesGame.com/youtube-video-sound*

Types of Videos

- **Animated Video** – Whiteboard animations are videos that draw themselves. They involve an animated use of images, shapes, characters, sounds, and voice-overs to create a clip. Visit www.PlayGooglesGame.com/whiteboard-animation
- **Explainer Videos** –
  o **Live Action Explainer Videos:** A real live promotional video explaining your business's product or service. Live action explainer videos are usually best for companies selling a product or service, such as a retail store or plumber. Having real people in your explainer video can create a connection for viewers, because we are drawn to other people.
  o **Animated Explainer Videos:** Animation is often the best format for explaining services or intangible products like computer programs. Also, some services like training include real objects.
  o **Whiteboard Explainer Videos:** Kahn Academy is a great example of a whiteboard video. This is an animation which is hand drawn and erased on a whiteboard.
- **Screen Capture Videos** – Screen capture tools can capture a screenshot of what you are looking at on your computer screen and explain what you are showing them online.
- **Slideshow Videos** – PowerPoint styled slideshows are good for quick voice overs or if you are shy in front of the camera. These are also great to transition in during your presentations in front of a group. Greg always records his presentations!

> ***Tip:*** *Converting a PowerPoint slide to a JPEG image is really easy if you know this technique. Learn More at:*
> *www.PlayGooglesGame.com/powerpoint-slide-to-jpeg*

- **Event Videos** – Event videos are more trustworthy than a scripted video because it's real world – gritty video. An event showcases the best things about your company, product, and culture.

- **How To Videos** – As seen in Greg's keyboard tray installation instructions example - create a tutorial explaining how to use your product.
  * Google loves these type of videos, so be sure and let them know by using the words "How To…." in the title of the video.

- **Video Interviews** – The best place to put an interview video is on your About page. This gives the owner a chance to reveal insider views of a company and is great for employee recruitment.

- **Presentation Videos** – Greg always films his presentations – ALWAYS. You should never, ever miss an opportunity to video yourself giving a presentation in front of a live audience.

Caution: While we can't give legal advice, beware of the legal issues surrounding using someone else's "likeness." Most attorneys will tell you that it's better to be safe than sorry and to get a model release from any person whose likeness you use, in still photography as well as video. This is especially true for employees. You never know when someone will leave your company disgruntled. And as far as your audience goes, as in the above "Presentation Videos," play it safe by filming from the back of the room, where you can't make out anyone's likeness from the back of their heads. It would not be practical to get a model release signed by everyone in your audience! Please consult your attorney for advice in this subject.

- **Product or Service Demo** – Most consumers enjoy and interact with product description or service demonstration videos. Most also say that product videos influences their buying decision. Showing a 360-degree view of your product helps your audience understand how it works and the features that will benefit them.

- **Customer Testimonial Videos** – This not only builds credibility for prospective customers, it's a great way to keep your current customers loyal and engage them after the sale. Ask your customers about their experience and get their permission (model release) to use their testimonial in your video.

- **CEO Testimonial Video** – People love a story, and a casual conversation with the owner or CEO explaining his passion for the product can be very reassuring for potential clients and customers. Observing how much passion and hard work went into the process of creating the product changes the way people look at it.

Tip: Your customers are a great source of ideas for the types of videos you can create. Do they keep calling you asking the same question over and over? Maybe it's time to create a "How To Video" that demonstrates how to install one of your products. See an example Greg did at www.PlayGooglesGame.com/youtube-how-to-video. This one instructional video has generated over 10,000 views and hundreds of sales over the years!

Editing Before YouTube Upload

Just like still images usually need a little cropping or light adjustment in a photo editing program, videos uploaded directly from the camera in one continuous segment are usually annoying and need a little tweaking. Every once in a while we get lucky and capture a great video in one continuous shot, but that is a rare exception. There is a reason that in Hollywood they say, "All the magic happens in the editing room." Even the pros know this!

There are three options for editing videos and they all revolve around the timing in the YouTube publishing process:

1. You can edit them on your computer, smart phone, or tablet right after you shoot them.
2. You can edit them on YouTube itself after you upload them, but before you publish them.
3. You can even tweak them after they have been published.

Editing before you upload usually gives you the most options and flexibility. This is of course dependent on the quality of the video editing software or app you are using.

> ***Tip:*** *Video editing is kind of a daunting task. If you are not comfortable editing your videos, there are lots of online choices and the prices are coming down. Some charge less than $200 for a short video. You shoot it, they edit it. For our favorite resources click here: www.PlayGooglesGame.com/video-editing-services*

Resolution and Aspect Ratio

YouTube uses 16:9 aspect ratio players. If you shot your video with a non-16:9 file video camera, it will be automatically processed and displayed correctly, with pillar boxes (black bars on the left and right) or letter boxes (black bars at the top and bottom) provided by the player.

The YouTube player automatically adds black bars so that videos are displayed correctly without cropping or stretching, no matter the size of the video or the player. For example, the player will automatically add pillarboxing to 4:3 videos in the new 16:9 widescreen player size.

> ***Learn More:*** *You can adjust the fit of your video in your player after uploading your video by using formatting tags during upload.*
> *www.PlayGooglesGame.com/video-editing-size*

Transitions Between the Clips

> ***Define: Transitions*** *– Transitions are a few individual frames that go between video segments. The segments can be videos or still images. The goal is to make the transition smooth, and not jerky or abrupt. This is usually accomplished by fading in and fading out.*

> ***Define: Frame*** *– Videos are just a bunch of still images (frames) all strung together. Just like old movie reels, when the frames are played at certain speeds, there appears to be motion, but it's really just a bunch of still frames.*

> ***Define: Clip*** *– The whole goal of a video editing program is to lay out and chop up (split) various video (or still image) segments along a timeline into shorter clips that you can manage.*

A transition makes for a smooth blending between the two segments, thus avoiding "jump cuts." There are various transition affects, but they all accomplish the same thing—smoothly fading out from the previous segments and fading into the next segment. Without transitions, the clips would abruptly jump from end and start, kind of slamming into one another; this is very annoying to the viewer.

Folks, this sounds like a daunting task, but it's really easy to use these video editing programs. They are all set up basically the same way—you can just drag and drop video clips and still images, then slice them up however you want. We use and like the editor right on YouTube (see below), Adobe Premier Elements for your PC, iMovie for iPhone, and KineMaster for Android. These video editing programs allow you to view your video in a timeline on a dashboard. This timeline can be sliced up into segments so you can work on each segment.

> ***How To:*** *See screenshots of some simple techniques and tips for Adobe Premier Elements at: www.PlayGooglesGame.com/adobe-premier-elements*

The value of being able to work on one segment at a time is that there will usually be parts (segments) of the video that you will want to crop out. Hollywood and TV has gotten us all accustomed to this. No one expects your video to run as one continuous shot end to end.

Transitioning Still Images Between the Video Clips

One of the best values of dividing your videos up into segments is that you can transition in regular photos. Maybe it's a company logo, an info graphic, product image, etc.

Transitioning in images makes a more interesting video and adds emphasis to what you are talking about. It's important to note that your voice, or the sound, is able to continue to play, when the image is shown. In the video editing program, you can control how long the image will stay there, usually by just dragging the ends of the image clip.

> ***Real World Example:*** *See how Greg embedded a still image of a map to show viewers where the business is located in Austin, Texas.*
> *www.PlayGooglesGame.com/youtube-ranking*

Convert Image Files into a Slideshow

Here's how you can easily convert photos into a slideshow:
- Visit the upload page on YouTube
- Click Create under Photo Slideshow
- Create a slideshow video
- Upload photos from your computer, or select photos from an existing Google+ photo album, and click Select
- Drag and drop the photos to rearrange them; when you're done, click Next
- Select an audio track from the library under "Audio", or select No Audio to have your slideshow play without music (You won't be able to upload audio files from your computer)
- Click Upload when you've finished making your slideshow
- Select the file format you'd like to convert:
  - .mp3, .wav, .jpg, .png
  - .mswmm (Movie maker project file)
  - .msdvd (DVD Maker project file)
  - .wlmp (Movie maker project file)

    o   .camproj (Camtasia project file)

    o   imovieproject, .dvdproj (iDVD project file)

    o   .rcproject (iMovie project file)

    o   .piv

Editing Sound

On the video timeline on the dashboard, there are usually separate lines running horizontally. One or two of these lines is usually the audio file. Just like still images, you can transition in audio clips. Often times, we like to just use music and turn off the audio in our video clips. These editing programs allow you to easily do this.

Sometimes there are good reasons to cover up your video recorded sound with music. Maybe the video was filmed outside and there is too much wind noise. Maybe you don't like the sound of your voice (practice makes perfect).

YouTube even offers copyright free music that you can overlay onto your video at the time you upload it—see their terms and conditions.

Tip: *Copyright Free music can also be found here: www.PlayGooglesGame.com.copyright-free-music*

Black Hat Warning: *We can't offer legal advice. However, almost 100% of all music is copyright protected; the same goes for any images or videos. Google is watching, and they are watching to see if you are uploading videos with copyright protected music violations. They figure if we are cheating here, then we are cheating elsewhere and they will penalize, or worse, ban you. It's against Google's and YouTube's terms of service to upload someone else's copyrighted music. Just because you bought a CD of your favorite artist, does not give you the right to upload that music for the rest of the world to hear. Please consult your attorney if you have any questions on this.*

Define: Exporting – *After all of the editing is done and you are happy with the way the video looks, then you "export" the video from your editor to a folder on your computer in a file format that will easily upload to YouTube. Click here for supported YouTube file formats: www.PlayGooglesGame.com/youtube-exporting-troubleshooter*

SEO Juice: Before you upload your final edited version of your video, rename the file name with the same keywords you use in the Title of the video.

Editing on YouTube After Upload – But <u>Before</u> Publishing

You have two options for editing your video during the upload process at the YouTube upload interface:

1. Editing your video directly on YouTube with YouTube's built in video editor
2. Tweak your video before publishing with Clickable Annotations, Text Overlays, etc.

YouTube's Built in Video Editor

So you don't have video editing software? No problem; YouTube has a video editor that you can use as you upload the video. This video editor keeps growing in functionality over the years and works very well now.

SEO Juice Alert: Google can more easily recognize edits in their own video editor, versus using a third party. This is especially important when it comes to overlaying text onto your video. Be sure and use your keywords!

This YouTube Video Editor is a great example, because it's basically a simplified version of more advanced video editors like Adobe Premier Elements.

- Sign in to your YouTube (Gmail) account
- Click the Upload button at the top of the page
- Click Edit on the right of the upload page, under "Video Editor"

With the YouTube Video Editor, you can do all of the things we recommend for editing:

- Combine multiple videos and still images you've uploaded to create a new video
- Trim, remove unwanted segments, and slice up your clips to custom lengths
- Add music to your video from a library of approved tracks
- Customize clips with special tools and effects

Using these tools, you can put together clips to create new videos and publish them to YouTube with one click.

Here's how to access the Video Editor: www.PlayGooglesGame.com/youtube-video-editor

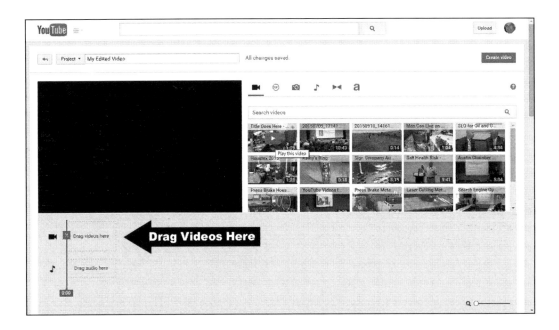

All of your previous video uploads are added automatically to the Video Editor and can be transitioned in as a clip on your new video. From your upload list you can drag the clip/image to the bottom of the timeline at the bottom of the editor, where it says, "Drag videos here to begin editing" when you start a new project.

Lengthen or Shorten:

Trim: Cut the length of your clip by moving your cursor over the edges of your video in the timeline. Drag the handles toward the center of the video to shorten. This shortens the length from either the beginning or the end, not the middle. See Cut/Snip below for removing segments from the middle of your clip.

Lengthen: Drag the handles outward from the center of the video to lengthen. Lengthening past the original length of the video will result in the video repeating.

Cut/Snip: Clips can be cut into portions. Move your mouse over the video and click the scissors icon to bring up the snip marker. Move this to where you want to snip the clip, then click on the scissors button to snip the clip.

Customize and Add Effects

Rotate: Rotates your video 90 degrees.

Effects: Apply Video Enhancements to your video to color correct, stabilize, and add filters.

Text: Apply a text overlay on the clip – **Use Your Keywords – and Add Your Phone Number and Website Address!**

Slow Motion: Modify the speed at which the clip plays. Move your mouse over a clip to bring up any of these options.

Add Music: You can add a new audio track to your video. Click the music note button in the upper left of the editor to bring up YouTube's library of pre-approved songs. The audio from an added track will overlap or replace your clips' original audio by default.

Customize the Thumbnail: You can do this either during the upload or after the video is published. See below for more details.

Editing on YouTube – <u>After</u> Publishing

There are many editing options available after you have published your video. One thing to note is that there is no way to replace an old video with a different version (even if it's just a slight revision of the same video) and keep the original view count, comments or ratings. Instead, you may want to try using clickable annotations or link to the new version of the video from your old video.

Go to your channel's Video Manager:
www.PlayGooglesGame.com/youtube-channel-video-manager

You will see a list of your uploaded videos. Find the video you want to edit, then click the little Edit icon in the middle of the video.

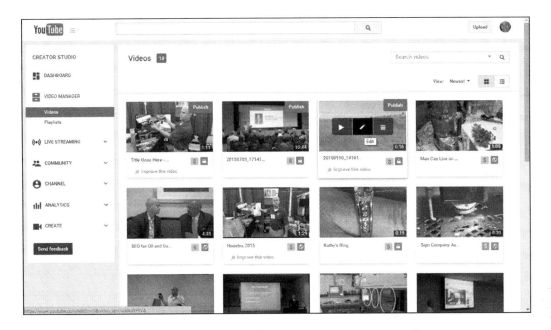

On the Info and Settings page, you'll see three tabs, depending on your account type:

Basic info: Change video title, description, tags, category, privacy. **Note:** You can use most characters to fill in the information in the video fields (like title or description), except angle brackets.

Monetization: See the options for monetizing your video. Learn more about monetizing your content.

Advanced settings: Change comments permissions, license, caption, video location, recording date, and 3D video options.

Caution: Be careful; changing a title that is already optimized and ranking well for your keywords is a big mistake!

Tip: Download the YouTube Creator Studio app for iOS or android. The app allows you to manage your YouTube Channel from your mobile device.

Enhancement Options and Features Available after Publishing

You can also make some changes to a video that you've already uploaded by using YouTube Video Enhancements. The Enhancement option is constantly adding features, so check it often for updates and ways you can tweak your video that has already been published.

Currently, in order to be eligible for YouTube Video Enhancements, your video must not have received more than 1,000 views; other restrictions apply.

Using enhancements, you can make some of the following improvements and edits to your videos. Note that on videos you have already published, you can't use Cut/Snip at this time to remove middle segments. This feature is only available before you publish the video. You can only use Trim to remove frames at the beginning or the end.

Auto-fix: Performs a one click-fix to enhance the video's lighting and color. You can also make manual adjustments to Fill Light, Contrast, Saturation, and Color Temperature by using the sliders

Lighting: Fill Light – Contrast – Saturation – Color Temperature

Stabilize: Adjusts the video to correct any shakiness

Slow Motion: Slow the speed at which your video plays (half speed, quarter speed, eighth speed)

Trim: Clip parts (frames) off the beginning and/or end of your video

Filters: This tab shows pre-set color filters that you can apply to your video to give them a stylish and unique look

Face blurring: Protect the anonymity of people in your video. Click on Special Effects to access this feature

Caution: *We can't give legal advice, but Face Blurring could be a great way to avoid model release issues. Consult your attorney for details.*

Custom Thumbnail: The video thumbnail is like the attention grabbing headline in a newspaper. It needs to have impact and grab the viewer's attention. Customizing your thumbnail, by replacing YouTube's with an image you can upload, almost guarantees it will look better than YouTube's randomly pre-selected thumbnail. For best results, your thumbnail should have a 1280 x 720 resolution with a 16:9 aspect ratio. Remember, Google tracks how often a video is clicked on as compared to other videos in the search results for those same keywords. If your video is clicked on more, then you are going to go up in the rankings. Make it stand out with a beautiful custom thumbnail. Your custom thumbnail image should be as large as possible, as the image will also be used as the preview image in the embedded player.

We recommend your custom thumbnails:

1. Have a resolution of 1280 x 720 (with minimum width of 640 pixels)
2. Be uploaded in image formats such as .JPG, .GIF, .BMP, or .PNG

3. Remain under the 2MB limit
4. Try to use a 16:9 aspect ratio as it's the most used in YouTube players and previews

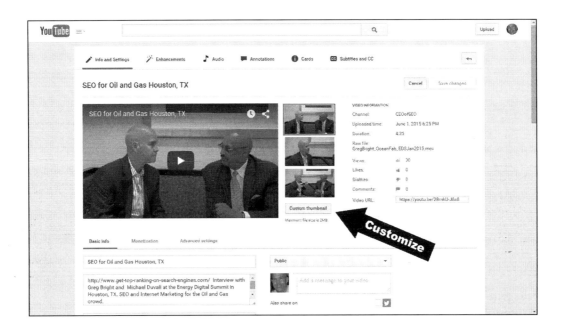

Preview how your video will look with the added enhancements in the video player by dragging the line in the middle to see a side-by-side comparison. To revert all changes, click Revert to Original.

> ***Caution:*** *Google tracks how long viewers watch your video and uses this information in ranking them on YouTube AND Google. If they see that viewers are bouncing right back to the YouTube search results after only watching a few seconds of you video, you get dinged. You must capture the viewer's attention in the first few seconds!*

Getting your viewers to act turns a single view into multiple views of your video. Do this by optimizing your clickable annotations and video descriptions to compel viewers to watch multiple videos, subscribe, or purchase items from your store, or visit your website. Used effectively, video descriptions and annotations can increase subscribers, watch time, and engagement.

> ***Caution: Give First*** *– Awesome videos have good subject matter. That's what makes a video interesting. If your video is interesting more people will watch it, and Google will reward you. If you simply make an ad about your business, or are overtly promoting yourself, that will turn people away faster than anything.*

SEO Juice Alert: *Most importantly, for our SEO efforts, Google is watching how many people subscribe, share, and comment on our videos. The more people that interact, the more Google rewards us with higher YouTube ranking and higher Google search ranking for our website for the keywords in our video titles, description, caption and clickable annotations.*

Tip: *At the end of the video, include a graphic or scene instructing folks to click on the link below to learn more at our website, or join the conversations on Facebook.*

Bright Idea: *When you want drive viewers to your YouTube from other platforms (blog posts and social media), instead of linking directly to YouTube, put links to a post on <u>your</u> website which has the video playing from your website instead of direct links to YouTube.*

Tip: *Whenever you make a blog post on your website that includes your embedded videos, also give them the direct link to your video on YouTube as well as the embed code for viewers to copy and place on their websites.*

Increase Customer Interactions with Your Video

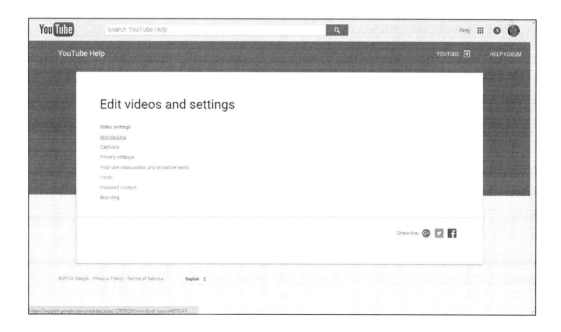

Annotations

With annotations you can layer text, links, speech bubbles, and hotspots over your video. They help you enrich the video experience by adding information, interactivity and engagement.

Annotations help you engage with viewers and make your videos more interactive by giving more information, and aiding in navigation. Be inventive! Creators consistently find new, innovative uses for annotations. Below are some guidelines, but use your best judgment to determine the timing, placement, style and number of annotations included in your videos.

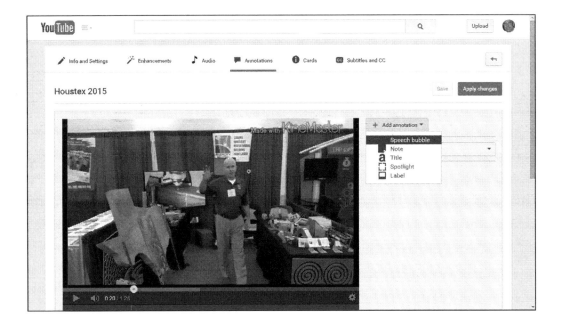

Learn More: *Advanced techniques for using annotations.*
www.PlayGooglesGame.com/youtube-annotations

Function: Clickable vs. Non-clickable

- **Clickable Annotations** – link to other videos, playlists, channels or full versions of shorter video clips.
    - o Consider creating a table of contents for long-form videos, or directing viewers of older videos to newly uploaded content.
    - o Highlight your dot com, merchandise store, or your social media presence.
    - o Place hidden "Easter eggs" or interactive games in your videos.
- **Non-clickable Annotations** – add text clarification to a specific part of the video.

Placement: Where should it be shown?

- Avoid annotations in the lower third of the video (unless you're creating an end-card); the advertisement overlay can obscure them.
- Also avoid annotations along the very top of the frame because the video player can obstruct them when shared outside of YouTube.
- Don't obstruct the actual content. Make sure annotations add value and do not get in the way of the viewing experience.
- Don't bombard the viewer.

Timing and duration: When is it shown and for how long?

- Be careful! Don't take viewers away from a video too soon.
- Repeat "subscribe" solicitations and other calls to actions at the end of the episode.

Some Types of Annotations:

- Spotlight Annotations – Spotlight annotations stand out because they allow creators to subtly create clickable areas within a video. The text only appears when viewers hover over it with their mouse: a light outline shows when viewers are not hovering. This is a great way to include unobtrusive but clickable annotations.
- In-Video Graphics – Eye-catching graphics can encourage subscribing, commenting, or sharing. Use the spotlight annotation to make these graphics clickable once the video is published.
- End-Cards – Create an end-card that directs viewers to act. Create a template that builds consistency into the end of your videos.

Add Subtitles and Closed Captions

Captions are YouTube's version of subtitles. Not only are they great for the hearing impaired and people who don't have their volume turned on, but the text you provide as a transcript is also read by YouTube's search engine. That means more opportunity to rank for more terms.

Add captions by choosing to edit a video and then selecting the "Captions" tab.

Subtitles and closed captions open up your content to a larger audience, including deaf or hard of hearing viewers or those who speak languages besides the one spoken in your video. They also act as metadata (keywords) that helps your videos show up in more places on YouTube. Learn more about these benefits with Creator Academy best practices or in our YouTube Captions and Subtitles video.

Cards

Cards allow you to add a new layer of interactivity to your videos. They are applied on a per video basis and are rendered on desktop and mobile devices. As seen in the images below, you can provide a destination URL from a list of eligible sites and, depending on the card type, customize an image, title, and call-to-action text.

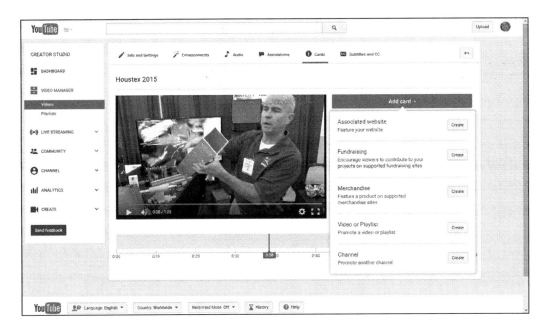

How Cards are Displayed in The YouTube Search Results

Cards are designed to be contextual to the video and should help creators reach their goals, while providing an enriched viewer experience. As the system evolves, Google plans to optimize it to rank the most relevant teasers and cards based on performance, viewer behaviour, and the device they are using.

Types of Cards

- **Merchandise card** – Merchandise cards can promote a creator's licensed merchandise directly from the video. If you haven't used merchandise annotations before, in order to create merchandise cards you need to accept the Terms & Conditions which will be presented to you during the setup. You can choose from a number of approved destination URLs and the card will display a top-level URL.

- **Fundraising card** – Fundraising cards can link viewers directly to projects on whitelisted fundraising sites. You can choose from a number of approved destination URLs and the card will display a top-level URL.

- **Video or playlist card** – This card can link to another public YouTube video or playlist which can be of interest to the viewer of the current video. You can also link to a specific time in a video or to an individual video in a playlist by entering a video or playlist URL directly.

- **Associated website card** – Link directly to your own "associated" website from a card. If you haven't used associated website annotations before, in order to create associated website cards you need to accept the Terms & Conditions which will be presented to you during the setup. DO NOT SEND PEOPLE TO A NON-ASSOCIATED WEBSITE!

- **Fan Funding card** – This card lets your fans show their appreciation for your videos by making a monetary contribution directly on the video page. Please note that you need to enable Fan Funding for your channel, before including the Fan Funding Card in your videos.

Scripted Shout-outs

Talk directly to the camera to get your audience to listen and act. See previous image.

Video Descriptions

Video descriptions serve two purposes: aid in the discovery of your videos in search (through your keywords placed there), and get viewers to take an action from the watch page. Remember, only the first few lines of your description will appear in search results or above the fold on a watch page, so make them count!

Get viewers to act:

The first 2-3 lines of your description (above the fold) should tell the story of what your video is about. Read the best practices in www.PlayGooglesGame.com/youtube-call-to-action

Let the viewer know about your channel by including links to your site and social media presence. Remember: if you send the audience off-site, you end their viewing session. Short viewer sessions negatively impact YouTube's "Suggested Video" feature and search ranking placement.

- Use short links to track the performance of these links (short links provide basic analytics).
- Link to sites, videos, or channels referenced in your video. Annotations don't appear on mobile devices.
- Mirror annotation links in the description.
- Any scripted calls to action should be represented in the description.

Additional uses for your video description:

- Include your channel's release schedule.
- Include links to time-codes in the video to help viewers navigate long-form content.

- Include a recurring keyword tagline. The keyword tagline is a group of sentences that describe your channel. They should include several search-driven keywords. Repeating this tagline in episode descriptions will inform first-time viewers about your channel.

REMEMBER THAT IT IS A VIOLATION OF YOUTUBE'S TERMS OF SERVICE TO USE MISLEADING METADATA ON YOUR VIDEOS.

Write video descriptions with two main purposes in mind: reinforce the story of the title and thumbnail in the first couple lines, and below that, let new viewers know that you have an entire channel full of great videos.

Get people to act, whether that means viewing more of your content, visiting your channel, or sending them to your website.

> ***Note:*** *Keep an eye on YouTube's <u>Live Streaming</u> and other live video streaming platforms that companies are just launching. Live Video Streaming apps – YouNow – GoPro (Meerkat) - Twitter (Periscope)*
> ***www.<u>PlayGooglesGame.com/youtube-live-streaming</u>***

Best Practices – Action Plan

1. Set up YouTube account:

_____

_____

_____

_____

2. Script: Think about the words you want to say. Type out the bullet points in large easy to read font, and practice:

_____

_____

_____

3. Film a practice video; consider: Lighting, Audio, and Background.

_____

_____

_____

_____

4. Video Editing – Add a couple of still images with transitions, upload to YouTube:

_____

_____

_____

_____

5. Write your Video Program procedures. Who will manage it?

_____

_____

_____

_____

Chapter 5

Get Backlinks... It's a Popularity Contest

Google loves links—But not just any kind of link

✓ Backlinks Made Google Famous
✓ Types of Links
✓ Anatomy of a Link
✓ Backlink Strategy

Before Google, search engines simply looked at the keywords in websites to rank them. The more keywords you had, the higher you got ranked. Google knew this was rife for cheating. People were coming up with all sorts of ways to stuff keywords into websites—thousands of them on a single page in fact. Tricks like making the keyword's text color the same as the background color, or the font so tiny that humans could not read them, but computer programs would pick them up and rank them high.

Because there was so much cheating, the public was growing disenchanted with all of the search engines. Those of us that are older have painful memories of all the times a website selling Viagra would pop when we just wanted to find the local pizza place…

The two founders of Google set out to make a better search experience by keeping the searcher in mind. This turned into their single mission, which still carries on today.

Google's idea was to turn search into a popularity contest. This simple idea spurred an empire and changed the world for the better. The world has become hungry for information and Google figured out a better way to make it searchable. That's why most of us love Google!

Highlights

Very Important:
- Create Awesome Content – Get Awesome Backlinks
- Keywords In Your Internal Links (URL Structure)
- No Link Sharing Farms

Important:
- Ge the Right Links
- Contact the Editors of Your Industry Trade Publications
- Build Links on Social Media

Helpful:
- Understand what Google wants
- Find all of your Backlinks through Google's Search Console

A Better Search Engine

Page Rank is Born

From Google: "PageRank is Google's opinion of the importance of a page based on the incoming links from other sites. (PageRank is an important signal, but it's one of more than 200 that we use to determine relevancy.) In general, a link from a site is regarded as a vote for the quality of your site.

The best way to get other sites to create high-quality, relevant links to yours is to create unique, relevant content that can naturally gain popularity in the Internet community. Creating good content pays off: Links are usually editorial votes given by choice, and the more useful content you have, the greater the chances someone else will find that content valuable to their readers and link to it."

Backlinks - It's a Popularity Contest

All of the experts agree the more *relevant websites* that link to your website the better. In fact, this is still one of the most important factors in SEO—as long as those links are natural links!

Google is all about *relevance*, and a backlink from a popular, authoritative website that has similar content as yours is the holy grail of relevance. Think of it as a positive vote for you and the fact that your website has something to do with that website's keywords. Google connects the dots.

This all makes perfect sense if you think about it. Google (and all the other search engines) view a link as a vote of approval among your peers. It's the equivalent of an online fan. The more fans you have (from related websites within your industry), the better your website must be, right? Your website must have something to do with the same keywords on those websites, and therefore it's relevant to those websites that are voting for you. It's a popularity contest indeed!

Notice that we emphasize relevant and natural links. Make no mistake about it, a large number of links from unrelated websites will not help you and can actually hurt you. Google will spank you for having *unnatural links*. We'll talk about steering clear of *link sharing farms* in Chapter 11, "Google Hates Cheaters". For a famous example of this penalty, Google this: "JC Penney Link Sharing". They got the spanking of their life!

> **Note:** *One exception to this "unrelated website" rule would be links from extremely popular websites like the New York Times – that kind of link is always good. ;)*

Off Page SEO vs On Page SEO

On Page SEO is what we do ourselves on our own web pages. *Off Page SEO* is what we (or others) do outside of the boundaries of our website. Backlinks are considered off page SEO.

Types of Links

There are three types of links on any website: links that go to pages within your website (*internal links*), links that go to a page on someone else's website (*external links*), and links that go to your website from another website (*backlinks*). All three links are very important places to include keywords; however in this chapter we'll be emphasizing links that point back to your website from someone else's—a *backlink*.

Link Structure

Note that the structure of both internal, external, and backlinks are all the same (they are all URLs), and the same keyword strategy should be used for all three in building the actual link itself. A good example of a keyword rich structure for a link is: www.keynamics.com/laptop-stand.html.

Let's break it down. The first half, www.keynamics.com is the domain name. The part after the forward slash (laptop-stand.html) is the individual webpage within the main website that you would land on when clicking the link. You can also tell that this is an individual webpage within a website because it ends with .html (it can also end with simply .htm). This is not the home page. The home page is where you would land if the link was simply www.keynamics.com.

It should be very clear, that particular page has to do with "laptop stands" right? Make a few notes here: **1.** Do not run the keywords together (i.e. /laptopstand.html); **2.** Do not use a blank space between the keywords (i.e. /laptop stand.html); and **3.** Always use a hyphen (dash) or underscore to separate the words!

Keywords in the Link URL Structure

Keywords placed within the actual URLs of the links (*hyperlinks*) are one of the best place to focus your SEO efforts. You will get more reward for your efforts here than just about anywhere else—it's super easy and often overlooked, or completely done wrong.

Just don't overdo it. The keywords should match the content of the page linked to. For example this would be horrible: www.keynamics.com/*buy-laptop-stand-hp-laptops-dell-laptops-macbook-stand*.

Anchor Text & Exact Match Anchor Text

Whenever any link is placed on a website, the text used to make the link visible is often not the actual URL itself. It can show up as any text. "Click Here," "Visit the Site," etc. This is called Anchor Text.

Google values the keywords in the anchor text, especially when it's an internal link on your own website. A link that uses your keywords as the anchor text is called an Exact Match Anchor Text Link. For External websites linking to you, in the real world, it's hard enough to get someone to link to you and even less likely that they will use your keywords in that link. See our caution below, because Google knows that hundreds of exact match anchor text links are unnatural and therefore, probably belong to a spammy website.

Exact Match Domains

If you really want to take the whole "keywords in the URL thing" to the extreme, new businesses should consider starting out by registering your main domain name with keywords in it; you can even separate the keywords by hyphens. This is also referred to as *exact match domains*. An example from Greg's laptop stand business is www.laptop-ergonomics.com. His laptop ergonomics website hardly gets any attention as far as SEO maintenance goes. However, it has consistently ranked on page one and in the top 5 for over 10 years for the search term "laptop ergonomics".

Please note—in fact, make a BIG note—purchasing an *exact match domain* for the sole purpose of ranking for that keyword will not help you if it only contains poor content. This doesn't mean having your main keyword in your real domain on your main website will hurt you, if done correctly and filled with great content; it will actually help you as long as you are creating the domain as your main domain for that endeavor. In Greg's example above, he wanted to show up high for folks looking to improve laptop ergonomics and educate them on the topic. Of course on that site he promotes his laptop stands. Creating sites using an exact match domain just to redirect people to your main site will absolutely hurt you!

Deep Linking

Deep links happen when outside websites link to your internal web pages—the pages other than the home page. Google tracks this and they analyze how many of your backlinks go to your homepage versus the number of internal backlinks.

Google knows that a website is more interesting if people are linking to internal pages more often than the home page; interesting is good! Plus, it looks more natural and that will have a positive effect on your rankings.

Deep Linking also enhances the user's experience. Your visitors will see exactly the information they are looking for, versus just seeing your home page, which might or might not be relevant to them. For this reason, Deep Linking also reduces bounce rate. When users see relevant pages that satisfy their goals, they are more likely to stick around and click on other pages of your website. It also reduces the chances that they'll bounce back to the search results. Google tracks this!

Backlink Strategy

Let's discuss some strategies for increasing your chances of getting a popular and relevant website to link to you. We call this *Fishing for Backlinks*, which is not to be confused with the internet scam artists who are *Phishing* to steal your identity and bank account!

This is a case of quality versus quantity, and the quality is far better. Therefore, do not just focus on getting lots of people to link to you, focus on getting <u>the right people to link to you</u>.

One thing to keep in mind is that it is not only the value of the backlink itself. Think of it as word of mouth advertising. You really are getting a vote of "approval" from someone who is interested in what you have to say—even if it's from yourself. For example, a backlink from your <u>business page</u> on Facebook will not help your search engine rankings. However, it will drive traffic to your website.

Fishing for Backlinks

Relevant incoming hyperlinks from other sites within your industry and with similar topics as your site are a high priority. Experts say it's still one of the highest priorities with Google.

> *SEO Juice Alert: When you are fishing for backlinks, be sure you are Deep Linking to the internal webpage, where that content is stored, versus your home page. This will enhance the experience of the user and grab Google's attention—in a good way.*

1. **Social Media** – Be active on social media sites. Just remember to "give first," which probably means that you don't want to just jump on to conversations with the obvious (and annoying) attempt to link back to yourself. That's just not cool, plus Google watches these interactions and they will notice your behavior, as it will be obvious by the reaction of the people you are engaging with.

   Tip: In order to drive traffic from your Facebook business page back to your website, always copy and paste the link from your website into the Facebook post. Rather than just making the post on your Facebook page. Facebook post will even pick up any images you have on your website page.

2. **Doing a Press Release** – Getting online editors from your industry trade publications to write a story about your business and put a link to your website is a great way to increase incoming links (*backlinks*). **Note:** A real press release, not an advertisement, is based around a newsworthy event. You will increase your likelihood of the editor picking up your press release if it is <u>newsworthy to their readers.</u> Editors will usually link back to your website from the story they post on their websites.

   Tip: Coincide your press release with a popular current event. One of Greg's best press releases coincided with JetBlue's inaugural "in-flight internet" flight. He just piggybacked on their historic flight with his press release, making his press release both timely and newsworthy. He stated that in-flight internet was the main reason he invented the Aviator Laptop Stand. Many editors asked for review samples to do stories, and they linked their story to his website. A link from the New York Times can do wonders for your ranking!

3. **Writing an Article or White Paper** – An interesting article can establish your authority in your area of expertise. Usually, websites that "post" your article on their website will also provide a link back to your website as the originator of the article. You in turn will want to link to the article from your website. This establishes your authority with your visitors. It's a win-win for increasing backlinks. Instead of submitting your articles to one of a hundred article submission sites, you will have more success by focusing on the leaders and trade publications within your industry. Just contact them directly. Your article must have enough impact and interest to grab their attention and be of interest to their readers.

   Tip: It is helpful to ask anyone that is linking to your website to make the hyperlink actual keyword text on their website. This is called including "Anchor Text" in the link. In other words, they should not just list your web address as the hyperlink on their site. For example, a good link for Greg's laptop stand would be the text "Ergonomic Laptop Stands", with this text being an actual hyperlink to his site, versus just making his web address (www.keynamics.com) the link. Most times you will not be able to get them to do this, but it's worth trying—beggars can't be choosy!

4. **Monthly Newsletter** – Newsletters not only keep your regular customers coming back for more, they can also increase your back links as long as you allow others to post your newsletters on their websites. Giving them permission to do so is a really good idea, but be sure to always request that they recognize the source of the article with a link back to your website.

5. **Curation or Article Scraping?** – Curation is looking for and sharing interesting articles that are already published and available for use or purchase from your industry trade publications, trade associations, or other influential sources. Curation in moderation is a good practice, especially when it brings value to your visitors.

   Please note, we can't give legal advice, but there is a huge difference between overtly copying others' content and reposting it as your own and reposting an article, summarized in your own words with a link back to the original source of that article. Copying verbatim (Article Scraping) is probably in clear violation of the original creator's stated copyrights. Also note that Google encourages you to create original content (this is why they want the business to do this in house) and discourages purely scraped content. You should lean on the side of original content!

   Furthermore, never, ever use blog scraping software for the sole purpose of scanning through a large number of blogs, searching for and copying content. Google will definitely penalize you for that!

6. **YouTube Video Links** – In Chapter 4 we showed you how to put a live link in the description area of your YouTube video. It's also helpful to overlay text in your video editing software onto the video itself, branded with your website domain. This will encourage others to reference your website with a link when discussing the awesomeness of your video to their friends and followers.

7. **Blog Posts** – In Chapter 8 we'll show you the importance of creating awesome blog posts. Be sure to always link to one of your internal website pages within your blog post. That way when someone else shares your awesome content, your link goes with it.

8. **Google Maps** – In Chapter 9 we'll show you how you can insert a link to your website on the map listings.

9. **Sitemaps** – Although not directly related to this chapter on incoming links, site maps do contain all of the internal links within your own site. Google states that a sitemap is a must have!

> *Define: Site Map – An area on a website that shows all of the links to all of the other pages within the website. For users, just like a regular map, it quickly and easily shows a user how to navigate the entire website. For Google, a sitemap is a file where you can list the web pages of your site to tell Google and other search engines about the organization of your site content. Search engine web crawlers like Googlebot read this file to more intelligently crawl your site.*

Trustworthiness

We all want to see websites that we can trust. Unfortunately, just because you "seen it on the internet" does not mean it's factual. Google takes trust very seriously. They only want to show trustworthy websites in the search results. There are many ways you can earn Google's trust and many ways you can ruin it.

Think like a Boy Scout: seriously, we know this sounds corny, but it works. Whenever you are optimizing your website with your creative content, ask yourself, "Does this feel right?" If it feels like cheating, it probably is cheating.

Of course this chapter is about increasing your popularity—in general the more popular you are, the more trustworthy you are.

Authoritative Links

Authoritative Links come from quality websites with good page rank. These types of links are always best. A bunch of links from spammy or low page rank sites can hurt you.

> *Real World Example: Here's an example of contacting an editor from Greg's concrete countertop business. He had just launched his business and did not have very much history in order to rank well. He knew he had to get the attention of the editor of his industry's main trade publication with something powerful.*

Knowing that she is always looking for interesting concrete techniques to share with her readers, he decided to give up one of his "trade secrets" to get her attention. The article proved interesting to her readers because it contained an unusual technique that no one had used before.

The article was posted along with the link to his website. Within a week, his Google ranking went through the roof! Plus, six months later, they published the article in their print publication—a double whammy!

Who Has Linked to Your Site?

It's pretty easy to determine all of the websites that are linking to you. You can choose between one of two ways: search your URL or use your account at Google's Search Console.

Link: Operator

To find a "sampling" of links to any site, you can perform a Google search using the ***link: operator***. For instance, a Google search for **link:www.PlayGooglesGame.com** will list a selection of the web pages that have links pointing to the that website.

Google says: "Note there can be no space between the 'link:' and the web page URL."

Since Google recommends the "no space" option, it's possible that Google has only associated the backlinks that show up under the "no space" option. In our experience that option shows the least results and more closely resembles what shows up in the Search Console.

We find different results using the link: operator all three of the following ways; you should try all three:

1. No Space
2. With a Space
3. Just search your domain name .com: keynamics.com

Use Google's Search Console Tool to See Your Backlinks

The Link: operator mentioned above might only supply a sampling of websites that link back to you. For a more complete list and many more details, use the Google Search Console.

The Links to Your Site report lists links that Googlebot discovered during its crawling and indexing process, as well as the most common link sources and the pages on your site with the most links. In addition, you can also see the most common anchor text found by Google.

On your Search Console, on the left side click "Search Traffic → Links to Your Site".

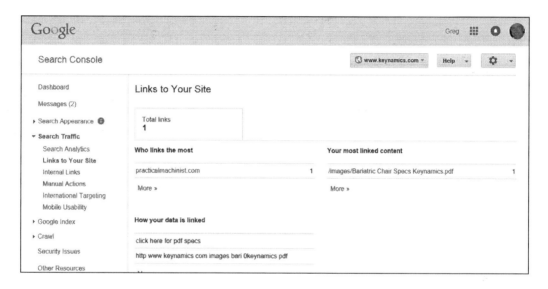

The Search Console tool is free, and at the present time you only need to have a Google account to log in. If Google decides to go the same route it did with their Keyword Tool, then we expect that you will eventually need an AdWords account to access the Search Console too.

You'll learn more about the Google Keyword tool (re-named Keyword Planner) in the next chapter. To use the Keyword Planner, they make you sign up for an AdWords account. You don't have to actually buy anything— for now anyway...

How to Set Up the Google Search Console

For a link to the Search Console to check links click here:
www.PlayGooglesGame.com/check-your-backlinks

Set up your Search Console account:

- Sign in to Search Console with your Google account. If you don't have a Google account, you'll need to create one.
- Once you sign in, click on Add a Site.

Verify that you're the owner of the site by doing one of the following (your web designer can easily help you with this, if you don't know how):

- Upload a file to your server
- Add a meta tag to your website's HTML
- Add a new DNS record
- Use your Google Analytics or Google Tag Manager account
- Easy GoDaddy verification, if GoDaddy is your host

Removing Unnatural Backlinks

Maybe your competitor subscribed you to one of those link sharing farms? Maybe you unwittingly hired an unscrupulous website designer or SEO Black Hat marketer? Or maybe you just did not realize it was against the rules.

Google realizes these are all reasons to forgive you for unnatural links. Forgiveness is enlightening even in Google's eyes. :)

However, you have to take action and it will take some work. We'll dive into this in Chapter 11, "Google Hates Cheaters". Just know that Google has some guidelines on removing unnatural backlinks. For the latest information click here:

www.PlayGooglesGame.com/removing-unnatural-backlinks

Link Schemes & Manipulative Linking is Cheating

Well, you might be guessing right about know how easy it would be for dishonest people to try and cheat the system. And cheat they did. And caught they got—just ask JC Penney.

Link sharing farms sprang up overnight offering to give you thousands of links. Others found very creative ways to cheat. It worked for a while, then it all came crumbling down. Remember what we said in the beginning. You are not going to outsmart Google, so spend your efforts creating amazing content that people want to link to.

It's Against the Rules

From Google: *Any links intended to manipulate PageRank or a site's ranking in Google search results may be considered part of a link scheme and a violation of Google's Webmaster Guidelines. This includes any behavior that manipulates links to your site or outgoing links from your site.*

The following are examples of *Link Schemes* *which can negatively impact a site's ranking in search results:*

- *Buying or selling links that pass PageRank. This includes exchanging money for links, or posts that contain links; exchanging goods or services for links; or sending someone a "free" product in exchange for them writing about it and including a link, also known as Link Sharing Farms.*
- *Excessive link exchanges ("Link to me and I'll link to you") or partner pages exclusively for the sake of cross-linking*
- *Large-scale article marketing or guest posting campaigns with keyword-rich anchor text links*
- *Using automated programs or services to create links to your site*

Additionally, creating links that weren't editorially placed or vouched for by the site's owner on a page, otherwise known as unnatural links, can be considered a violation of our guidelines. Here are a few common examples of unnatural links that may violate our guidelines:

- *Text advertisements that pass PageRank*
- *Advertorials or native advertising where payment is received for articles that include links that pass PageRank*
- *Links with optimized anchor text in articles or press releases distributed on other sites. For example:*

"There are many <u>wedding rings</u> on the market. If you want to have a <u>wedding</u>, you will have to pick the <u>best ring</u>. You will also need to <u>buy flowers</u> and a <u>wedding dress</u>."

*(**Note:** The underlined words are hyperlinks in the previous sentence.)*
- *Low-quality directory or bookmark site links.*
  *(**Note:** These are spammy directories set up only for the purpose of selling local links. In Chapter 9 we talked about the importance of having listings in local directories – just be sure they are legit!)*
- *Keyword-rich, hidden or low-quality links embedded in widgets that are distributed across various sites, for example:*
- *Widely distributed links in the footers or templates of various sites*

Caution: *Exact Match Anchor Text – Google says: "Links with optimized anchor text in articles or press releases distributed on other sites" <u>can be considered a link scheme</u>. We know that Anchor text is becoming overtly overused and now Google considers this a spammy tactic. While Google thinks it's fine to have a few links that are exact match anchor text, Google also knows that it's unnatural to have hundreds or thousands of text links that exactly match your keywords. Be cautious and don't overdo it. The truth is most outside websites are not going to give you an exact matched anchor text link anyway, and Google knows that. To learn more: <u>www.PlayGooglesGame.com/exact-match-anchor-text-links</u>*

Define: Link Velocity *– Link Velocity refers to how fast links are built to your site in a given period of time. High link velocity could be a bad thing. It's a sure sign that you just bought a bunch of incoming links from a link sharing farm.*

Back Links Are Not Dead

With all of the link manipulation going on, Google would probably like to do away with links all together, and maybe one day they will refine their algorithms to the point that they can, but they're not anywhere close yet.

For now it looks like Google will continue to stick with its roots and embrace backlinks. Just know that they have figured out all the angles for cheating. Therefore, spend time building amazing content, and they will come....

Best Practices – Action Plan

1. Plan to visit blogs or discussion forums to post comments, give expert advice or answer technical questions? Be sure to link back to your website (for further details) when doing so.

_____

_____

_____

_____

2. What valuable insight do you have within your industry, which you could share?

_____

_____

_____

_____

3. Ongoing plan for writing newsworthy Press Releases, Articles and Newsletters.

_____

_____

_____

_____

4. Create a site map.

_____

_____

_____

_____

5. Check your backlinks with Google and Yahoo.

_____

_____

_____

_____

Chapter 6

Good Content is All Google Cares About

Build amazing content, and they will come...

✓ Text | Images | Video
✓ Lack of it Nullifies All Other Efforts
✓ Google Watches Our Content Everywhere
  Across the Internet

Google loves good content... people like it as well. The most important point to make in this chapter is that not one single keyword strategy in this book will be effective unless you reinforce those same keywords within the content on the pages of your website, on social media platforms, on

Google Images, and on YouTube.

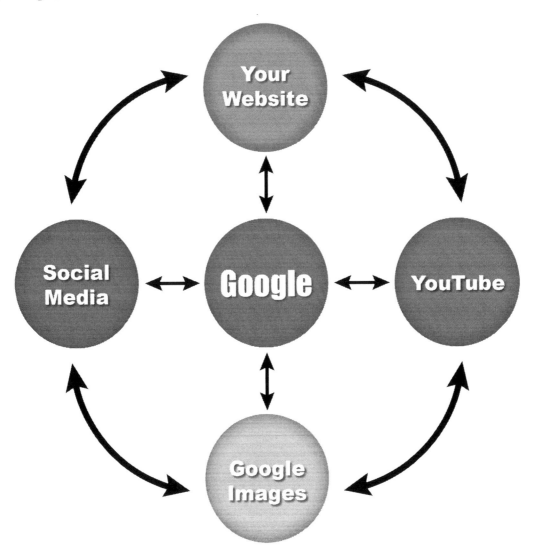

Google has had one consistent message about SEO: "Provide Good Content." There is some misunderstanding out there that content is only the "textual" content on your website. In Google's mind, content consists of Video, Images, and Text that you engage with <u>anywhere on the internet</u>. This book revolves around good content—it's a fundamental law of SEO and remains constant.

Highlights

Very Important:

- Google's success depends on only showing websites with good content.
- Content = Written Text, Images, Video
- Your content can be, and should be, located anywhere on the internet
- Place your content on all of Google's platforms

Important:

- Place your content on Social Media
- Understand what differentiates good content from content that's meant to influence search engines

Helpful:

- Look at your website through Google's lens

The Fundamentals Never Change

Even as every new Google algorithm comes out, their message about SEO has been consistent over the years:

Offer interesting content that compels the visitor to share it with their friends, bookmark it, and want to come back for more. Google tracks all of this.

"First and foremost we care about trying to get the stuff that people really will like, the good, the compelling content in front of them." - quote by Matt Cutts, Google's voice on SEO and head of Google's Webspam team.

Actually when Google tweaks their algorithms, they are just trying to enhance their ability to detect websites with good content versus websites with low quality or spammy content.

We know that everything Google does focuses around the end user—the searcher. Google even adheres to this philosophy with their money making advertising division *Google Adwords*, where the end user (not the advertiser) is priority number one. This is proven by how Google ranks the order of the ads as they appear along the top or side bar; it's just as much about how many searchers clicked on the ads, as it is how much advertisers are willing to pay for the ads. Simply paying more does not guarantee a higher rank in Google Adwords. They instill this "end user" philosophy into every single employee.

Caution: Textual content should be written for the benefit and enjoyment of your visitors. Text should not be written simply to influence the search engines. Google has very sophisticated programs that can sniff out spammy text that is only written to influence search engines. Google will reward you for writing content that your users enjoy, engage with, share with their friends, and come back for more. Ideally content is remarkable, wonderful, incredibly fascinating, and useful. When it's that good, your visitors will amplify it for you everywhere on the internet! It's that amplification that Google tracks.

Good Content - According to Google

Again – repeated from Chapter 1 (Yes, it's that important) Here are Google's guidelines:

1. People find it interesting enough to stick around for a while, compelled enough to tell their friends, and come back for more. Google tracks how fast visitors bounce right back to the search results or any previous website. (The average *bounce rate* is 3 seconds—you have to get their attention quick!)
2. Relevant to your business. Therefore it revolves around your keywords and contains both incoming and outgoing hyperlinks to authoritative websites relevant to your industry.
3. Fresh & Original – it's created by you, the owner (or manager), not some sponsored content, paid guest blogging service, or worse, copied and pasted from another website. Keep it fresh and create something, anything—a new image, some new text, or a video once a week. Just be sure whatever you create focuses on your keywords.
4. Your text copy is written for the enjoyment of people and not to influence the search engines.

   - **Readable** – Is your content written for humans, or just to influence the search engines?
   - **Compelling** – Do your visitors want to share it with their friends after visiting you website? Is your content arousing their interest, attention, and admiration in a powerful and captivating way?
   - **Informative** – Is it interesting? Is it helpful? Does it answer any questions or concerns they might have?

Black Hat Warning: Never repeat or stuff a bunch of keywords anywhere, especially in your content elements. Google watches out for this. Your visitors can also tell when keywords have been crammed in because the text reads funny and Google can tell too. Remember, Google wants your content to be Readable, Compelling, and Informative!

Play Google's Game

Participate in every platform they own, spread your awesome content everywhere. By the way, have we mentioned—it's all free.

- YouTube (a search engine of videos)
- Google Image Search (a search engine of images)
- Google+
- Google My Business (Maps)

SEO is not just one single thing you can do. There is no silver bullet; it's the many things you do, all working together—a holistic approach.

In order to determine how "interesting" or "compelling" our content is to their customers (the searching public), Google watches what we do and how engaged we are with the users on entire internet, both on our website and off our website. Google watches us on Social Media and Blogs. They look at our on-page and off-page text Videos and Images. "Play Google's Game."

Focus Your Content on Something You Can Win At

It's better to be a big fish in a small pond… Win by focusing your keyword strategy on a niche, specialty, or geographic area. It's also easier to win by being a big fish in the following underutilized areas.

- Win with Google Images. It's much easier to get high ranking for your keywords on a Google Image search (versus a regular Google search), because most of your customers are not optimizing their images for this search engine.
- Win with YouTube – it's also easier to rank higher here (versus a regular Google search) by optimizing your YouTube videos for your keywords. Plus, being active on YouTube will help your regular Google search ranking for those same keywords.
- Win with Blogs – Google loves blogs on our websites. In fact, they favor websites with blogs. It's also our best opportunity for great "fresh" content. More on blogs in Chapter 8.
- For Local Business – Win with Google Maps (Google My Business): it's easier to be a big fish in your city, than trying to be a big fish in the oceans of the world!

Fresh Content

Google loves fresh content because users love fresh content. Think about it; how long do you stick around when you land on a page and realize it hasn't been updated for 5 years?

We're noticing an increase in the number of listings on the SERP that have been updated in the last week—some in 24 or less! Most of these revolve around blog posts, which we will dive into in Chapter 8, "Google Loves Blogs".

In the example below, notice the top listing is a blog post Greg made six days prior to capturing this screen shot. The point of this example is how fast Google can pick up a webpage. We know that no one would ever search those exact terms, but the fact that Google did pick up a page for those terms in the title in six days or less, and ranked it #1, shows the value of fresh content.

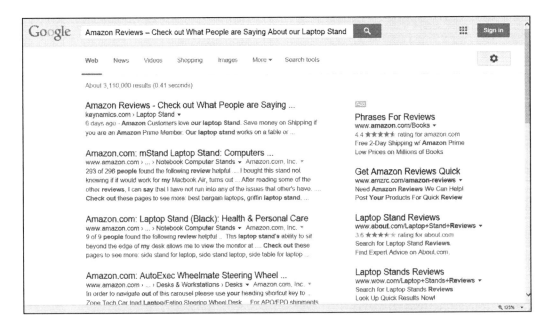

Let's compare updating your website to one of those changeable marquees on the outside of a "brick and mortar" business. Imagine if the owner left the same message on the sign all year. People would just drive by without paying attention to it. Nobody likes a stale message.

Greg had those changeable message boards on his family owned Ace Hardware stores in Houston, Texas. Growing up, Greg's dad was adamant about him getting up on that ladder every week to change the letters. His dad told him that people would pay attention to their messages/advertisements as they drove by if they were fresh. The same goes for your content. Keep it fresh—Thanks Dad!

The bottom line is that you should make a new blog post, share something on Twitter or Facebook, upload a new image or video at least once a week! If you don't, you will be left in the dust!

Google's Secret Code – The Rules

Google is very secretive about the *algorithms* they use to index and rank websites for any particular keyword. *Algorithms* are simply the rules that search engines use to rank webpages. Their algorithms are plugged into computer programs, also referred to as *spiders*. These are programs that take a snapshot of our websites, looking through all of our programming code for our keywords and deciding how to rank us for those keywords. They read every bit of programming code including the text, images, and video on our website. Here are a few points to keep in mind.

These spiders are not only searching for our individual keywords, they are also taking a holistic view of all of the elements on the webpage. They want to know the true meaning of our words. Therefore, they use syntax and semantics to look at the context and the sentence structure of the other words surrounding our keywords. Google is looking for the relationship and cohesion between our words and how they fit in with our keywords, images, and videos on the rest of the page.

Simply put, is it grammatically correct, logical, and using words that one would expect to find on similar websites with the same topic? This is exactly why stuffing a bunch of keywords into your content does nothing but hurt you.

They also look for any changes since the last time they crawled our websites— change is good; it means the website has fresh content. They follow our hyperlinks to other websites on the internet and scan them as well to see how they relate and interact with our keywords. Ultimately they are trying to decide how to rank us for those keywords, based on the rules set out in the algorithms and the overall relevance our site has to those keywords. This all happens in a split second and with regular frequency. We notice that our websites seem to get crawled once a week or so.

Guess what—no one but Google has the secret algorithmic code. Their secrets are locked away tight in the Google vault!

However, Google has had one consistent message over the years: "Provide Good Content." As discussed in previous chapters, once you start using Google's Search Console, you will notice that everything revolves around good content that pleases Google's users. All we know for sure is that the algorithms are designed around this basic concept.

> **Caution:** *As previously discussed, your Title tag is the most important place to put your keywords. However, if you do not reinforce those keywords with more of them in the content of your website, you will get zero value from the keywords in your Title Tag.*

Latent Semantic Indexing

Note that Google employs something called *LSI* or *Latent Semantic Indexing* to catch people who are simply writing content for search engines and not people. LSI identifies patterns in the relationships between the keywords and concepts contained in your textual content. Google is trying to make sure that your text is relevant and that it is logical, based on your keywords.

Google is looking for unnatural relationships between your words. LSI is based on the principle that keywords that are used in the same contexts on other websites tend to have similar meanings. A key feature of LSI is its ability to extract the conceptual content of a body of text by establishing associations between those keywords that occur in similar contexts.

In simple terms it just means that Google is looking for natural content that a human would enjoy reading. They don't look at the number of times a keyword is repeated on a page; they look at how the keyword is associated with the "theme" or context of the page as compared to similarly themed pages throughout the internet.

Google will give more weight to a site's central theme than a particular keyword.

This does not mean that you should not sprinkle your keywords throughout your text. In fact you absolutely should. However, you should do it in a way that looks and reads naturally. Google gives an example of unnatural text:

> *"There are many <u>wedding rings</u> on the market. If you want to have a <u>wedding</u>, you will have to pick the <u>best wedding ring</u>. You will also need to <u>buy wedding flowers</u> and a <u>wedding dress</u>."*

Writing this way will cause Google to flag your website as a spammy, low quality website and you will never rank high.

As described through this book, as long as you write naturally and for the enjoyment of your readers, you'll be fine. As in the above example, it will be obvious to your readers and to Google when you are simply stuffing as many keywords in as many places that you can.

> *SEO Juice Alert: Be sure to place your keyword or keyword phrase close to or in the first sentence and the last sentence on a webpage. This is what the Google spiders see first. This is also natural. Remember good writing structure from English class?*

1. *Tell them what you are going to tell them.*
2. *Tell them.*
3. *Then tell them what you told them.*

Greg's Moment of Clarity

Greg has been doing SEO since 2003. It wasn't until recently that a light bulb went off about this whole content thing. Yeah, yeah, Google has always been saying "Provide Good Content".

Clarity came when Greg thought about the history of the Google algorithm changes as it relates to how Google tries to identify websites with good content. He put himself in Google's shoes and was able to start looking at everything through Google's lens.

In the beginning, search engines were all about "keywords in the content;" then people started abusing keywords, so they tweaked their algorithm to catch people cheating, using tactics like invisible text, super small fonts, and keyword stuffing.

Then Google came along and started looking at the popularity of "Backlinks to the Content". Google figured it was like a popularity contest. Then people started selling backlinks and Google figured out an algorithm change to catch them.

Today it's about how many people are "engaging with our content" on our websites and on other internet platforms. Today it's Facebook, Twitter, LinkedIn, and others; who knows what it will be tomorrow.

So, look at your website through Google's lens.

- Does it have interesting content? Well, let's see, are people talking about it and sharing it (backlinks)?
- Are people talking about it on Social Media?

- Is the business itself talking about it through their blog page?
- Are people clicking on your images from Google Image Search; are they then clicking through onto your website from Google Image Search?
- Are they commenting on your YouTube videos, liking them, sharing them, and clicking through to your website from them?
- And most importantly, do visitors like it so much that they come back often?

Do It Yourself or Hire a Pro?

As discussed in Chapter 1, Google prefers that the bulk of your content is created by you. They know that the business owner can create original content by sharing their industry knowledge and real world stories.

However, we realize that for some business owners, creating content is kind of a daunting task, especially in the beginning. Maybe you're not that comfortable writing copy, communicating on social media platforms like Twitter or Facebook, taking pictures, or creating video.

> ***Learn More:*** *For our favorite resources to help you create awesome content, or least give you a head start click here:* <u>*www.PlayGooglesGame.com/website-content-creating-services*</u>

When hiring someone else to do this for you, just make sure that you are involved in the process and communicating with them. We wrote this book with the hope that your increased knowledge would enable you to have these conversations with the services you hire out.

You must also realize that people can tell whether or not content is original and natural. If it's not, they will just click the back button and bounce right back to the page they were before. Google will take note of this lack of interaction and ding you for it. You will lose trust with Google and your potential customers. Worse, you won't sell anything!

Therefore, if you need to outsource content, then be sure that you are hiring writers, photographers, and videographers that understand your business industry and your business goals. Be sure they are capable of producing original content that reflects your unique business and that you are proud to publish anywhere in the internet.

Best Practices – Action Plan

1. What's your ongoing strategy for updating with fresh content?

_____

_____

_____

_____

2. Do you have your content on all of Google's platforms? YouTube? Google Images?

_____

_____

_____

_____

3. Do you have a blog page (see Chapter 8)? How often do you create a new blog post? Do you embed new images in that blog post? Embed YouTube videos?

_____

_____

_____

_____

4. Do you have a Facebook business page? Are you posting your blog post URLs on your Facebook Page—hopefully driving traffic back to your webpage?

_____

_____

_____

_____

Chapter 7

How to Get Chosen from the Search Results

Top Rank does not guarantee a click through to your website

✓ Attention Grabbing Headline
✓ Your Call-To-Action
✓ Google Tracks Your Clicks

High ranking is the ultimate goal of SEO. However, most SEO marketers and website designers completely overlook this opportunity.

Just because you are in the #1 spot does not guarantee that you will be picked. The searcher is presented with a lot of choices on the *search engine results page*; sometimes as many as 50 or more options that they can click on, including maps, images, videos, ads, and the other free listings we are competing against for the #1 spot. Many times a searcher will choose a lower ranked listing, just because it stands out, grabs their attention, and is more compelling to click on.

The ultimate goal? You want the searching public to pick **you** out of the top ten websites that are displayed in front of them.

> **The Double Whammy:** *The more that you are picked, the higher you will be ranked for those particular keywords—Google tracks this. Self-fulfilling!*

Highlights

Very Important:
- Title Tag = Headline
- Description Meta Tag = Call to Action

Important:
- Put your phone number in the description Meta Tag
- Realize that Google is watching and rewarding you for more clicks

Helpful:
- Understand what motivates your customers and use that in your headline and your call to action

Advertising 101 – Headline & Call to Action

We recommend that you use the same simple strategy that has worked in print advertising for hundreds of years. First, use an *Attention Grabbing Headline* and second, have a *Call to Action*—it's basic advertising 101.

Think of the Search Engine Results Page as the front page of a newspaper, and just like a newspaper, your copy should be short and have impact. Your words should be chosen carefully based on the needs of your target audience. Find out what their "pain" is and address it. What are they looking for?

The search engine results page is laid out perfectly for this headline/call to action scenario. It might help to see this by doing a live Google search right now so you can follow along.

The Title Tag and the Description Meta Tag in the code of your website form what's called your snippet area on the SERP. Think of this as your little space to put your advertisement on the page.

The Attention Grabbing Headline

On the ten free search results, notice that they all begin with a bold blue line of text that is underlined. This is at the top of the area referred to as the *Title Line* of your *Snippet Area.*

Google grabs this from your *Title Tag* in your programming code. Remember back in Chapter 2 we said that the title tag is the number one most important place to put keywords on your website? Well, it's also very important because you want use it to grab attention here.

This is the most visible line of text! The title also shows up on the very top line in your browser. You only get a few words and Google truncates the rest, so play around with it.

Therefore, we have a balancing act:

1. We have to work in our most important keywords in the first two or three words for proper SEO; remember that the first words count more.
2. We have to use the rest of the words in the title line to grab attention.

Google will display about 55 to 60 characters on this first line and will truncate anything else. Therefore, you must accomplish these two goals within the first 55 to 60 characters.

As discussed previously, every page on your website should have a different title, and description meta tag. It amazes us to see how many prominent websites are not doing this properly. Some Examples below will give you an idea of the proper way:

- **Home Page (local business)** = City Name | Most Important Keyword | Something Attention Grabbing
- **Home Page (non-local)** = Most Important Keyword | Something Attention Grabbing

- **About Page** = About Us | Most Important Keyword | Something Attention Grabbing
- **Contact Page** = Contact Us | Most Important Keyword | Something Attention Grabbing

Real world Example: Let's look at a recent example from Greg's laptop stand business. On his laptop stand landing page, his title tag reads:

Laptop Stand | $19.99 | Recycled | Lightweight | Pink Donations

Let's break it down. The keyword (phrase) "Laptop Stand" are Greg's most important keywords, so they always go first. Next, Greg used a compelling price point of $19.99. Then, hoping to ride the wave of folks concerned about the environment, he used "Recycled". Many laptop stand users are mobile, therefore, weight is a concern. And finally, he highlights that he will donate to charity if they order a pink laptop stand.

Tip: Use the "pipes" key to separate your words in the title—it looks and reads better.

Note: If you don't do this properly, or you don't create your content properly, then Google might display a different Title and Description than you created in your Meta Data. Especially if they think their version fits the description of your site better. Create awesome content and you will be fine.

The Call to Action

Look again at your live Google search that we asked you to do earlier, and notice that under the first bold blue underlined text are a couple of lines of black text. Google places your *Description Meta Tag* in this snippet space and we call it the *Description Line*. You get about 150 to 160 characters and Google truncates the rest.

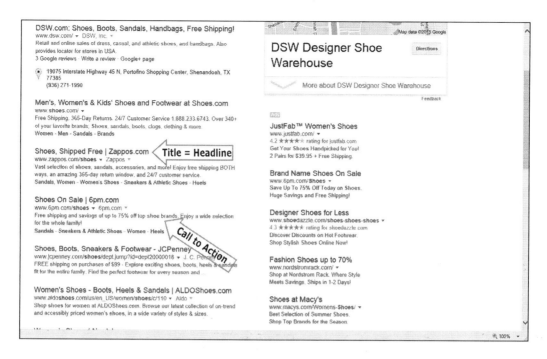

The real value of this space is to create a compelling call to action. Place words here that would encourage the searcher to click through to your website to see more or "Find Out How." There are many words you can use to do this: "Free Shipping", "On Sale Now", "Discounts for Our Facebook Fans"… You get the point.

Notice the screen shot above. Zappos did a good job with their title tag and 6pm did a good job with the description offering 75% off.

Description Meta Tags are not as important for search engine rankings as they are in gaining user click-through from SERPs, which ultimately help your rankings. This is your opportunity to promote your content to searchers and to let them know that your content is more awesome than others listed.

Using keywords in the Description Meta Tag is not as important as compelling the searcher to click. Of course, by nature, that will probably include some of your keywords. The description should optimally be between 150-160 characters. Just like any content, it's best to make it as natural as possible.

Phone Number in the Description Meta Tag

Many times people will never even click through to your website. They are simply calling everyone down the list, right from the search engine results page. This is especially true for mobile phone users because all they have to do is touch the phone number on their screen and it calls instantly from their phone.

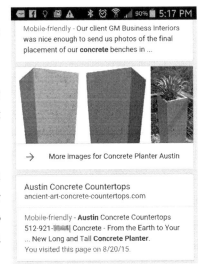

If you don't want to miss out on these types of searchers, then place your phone number in the description Meta Tag.

For Local Business (Local SEO) this also helps build trust for customers wanting to do business with someone they might trust more locally.

It also helps Google trust your information and reward you with higher ranking on the Google Map listings. Your local number in your description meta tag must match the number you gave to Google when you verified your map listing, as we'll discuss in Chapter 9 on the Google Map Listing (Google My Business).

Best Practices – Action Plan

1. Title Meta Tag = your Headline. What does your Homepage say? Your Products or Services Page?

_____

_____

_____

_____

2. Description Meta Tag = your "Call to Action." What compels your customers to take action?

_____

_____

_____

_____

3. What titles and descriptions are your competitors using?

_____

_____

_____

_____

4. Put your Phone Number in your Description Meta Tag if you want people to call.

_____

_____

_____

_____

Chapter 8

Google LOVES Blogs

Google employees live in a blog world

✓ Spiders Come From Geeks
✓ Benefits of a Blog
✓ WordPress Wins

If we could only pick one technique in this entire book that would help you win more business, it would be this chapter. Creating a blog page, while using the WordPress website building platform, forms a foundation to easily implement every tip and technique in this entire book. It's like getting a head start!

OK, right about now you're probably thinking… "None of my customers use those blogs;

those things are only for geeks. Plus, I don't have time to make all those blog posts and you can just forget about me answering all those comments that people will make!" Or, maybe you're thinking, "What the heck is a blog?"

No worries—we agree, the word blog is kind of geeky. So label it whatever you want. You don't have to call it a blog. We actually prefer to title the blog page something like "News", "Current Events", "New Arrivals", or "Current Projects". See the screen shot below from the Greater Houston Manufacturers Association (managed by the author). We list the blog posts as "Manufacturing News".

As far as your time goes, we're talking a couple of posts per month; once a week is ideal. Unfortunately, few visitors (if any) will take the time to respond with a comment. Consider yourself lucky if you start to get that kind of following.

Highlights

Very Important:
- Google Identifies All Blogs and Gives them a Boost in Rankings
- Mobile Friendly is now Mandatory
- Blogs Provide Fresh, Engaging Content (text, images, and video)
- Put Keywords in the Blog Title
- WordPress Wins – Game Over
- Most of Your Competitors Are Not Blogging – You can Win!
- Blogs Give You a Head Start for Implementing All Techniques in this Book

Important:
- Ease of Creating a Blog Post
- Ease of Updating & Changing Themes (templates)
- Open Source – Not Married to One Web Designer
- Give First – Never Overtly Advertise
- Share Your Industry Knowledge

Helpful:
- SEO & Other Plugins
- Insert Links to Your Blog Post into Facebook, Twitter, etc.
- Ideas for Blog Post Content
- Anatomy of a Blog

Why are Blogs So Important?

Rest assured that the quantity of your blog posts and the number of people commenting is not what this is about. First and foremost, it's about Google identifying your website as one that contains a blog page and the regular, original, fresh content that you can easily pop in. Once set up, a blog post just takes a few minutes to add. Remember, Google rewards you for fresh content.

Second, it's about your visitors enjoying the experience of being on your website and coming back for more. They crave the informative content of the post itself. Business owners are experts in their field; they have lots of great information, advice, and tips to share. While we might think it's mundane, potential customers value this expertise and will keep coming back if you provide interesting content. At the very least, it establishes your credibility and proficiency in your field.

Folks, this can't be stressed enough. A blog post is the easiest way for a non-technical person to implement most of the techniques that we teach in this book. If you can type, and you have some industry knowledge to share, then you can create an interesting blog post in just a few minutes. Google will love you for it!

Again, if we had to choose only one technique in this entire book to recommend, it would be to launch a blog page within your website, and to use WordPress to design your entire website— period.

Spiders Come From Geeks

In addition to the whole *fresh content* thing, Google loves blogs because their employees love blogs. The Google programs (spiders) that crawl the internet were written by humans. Those humans are computer geeks who grew up reading and creating blogs, and they live in the blog world. Therefore, they prefer blogs over regular websites and have written their programs to rank websites that contain blogs higher than ones that don't (generally speaking).

We are seeing blog posts ranked within minutes of being posted, many times right on the first page of Google. Those Google spiders have identified all of the blogs, and are sitting there just waiting for a new blog post to be made. Once the post is made, it's snatched up and displayed on the search results, almost instantly!

Folks, we have really become vocal about this in our presentations and classes. The bottom line is, if you don't have a blog page on your website, it's like fighting the SEO battle with one arm tied behind your back. Yeah, you can be somewhat successful without it, but everything we talk about is exponentially more effective when you have a blog. You can use your blog post for most of the techniques we teach. Simply drop in your optimized images, videos, articles, content, and keywords. A blog post is the easiest way to accomplish this on a regular basis.

What is a Blog?

For this book we'll define a blog as is a professional series of individual posts including knowledge based articles, news events, and product/service descriptions. We are not going to be discussing the type of blog that is a personal diary.

A blog post is located on a standalone webpage, and this page can be integrated within your main website (as one of the internal pages) or as a separate website all by itself; integrated within your main website is best. These posts are ordered as reverse chronological entries—newest being at the top of the page.

This is an opportunity to share your expert knowledge, or other information relative to your business or keywords. These posts should add to the experience of your visitors. A blog is similar to the Facebook wall or the Facebook news feed, in that visitors can comment and share your post, by just copying the link to your post.

Your visitors are demanding this information, and if they can't get it from you, they will just move on—within seconds. Forrester Research did an in-depth study of internet buyers in 2014, and the information and content contained within a website was ranked above or equal to price in the customer's buying decisions.

The word *blog* is a blend of the term web and log. Wikipedia says a blog is a type of website, or part of a website that is supposed to be updated with new content from time to time. For our business websites, we are only interested in making a blog page as a standalone page contained within our website. Some blogs are simply a website consisting of one page (the blog itself). A separate, stand-alone blog website is no value to us. Our blog webpage should be incorporated in the header of our website along with all the other important pages of our website: the *Home Page*, *Contact* page, *About* page, Products and Services page, etc. You can even choose to have your blog page as your homepage, as seen in the Greater Houston Manufacturers screen shot previously.

> **Bright Idea:** *If you are lucky enough to spark that interaction between you and your customers on your blog page and you actually do start getting lots of comments, you should hire a ghost blogger or have an employee answer them if you don't have time. What a great opportunity!!! However, it's better if the owner does it.*

Blogs are usually maintained by an individual with regular typed entries (posts) including commentary, descriptions of events, industry news, how to, instructions, and other material such as graphics, audio, or video. Entries are commonly displayed in reverse chronological order. Blog can also be used as a verb, meaning to maintain or add content to a blog.

Although not a requirement, most good quality blogs are interactive, allowing visitors to leave comments and even message each other via *widgets* on the blogs, and it is this *interactivity* that distinguishes them from other static websites.

Many blogs provide commentary on a particular subject; others function as more personal online diaries. A typical blog combines text, images, audio, video, and links to other blogs, web pages, and other media related to its topic.

The ability of readers to leave comments in an interactive format is an important part of many blogs. Most blogs are primarily textual, although some focus on art (art blog), photographs (photoblog), videos (video blogging or vlogging), music (MP3 blog), and audio (podcasting). We highly recommend that you always include images or videos in your blog posts, for all the reasons we talk about in the chapters dedicated to images and video. Remember, Google loves images and video so much that they have a separate, dedicated search engine for each one (think YouTube). Research shows that including and image or video greatly increases the chances that a blog post will be read.

The first blogs started in the 1990s as online diaries about the blogger's life and opinions. This was strictly a one sided conversation. As blog software evolved, interactive features, such as the ability for anyone to comment on the blogger's post, were added to create a two way conversation— this is what they refer to as web 2.0. This more social feature gave rise to the immense popularity of blogs.

It's very important to think of each blog post as a standalone website page. The post is listed reverse chronologically as a small section on the main blog webpage. However, clicking on that smaller section opens a new page, where only the blog post is shown on an entire page by itself. **The most important thing to note here is that Google treats those as individual web pages and ranks them for the keywords placed in the elements of the post.** Google looks at the keywords in the text, the file names of the images and or videos in the post, as well as the name of the *category* you assign the post to. All of these elements in the post relate to each other and Google connects the dots to rank you for those keywords. We'll discuss all of these *post elements* later in this chapter.

> ***Learn More:*** *There are programs that will automate re-posting of a blog post for you, or you can simply copy and paste the blog post URL into LinkedIn or your Facebook Business Page and it will show an abbreviated version with a thumbnail image of your choice from your website. This helps drive folks from Facebook back to your website. Plus, Facebook posts can be set to automatically post to your Twitter feed. Visit www.PlayGooglesGame.com/blog-seo for detailed instructions on how to leverage your blog posts on other platforms. See Chapter 10 for more information on Social Media Marketing.*

Benefits of a Blog

Each new blog "post" is the perfect way to introduce fresh content into your website and build credibility in your field. Google rewards websites for fresh content and penalizes websites that are not updated very often; see Chapter 6 for more info on the value of fresh content. A blog post is an opportunity to get the two way conversation going between you and your customers. This interactivity is the whole point of *web 2.0*—a break from the old school, one way communication.

Today's consumers want to participate on your website by contributing, sharing, or giving feedback. Just be careful with your blog post not make it feel like an advertisement. Visitors will spot that a mile away and leave to never come back.

Forester Research did a survey in 2014 of B2B buyers and their online purchasing trends. Survey after survey showed that information and content was either equal to or in some cases more important than price. For repeat return business price was actually second behind informative content.

Your customers that enjoy reading blogs like the fact that the information is current. Some like it so much that they will want to get notified whenever you make a new blog post. They can get notified with an RSS Feed. (We'll discuss RSS Feeds later in the chapter). Even if your customers don't use blogs, they expect to see one on your website. This reassures them and builds trust.

Use your blog to keep your customers up to date on your products and services, highlight your press releases, and make your company seem friendlier. Blogs are one of the best ways to find out what your customers think of your company by paying attention to their comments.

Top 20 Benefits of a Blog

1. Posts are the easiest way to implement all SEO techniques.
2. Business websites with blogs get double the amount of Backlinks.
3. Establish your expertise, authority and trustworthiness.
4. Build a community, or leverage your social media community.
5. Deepen customer relationships.
6. Business websites with blogs get 126% more leads.
7. B2B websites with blogs generate 67% more leads.
8. Your blog is selling 24/7.
9. It's free—all it costs is your time.
10. Blogs are rated the 5th most trusted source of information.
11. Companies that blog have 55% more visitors.
12. 75% of people use blogs.
13. 61% of consumers have made a purchase based on a blog post.
14. 82% of consumers enjoy reading relevant content about brands.
15. 70% of consumers learn about a company through articles, versus advertisements.
16. Facebook has made blogs more acceptable.
17. Drive traffic back to your website by placing the blog post into Facebook, LinkedIn, Twitter, Google Plus, etc.

18. Build Your Brand.
19. Allows a user, even with limited expertise, to add, modify and remove content from a website without relying on the original website designer.
20. Fresh Content – Fresh Content – Fresh Content!

> **Bright Idea:** *Give First – Always keep this in mind when writing a blog post. Never, ever use a blog post as simply an advertisement. Or to simply stuff a bunch of keywords in – that will make a visitor leave faster than anything. People love stories and hate advertisements.*

Anatomy of a Blog

Most blogs are built using computer applications called CMS (*Content Management Systems*). These systems allow a central interface (*dashboard*) for maintaining and editing all of the content, pages, posts, comments, and overall layout of the website. Popular CMS platforms are WordPress, Drupal, and Joomla.

As discussed in Chapter 1, a website is nothing more than a bunch of files strung together. A CMS stores and organizes these files, allowing for the publishing, editing, and modifying of the content of our websites.

We've previously discussed that a blog is a standalone webpage that holds the individual posts. Let's now discuss the general layout of that page.

Blog Page Layout

Just like a regular webpage, a blog page can be laid out in just about any format you want. However, from a *usability* standpoint, it's best to lay it out in a format that your visitors are familiar with.

The ***header*** area at the top should be exactly the same for all pages of your website. It usually contains a header image: a wide eye catching graphic that stretches across the entire top of the page. Think of this graphic as your attention grabbing headline in the newspaper. Remember, you only have about 3 seconds to grab their attention before they bounce right back to the search results, and you've lost them forever!

Either directly above or directly below the header image should be ***text links*** to the main pages of the website: "Contact" | "About" | "Products" | "Services". It's also a good place to put a *search box*, where visitors can search your entire website. Search boxes are really good for repeat customers, who are coming back and know what they want. Maybe they're making a repeat purchase and just want to search for the topic they read about previously.

A ***sidebar*** is a column that is tall and narrow, and runs down the entire length of either side of the page. Most sidebars are located on the right hand side of the page. Sidebars are a great place to put important information that you want to feature: maybe an image of a product line you want to feature, a new product, links to *categories*, a video, a *search box*, links to other important pages within or outside of your website.

> ***Tip:*** *Now that most people are searching the internet from mobile devices, using more than one sidebar is not a good idea. It's hard enough to get one column to show correctly on a mobile device.*

The **main body** of the page is the area that actually contains your reverse chronological list of posts. In order to feature several of your posts *"above the fold,"* it's best to only show a few enticing sentences along with good image on your individual post. You can do this by inserting a link at the end of the last sentence to "Continue reading." Once visitors click that link it will take them to the standalone page that contains the entire post.

The ***footer area***, just like the header area, is the same for all main pages of your website and is useful for copyright information and repeating links to all of your pages within your website. But most importantly, if you want local business, **you must put your physical address and local phone number in the footer**. We'll discuss more about this in Chapter 9 (Google Maps and Google local search).

Posts versus Pages

Blog posts are actually located in two places. First, they are contained as a list, by date, within the main blog page on your website. Usually, this main blog page only shows the first portion of the actual blog post, with a link to "read more," kind of like a teaser. One reason to only list a short section of the post is that visitors can quickly scan down the entire list of posts without having to scroll all the way to the bottom of each post to get to the beginning of the next one. Being able to quickly scan down the list is better from a usability standpoint.

Once they follow that link to read more, it takes them to the entire, full post. **It's very, very**

important to understand that this page that contains the entire post is actually a standalone webpage, with its own URL, that can be picked up and ranked by Google in the search results. This is also referred to as the *permalink* of the blog post.

A "Page" refers to a permanent, static web page on your website. While a post is dated and "time-sensitive," a page is not. For Example, the "Contact Us" or "About" page is a permanent page with information that changes infrequently.

This is a tad bit confusing, because the permalink containing the full blog post is actually a standalone web page. However, when most people refer to website page, they mean the traditional static pages that do not contain the blog posts.

Blog Post Elements

Breaking down the post into its elements will help us understand why Google treats the entire post as an individual web page. Google is determining the ranking value of the post by looking at the keywords placed in the title of the post and in text with the body of the post. Google also looks at the keywords in the images and or videos in the post, as well as the *category* you assign the post to. All of these elements in the post are connected, and Google connects the dots to rank you for those keywords.

Post Title

Just like everything else we talk about in the book, it's all about the keywords. **You must put your most important keywords in the *Post Title*** (aka - the headline) of the blog post. This is paramount!

FYI: Most blog platforms like WordPress are automatically set to use the words in the post title as part of the URL (after the ".com/") by automatically separating the words with hyphens. We already discussed the benefit of this in the keyword chapter.

> *SEO Juice Alert: The order of the keywords is important when you are stringing together multiple keywords or in a series of words like the title of a blog post. Therefore, if you have more than one keyword (a keyword phrase), always put your most important keywords first. For example, if you want local business, your city or town name should be heavily incorporated into your keyword strategy and start the keyword phrase with the name of your city!*

Body/Content Section

The body is the main section of the blog post where you can insert content in the form of text, images, and video.

Just as we talked about in the keyword chapter, reinforce the keywords in your title by using those same keywords in the body of the blog post. Include some images in the body with file ".jpg" names containing those same keywords. (See Chapter 3, "Be Found on Image Search", for more details on making your images findable. Embedding your YouTube videos in your posts by copying and pasting the embed code (provided by YouTube) is also huge for your ranking!

> **Bright Idea:** *Always include a live hyperlink to another page within your website from your blog post. This way, whenever someone copies your blog post and pastes it onto another website, a link to your website will usually go with it.*

Categories

In WordPress you can assign your post to various predefined *Categories* at the time you first create the post. Be sure to assign a category to all posts; if you don't the post will, by default, go into "Uncategorized". You must initially set up your various categories by **naming them with your most important keywords!** Many times our blog posts that are assigned to a category are ranked #1 for the keywords of the category itself.

Think long and hard about naming your categories. You probably don't want to water down your keywords too much, so limit the number of categories to 10 or so. It's fine to name your category with a keyword phrase.

Need Ideas For Blog Posts?
"People like to hear stories—they ignore advertisements"

We're all busy running our businesses, right? Who has time to write those silly blog posts? And who has time to answer all the comments people will make?

Not to worry. The good quality content that Google implores us to create already resides within your head: your business expertise and your ongoing experiences living and learning your craft. For example, discussing a special technique that differentiates you from your competition.

Think about all of the industry knowledge that we can share. How about a newsworthy event or new technology? Even though we tend to think it's mundane and that no one would be interested, the fact is that customers love that sort of stuff, and Google rewards us for creating it.

Your visitors don't expect a polished professional writer; in fact they prefer a more real world experience. Don't get caught up on a 1,000 word dissertation; keep it short and to the point—less is better!

Bright Ideas

1. Give First.
2. Keep an eye out for something unique and interesting.
3. News – Trends – Seasonal Events.
4. Solicit guest posts from customers, vendors, or industry experts.
5. Ask a question in the title of your post.
6. Encourage engagement.
7. Find your customer's pain points and answer them.
8. Share both your successes and trials.
9. Tell Stories.

Trade Journals

There is a wealth of information in your business and industry trade journals that you can share. Just be careful to paraphrase the article in your own words and then place a link to the article. If you simply copy and paste the content of the article, you could be flagged as a *scraper site* for simply copying and pasting someone else's work, plus you could be liable for copyright infringement. Please pay attention to their copyright policies so you don't get in trouble.

Google News Alert

Setting up a Google news alert is super easy. Just make sure you are logged on to your Google account (registering for a Google account is the first step in Playing Google's Game – it's free).

Set some news alerts for your specific keywords, or topics in your industry, specifically related to the interest of your visitors. Read the article. Write up a synopsis of the highlights in your own words. Relate it to your business or audience, and put a link to the article. Again, please be careful here not to copy and paste verbatim, as you will be identified as a scraper website.

Subscribe to Newsletters and RSS Feeds

Follow the leaders in your industry by subscribing to their email newsletters or RSS feeds. If the person or platform you want to get information from has RSS feeds available, it will alert you whenever they update their blog or news entry. Again, just paraphrase the highlights of their content and be sure to note the source, paying attention to their copyright policies so you don't get in trouble.

> ***Quick Fact:*** *RSS (Rich Site Summary; originally RDF Site Summary), often called Really Simple Syndication, uses a family of standard web feed formats to publish (or subscribe to) frequently updated information: blog entries, news headlines, audio, video.*

Embed YouTube Videos

YouTube allows you to embed their videos into your website by providing you with the *embed code*. This is great because the embed code puts a little video player right on your website. Visitors love it; they can just click and watch, and never leave your website. These can be instructional videos from your YouTube channel or anyone else's YouTube video, as long as they have opted to allow embedding (most do). Of course it's best to create your own YouTube videos, as explained in Chapter 4, but any YouTube video which is relevant to your keywords will do. You can see an example of the embed code from the YouTube screenshot below. It's the HTML code underneath the word "Embed". Just copy and paste it into your blog post as shown in the next screen shot.

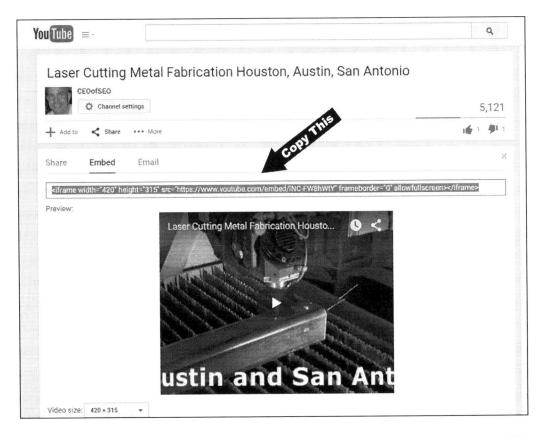

Be sure and place some text in close proximity around the video in the blog post. Relate it back to your product or service, and of course work in a few of your important keywords. It would be very helpful if the video title had those same keywords. See Chapter 4 for techniques to optimize YouTube videos.

Bright Idea: *On your own YouTube channel, you should allow embedding. Wouldn't it be great if lots of other websites embedded your video! We'll show you how you can brand it and link it back to your website in Chapter 4.*

Embed Still Images

An image can quickly and easily be embedded into a blog post. The blog software allows you to easily justify it to the left, right, or center area of the blog post. You can resize the image as needed. Be sure to see Chapter 3 for instruction on how to properly name the image file and give it an ALT and Title Tag so you rank high on the Google Image Search Engine.

Tip: *Infographics are a great way to communicate a lot of information within one image. Infographics are graphic visual representations of information, data or knowledge intended to present information quickly and clearly.*

Real World Example: *Greg accidentally discovered a great way to introduce an image into a blog post, which displays very nicely within the Google Image search results. Insert an image of your business card!*

WordPress Wins

WordPress is the mother of all *blog software* applications, plus it's a very powerful and flexible website design program for your entire website—not just the blog page! In fact, it's the most popular website design software in the world. One out of every five websites is designed entirely with WordPress.

Of course there are always exceptions, and if your business can afford to hire programmers to custom code a blog into your main website, then more power to you! However, as of today, there is no simpler, more effective, nor cheaper way to design a fully functional website than using WordPress.

Some still say that WordPress is just for building a blog and not your entire website. Well, tell that to NASA, Reuters, The New York Times, CNN, Forbes, GM, Sony, Best Buy, and on and on...

Blog Software Applications

Blogs are built with programs much like any website is built. Most websites use website design programs to build the site in HTML programming language, while most blogs use applications with content management system software like Joomla and Drupal using PHP programming language; sounds scary right?

Well, it doesn't have to be. Those applications listed above are for programmers who custom code websites line by line. Most small business owners do not need this level of customization, plus it's very expensive to custom code a website and we have already talked about the problem of being married to one website designer if they custom code it—and they probably own the code anyway!

Leave the custom coded blogs to the large corporations. Using WordPress is easy and requires little to no programming skills.

From WordPress:

WordPress powers more than 23% of the web—a figure that rises every day. Everything from simple websites and business ecommerce sites to blogs, to complex portals and enterprise websites, and even applications, are built with WordPress.

WordPress combines simplicity for users and publishers with under-the-hood complexity for developers. This makes it flexible while still being easy to use.

The following is a list of some of the features that come as standard with WordPress; however, there are literally thousands of plugins that extend what WordPress does, so the actual functionality is nearly limitless. You are also free to do whatever you like with the WordPress code; extend it or modify in any way or use it for commercial projects without any licensing fees. That is the beauty of free software: free refers not only to price but also the freedom to have complete control over it.

Features of WordPress

1. **It's Free**.
2. **It's Everywhere:** Find someone to help you build, maintain or fix your website with an ad on Craigslist. There is literally a ton of support around every corner! This usually translates into big money savings.
3. **Easy To Use:** Writing a blog post is just about as easy as typing a letter on a Word document, and dragging and dropping images from your computer into the WordPress image uploader. No coding necessary! By default, the WordPress interface uses WYSIWYG (what you see is what you get) designing, although knowing some code basics will make your life easier if you want to dive into maintaining the various pages of your website.

   Folks it's really not that hard, once you give it a try. This will save you a ton of money. You don't want to have to call your website designer just to have them make a blog post for you. That would be very expensive and untimely! Plus, if you ever get stumped, just Google your question and you'll get your answer in seconds.

   Learn More: See our Top 10 Code Snippet Examples. It's as easy as copying and pasting the code snippet, which is what most professional programmers do anyway.
   www.PlayGooglesGame.com/top-ten-code-snippets

4. **Open Source:** You are not tied to your original website designer, in case you want to leave them, they disappear, or you need to maintain it in their absence. Note: Be sure to get the rights/ownership of your code, domain name, and content when you first get a website designed. Get this in writing!

   Caution: It's the old 80/20 rule with website designers. 20% are really good, professional business folks and 80% are less than par. We hear so many negative stories about business owners being tied down to the original website designer. When things go bad, or the original website designer moves away, you're either stuck with something you can't use and maintain, or left with nothing at all. This can happen in one of two ways: 1. The original website designer designs the website in something other than WordPress (custom code that is hard to maintain by anyone else); 2. They actually own the copyright to the code, content, images, text— everything. You can leave them, but you can't take your website with you! By the way, the 20% that are good are typically using WordPress, and for sure they don't mind handing over the ownership rights to your website.

173

5. **Simplicity:** Simplicity makes it possible for you to get online and get publishing, quickly. Nothing should get in the way of you getting your website up and your content out there. WordPress is built to make that happen. This also translates into big money savings.

6. **Flexibility:** WordPress is not just for building a blog website. With WordPress, you can create any type of website you want: a personal blog or a full blown website, a photoblog, a business website, an ecommerce website, a professional portfolio, a government website, a magazine or news website, an online community, even a network of websites. You can make your website beautiful with themes, and extend it with plugins. You can even build your very own application.

7. **Publish with Ease—Save money and Do It Yourself:** If you've ever written an email, made a Facebook post or created a Word document, then you're already a whizz at creating content with WordPress. You can create Posts and Pages, format them easily, insert media (images and videos), and with the click of a button your content is live and on the web.

8. **Publishing Tools:** WordPress makes it easy for you to manage your content. Create drafts, schedule publication, and look at your post revisions. Make your content public or private, and secure posts and pages with a password.

9. **User Management:** Not everyone requires the same level of access to your website. Maybe you want to hire a summer intern, or even a high school student (yes it's that easy) to make posts for you. Administrator level can manage the entire website, Editor level can work with content, Authors and Contributors can only write the post content, and—if you allow it— subscribers can have a profile that they can manage. This lets you have a variety of contributors to your website, and lets others simply be part of your community.

10. **Easily Add Images and Videos:** As discussed in Chapters 3 and 4, if a picture is worth a thousand words, videos are worth 10,000, which is why it's important for you to be able to quickly and easily upload images and media to WordPress. Drag and drop your media into the uploader to add it to your website. Add ALT text, captions, and titles, and insert images and galleries into your content. WordPress even has a few image editing tools you can have fun with.

11. **Full Standards Compliance:** Every piece of WordPress generated code is in full compliance with the standards set by the W3C. This means that your website will work in today's browser, while maintaining forward compatibility with the next generation of browser. Your website is a beautiful thing, now and in the future.

12. **Safe – Stable – Secure:** The WordPress community is enormous and worldwide, with many checks and balances. New versions and updates are vetted more than any other program on the planet before they are released into the public. You can rest assured that the chances it will break, or cause security issues is less than any other program available because it's been thoroughly tested before it is released. Whenever the latest security hack makes the news headlines, WordPress is quick to respond with an updated revision and security patch. With

a simple mouse click, it literally takes seconds to update to the latest version of WordPress, and you will get fair warning that you need to update whenever a new version comes out.

Caution: Always, ALWAYS back up your website regularly, and especially before applying any WordPress updates or major changes to your website. WordPress makes it super easy to back up. See www.PlayGooglesGame.com/wordpress-backing-up for more details.

Caution: Two common threats with blogs and Wordpress (or any website): 1. Spammy comments; 2. Security and Hacks.

For the latest plugins to reduce spam and help protect your website from being hacked click here:
www.PlayGooglesGame.com/comment-spam
www.PlayGooglesGame.com/wordpress-security

13. **Easy Theme System:** Themes affect the overall appearance of your website, allowing you to easily customize the layout, colors, menus, navigation, etc. WordPress comes bundled with two default themes, but they are very plain and vanilla. You should spice up the look of your site using the WordPress theme directory, which contains thousands of themes for you to create a beautiful website. None of those to your taste? Upload a theme you have bought from a designer with the click of a button. It only takes a few seconds for you to give your website a complete makeover. Within seconds you can also switch back and forth until you find one you're happy with. More money savings!

Note: You can change your theme without affecting the content of your website. Changing a theme retains all of your posts, comments, images, video etc. All it does is rearrange them into a different appearance. Usually you will also have to upload a new header image when you change themes.

14. **Extend with Plugins: Plugins add special functionality without having to hire someone to custom code it. You can even get a plugin that helps you with SEO!** WordPress comes packed full of features for every user; for every other feature there's a plugin directory with thousands of plugins. Add complex galleries, social networking, forums, social media widgets, spam protection, calendars, fine-tune controls for search engine optimization, and forms.

15. **Built-in Comments:** Your blog is your home, and comments provide a space for your followers to engage with your content. WordPress's comment tools give you everything you

need to be a forum for discussion and to moderate that discussion. It's this engagement that Google loves!

16. **Search Engine Friendly:** WordPress is optimized for search engines right out of the box. For more fine-grained SEO control, there are plenty of SEO plugins to take care of that for you.

SEO Juice Alert: Even though there are great plugins for SEO, and we highly recommend you install one, nothing about SEO runs on autopilot! You still have to work it, apply the proper techniques, and constantly tweak it.

Caution: Many website designers will "include" an SEO plugin and they'll tell you that the website they designed you "includes" SEO. While this might be true, it is a little misleading and gives a false sense of security. Did they optimize your images for Google Image search? Did they place YouTube videos on your website? The truth is you're probably not paying them enough to do all that. It's really up to you; just follow the advice in our book. :)

17. **Multilingual:** WordPress is available in more than 70 languages. If you or the person you're building the website for would prefer to use WordPress in a language other than English, that's easy to do.

18. **Mobile Friendly:** In Chapter 11 we talk about the importance of having a mobile friendly website. Most searches are done on a mobile device these days, and Google has officially announced that non-mobile friendly websites will be penalized in the search rankings. Out of the box, WordPress is mobile friendly—just be sure to select a theme that supports *responsive design.*

19. **Easy Installation and Upgrades:** WordPress has always been easy to install and upgrade. Most popular website hosting services (we like GoDaddy and Host Gator) make it super easy to upload and launch a WordPress website; it only takes a few minutes to install the WordPress database.

20. **Import Your Old Blog:** Using blog or website software that you aren't happy with? Running your blog on a hosted service that's about to shut down? WordPress comes with importers for Blogger, LiveJournal, Movable Type, TypePad, Tumblr, and WordPress. If you're ready to make the move, they've made it easy for you.

21. **Own Your Data:** Hosted services come and go. If you've ever used a service that disappeared, you know how traumatic that can be. If you've ever seen unauthorized advertisements appear on your website, you've probably been pretty annoyed. Using WordPress means no one has access to your content. Own your data, all of it—your website, your content, your data. Just be sure that you obtain a written document if someone else designs your WordPress website that says you own it.

22. **Freedom:** WordPress is licensed under the GPL, which was created to protect your freedoms. You are free to use WordPress in any way you choose: install it, use it, modify it, distribute it. Software freedom is the foundation that WordPress is built on.

23. **Community:** As the most popular open source CMS on the web, WordPress has a vibrant and supportive community. Ask a question on the support forums and get help from a volunteer, attend a WordCamp or Meetup to learn more about WordPress, or read blog posts and tutorials about WordPress. Community is at the heart of WordPress, making it what it is today. We find that a simple Google search is the fastest and easiest way to get help, if you ever get stumped.

How To: You are usually working within a theme when making changes to your website. If you get stumped, Google "your theme name and your question".

24. **Contribute:** You can be WordPress too! Help to build WordPress, answer questions on the support forums, write documentation, translate WordPress into your language, speak at a WordCamp, and write about WordPress on your blog. Whatever your skill, they would love to have you!

25. **User Experience Wins:** WordPress has usability built in by keeping things simple with a layout that users are familiar with.

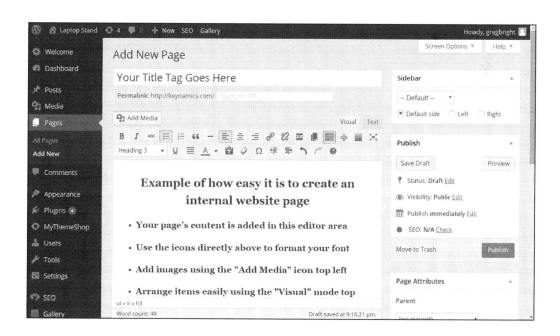

Easy to Host

The WordPress program can be hosted on popular hosting sites like GoDaddy and Host Gator and is easily scalable and can grow with your business, because it's built on a database platform. Pardon the geeky talk here, but trust us, this is a good thing because your website can continually be expanded (usually without starting over) as the needs of your business grow. Also, recent versions of WordPress have focused on making it even faster and lighter so it loads quickly for viewers (Google rewards quick loading websites; see Chapter 12).

> ***Learn More:*** *See screen shots on how to set up a WordPress website on GoDaddy and HostGator, install a popular theme and the latest "must have" plugins. It's "paint by numbers" easy.*
> *www.PlayGooglesGame.com/wordpress-godaddy*

Most Website Designers are Using WordPress

Most "good" website designers are using WordPress because they want to provide their clients with a website that can be found and that looks good. As mentioned before, "What's the point of a beautiful billboard in the middle of the desert, if no one can see it?" Plus, the fact that it's open source usually means that it's portable and you can easily take it with you*, transitioning to another website designer, if you need to.

> **As noted throughout this book, get this in writing! Who owns the copyright to your website? If you don't get these things in writing, you might not be able to take your website anywhere! We prefer to own the copyright of our websites and contract designers who will release the copyright to us—in writing. As always, consult an attorney on this, because we can't give legal advice.*

All of these features translate into huge benefits and money savings. With WordPress you get a double whammy. All of the SEO magic that comes with creating a blog post, plus a beautifully designed, fully functional, selling machine. Oh, did we mention that WordPress is free?

You might still hear people say that WordPress is only for building a blog website and not a "real" business website. Whenever anyone makes that claim, we are highly suspect of what their real agenda is. Do they want to be able to hold you hostage, by creating proprietary code? Do they want to make it difficult for you to leave them? Do they actually want to own your website outright?

Don't be fooled, those are usually people who are trying to sell you custom coded websites. While it's true that WordPress did originate as purely a blog design platform, it has evolved over the years into a full blown *web development program*. Almost any website can be designed entirely by using WordPress, including an *ecommerce* site. Not only is WordPress the king of blogs, it is designed to be search engine friendly. Because of this and its history in the blogging world, Google favors websites designed in WordPress. Those Google spiders have identified all of the WordPress blogs and sit on top of them, waiting for a post to show up, only to be snatched up and placed on the Google search results.

If your current website is not designed in WordPress, you should seriously consider changing it as your long term strategy. **If you are about to launch your new website, we implore you to have it designed in WordPress from the start!**

> *From Wikipedia: "WordPress is a free and open-source tool and a content management system (CMS) based on PHP and MySQL. Features include a plugin architecture and a template system. WordPress was used by more than 23.3% of the top 10 million websites as of January 2015. WordPress is the most popular blogging system in use on the Web, at more than 60 million websites."*
> *Source: http://en.wikipedia.org/wiki/Wordpress*
> ** Please support Wikipedia with a contribution.*

The best thing about WordPress its immense popularity, with tons and tons of support, ranging from online forums to millions of "How To" articles and posts. You can easily find someone who will design your website in WordPress, as most web designers are using this now. This is really important because you want to have a website that can be maintained and updated easily, both from a cost savings aspect (self-maintenance) and in case you need to find a new website designer (it happens). Help is only a Craigslist ad away!

Your WordPress-designed website is limited only by your imagination. WordPress is fully customizable, has thousands of free *plugins* and thousands more free templates (*themes*), which allow users and developers to extend its functionality beyond the features that come as part of the free WordPress install (out of the box).

The Two Most Popular Features of WordPress:
Themes & Plugins

By nature, WordPress is SEO friendly because it is designed to be lean, to maximize flexibility and minimize *Bloat*. Themes and Plugins offer custom functions and features so that each user can add only what they need. The best news: most are free, they are super easy to use, and they take less than 10 seconds to install!

Plugins

WordPress is noted for its rich *plugin* architecture which allows users and developers to extend its abilities beyond the features that are part of the base install. Plugins greatly extend the functionality of WordPress as it comes "out of the box," without the web designer having to perform one bit of custom coding.

If you can imagine it, someone probably has developed a plugin for it. Maybe you like a neat "Contact Us" form? Or how about a plugin that automates many of the SEO tasks that we talk about in this book? Plugins could be compared to Apps on a mobile phone. WordPress has a database of over 37,000 plugins.

Themes

While plugins are usually reserved for customizing individual areas within your website, *Themes* allow users to change the overall appearance and functionality of the entire WordPress website. Much the same as Plugins, Themes allow for customization of a WordPress website with little to no programming involved.

WordPress is pretty basic as it comes "out of the box." A theme gives the web designer a template where they can just copy and paste in the various *Elements of a Website* like Pictures, Videos, and Text. A theme can greatly enhance the look and feel of the basic "out of the box" WordPress website with a beautiful *Color Scheme* and *Page Layout* including: *Column Layout*, *Header Area* and *Sidebar* customization, and the main *Body* of the website.

Fundamentally, a WordPress Theme is a way to "skin" your website. WordPress Themes provide much more control over the look and presentation of the material on your website. Themes give us business owners the ability to create beautiful, professional level websites with the click of the mouse.

How To: *If you ever get stumped when making a change on your WordPress website, just do a Google search for your theme and your quandary and you will find your answer in seconds. We find that using a Google search is much faster and easier.*

From WordPress: *"A WordPress Theme is a collection of files that work together to produce a Graphical Interface with an underlying, unifying design for a weblog. These files are called template files. A Theme modifies the way the site is displayed, without modifying the underlying software..."*

The absolute best thing about themes is that there are thousands of them, most are free, and some are low cost. This immense popularity means that help is only a Google search away. If you get stumped or have a question, chances are that many others have the same question and someone has already answered it.

WordPress is already intuitive and easy to use, including a WYSIWYG feature, requiring little to no programming skills. Adding a theme to it gives the average business owner easy access to professional level design.

Real World Example: *Greg thought his WordPress theme was mobile friendly. It looked fine on a mobile phone. Well, when Google announced their Mobile Friendly Test Website and Greg plugged his URL into the tester, it failed! Greg quickly found a new theme that was mobile friendly (responsive) and it only took a few seconds to install and activate the theme and about an hour to reconfigure some of the images and layout. Try doing that kind of makeover with any other program and you're talking weeks and a ton of money! Read more on Mobile in Chapter 11.*

Integrating Your Blog versus Just Linking to Your Blog

Your best option is to create your blog page as one of your main *internal pages* within your main website versus having it as a stand-alone platform on a separate website like **www.blogger.com**. Blogger is a blog publishing service which cannot be loaded on your server like WordPress can. Some of these stand-alone blog publishing programs allow you to embed the blog post into your website. Embedding a blog from another platform brings little to no SEO juice to your main website.

Linking To Your Blog

Simply supplying a link from your main website to the external website that hosts your blog also brings zero SEO juice to your main website, because all of the SEO juice happens on the blog website. To make matters worse, when Google ranks one of your blog posts, searchers clicking on it will only go to your blog website and not see any of the products and services on your real website.

By integrating the blog page within your main site, we mean that it will appear as one of your internal pages, also referred to as a static page. You should list it right along the top header area along with your "Contact Us" and "About Us" pages. The link will look something like www.yourdomain.com/blog. This format also looks more professional.

With WordPress, you can set it up the blog page to be your home page. The location of the blog page within your site is personal preference. Locating it on the home page can have advantages with the look and feel of a news feed or current events if done correctly. We favor putting it on the home page.

Embedding – Creating a Window to Display Your Blog

Another option for incorporating a standalone blog into your main website is to create a placeholder or window frame/box to hold and display your blog posts.

An **iframe** is a little bit of programming code that displays the blog website in a smaller window within the main website. Visually this might look OK, but you are still not getting the full SEO juice value, because it's still a standalone website. It just appears that it's part of your main website to human eyes, because it's "framed" into a page.

RSS Feed Widget: This is another way to create a placeholder/box to display your standalone blog posts on your real website. While RSS is a great tool to subscribe to others' blogs, using it to create a placeholder for your own blog within your website does little for your SEO ranking.

Simple is Best: Create Your Entire Site with WordPress

Most of the options above involve complicated programming and extra steps. Some might even dictate a whole team of internal software engineers to maintain it! Why not just use WordPress to build your entire website in the first place—and you're done!

WordPress has evolved into such a powerful website design program that you can use it to create your entire website, including the actual blog page. You will be able to create all the pages you need: Home page, Contact Us page, Product pages, and ecommerce pages.

Your Challenge and Your Opportunity

Most of your competitors are not making any efforts to create a blog on their website. It never fails; whenever we encourage a business owner to develop a blog page within their website and make their own posts, the first words out of their mouths are, **"I don't have time to be making all those blog posts, I have a business to run."** The second thing that comes out of the business owner's mouth is, **"I don't have time to be answering all of those comments to my posts."**

Your opportunity is that the majority of businesses are not blogging, and we'll bet if you analyze your competitors, they are not blogging either. If they are, you better catch up quick!

> **Black Hat Warning:** *If all you do is repost or simply copy and paste text from other websites without contributing your own unique content, then you might get penalized as a <u>Scraper</u> website. The Scraper penalty was rolled out with Google's Panda algorithm update. See Chapter 12 for more info on the Panda update. Try to reword the posts in your own language and give them credit and link to them.*

> **Caution:** *Be sure your posts are interesting, newsworthy, entertaining, and enjoyable. For sure they can't just be an advertisement; viewers can spot that a mile away! You want the reader to think, "I have got to share this with my friend..." Keep this one little thing in mind: "Give First." You can even link to another article or news story from another website relevant to your industry after you have added your own original content.*

Better Late Than Never

It's never too late to start. Greg was a late bloomer coming to the blog world. In fact, even today, he is not an active subscriber to blogs. Greg first witnessed the power of a blog when a friend and fellow concrete countertop artisan decided to launch his own website.

You might guess that Greg has dominated the ranking for concrete countertops in Texas for many years now. Plus, he is well aware of his competitors' attempts to outrank him. Well, this friendly competitor did launch a website and they used the WordPress website design program to build it. Greg was amazed. Within a few weeks, that new WordPress website was outranking almost everyone (except Greg's of course) on page one of Google! It had taken years for some of Greg's competitors to get to where this one got in a couple of weeks.

Please note, most of us can't expect this kind of result so quickly, but that was proof positive for Greg. He immediately started converting his other websites over to blogs using WordPress.

> **How To:** *For our Top 10 Must Do WordPress Tweaks, visit:*
> *www.PlayGooglesGame.com/top-ten-wordpress-tweaks*

Best Practices – Action Plan

1. If you are a larger enterprise, hire programmers to code and maintain your blog/website (expensive). Be sure and budget for professional level custom coding for any ongoing maintenance.

_____

_____

_____

_____

2. If you are a small to medium size business, use WordPress to build your entire website, blog included (very smart).

_____

_____

_____

_____

3. Implement a Content Development Program, including schedules for regular postings and sources for interesting articles. Incorporate your image development program as discussed in chapter 3 and your video development program from Chapter 4.

4. If you are starting over and converting from a non-WordPress website, be sure to spend a lot of time checking for any high ranking pages and images (Google Image Search) before you shut the old website down. It would be a shame to lose any of that. Make a note of the exact URLs and sizes, ALT tags, etc. of the pages and images; keep them all the same and be sure and place the image back on the same page (URL) when you re-launch. Leave the image files where they are on your server—especially if they are stored in the "images" file folder.

5. Interview website designers who use WordPress; get referrals and testimonials. Ask them who will own the code as well as the content. Will they provide that in writing? Will they show you how to make posts on your own, and make simple changes like uploading new images to the various pages?

6. Watch YouTube videos on how to make WordPress blog posts and using the WordPress Dashboard.

7. Two main goals are creating quality content and driving as much organic traffic as you possibly can to your site.

_____

_____

_____

_____

8. Plan to drive traffic back to your website by posting your post on Facebook and Twitter.

_____

_____

_____

_____

Chapter 9

Google Map Listings

*Local Search is Extremely Important
if You Want Local Business*

✓ Claim Yours
✓ Get Listed
✓ Get to the Top of the Map

Google's local business map has evolved over the years, and sometimes the frequent changes are enough to make your head spin off. As we write this book, the dust is still settling on the latest change which moved Google Places to Google+ and renamed it *Google My Business*. Google My Business connects you directly with customers, whether they're looking for you on Search, Maps, or Google+.

When you add your business using Google My Business, you'll create a Google+ Page for your business. Just know that this is one of the first steps in "Playing Google's Game"—and it's free.

As frustrating as all of these Google local business changes have been over the years, there is no getting around it; if you want to attract local customers then you must continually tweak and work on your Local Search SEO.

> ***How To:*** *With all the changes, we thought it would be a good idea to offer a resource with the latest links to Google's guidelines for Google My Business and Google+ business pages:*
> *www.PlayGooglesGame.com/google-local-business-listings*

Highlights

Very Important:
- Confirm the accuracy of your name, address, and phone number on every website that it shows up on, all over the internet.
- Claim your business listing before someone else does.
- Start all of your keyword phrases with the name of your city.
- Put your physical address and local phone number in the footer of every page.
- Only use a local area code in your real business phone number—no 800 numbers!
- Put your city as the first word in your home page Title Tag.

Important:
- Do not use a USPS Post Office Box (UPS Store OK—only if it's a Service Area or Brand Page).
- Link your YouTube Channel to your Google+ Page.
- Update your business Google+ Page often; Google has announced they will un-verify inactive Google+ Pages.

Helpful:
- Don't be complacent if you notice you are already on the map. Be proactive and claim it!

Evolution of Google Local Business

At the present time on Google, you can be found in one of three ways to grow your local business. Being found in all three ways is ideal:

1. In Google Maps
2. In Google+
3. Within the regular (natural/organic) Google search results for a search of your keywords and your city name.

For popular headings, if you are logged onto the internet in the city you are searching, you don't even have to put in the city name; Google knows where you are located and shows you the results of that city.

> **Note:** *Yahoo (Yahoo Small Business) and Bing (Bing Places) have similar local business/map programs and you should register there as well.*

Google launched *Google Local* back in 2004. Since that day Google's version of local business has always been tied to their *Google Maps* division.

Each new version of Google Local Business strives to organize local business by business type or category and then display all of the businesses of the same category into a map which pops up in the search results. Think of it as the internet's version of the Yellow Pages on steroids, with the added benefit of the business locations on the interactive map.

> **Quick Fact:** *Many local searchers never even make it to your actual webpage. They simply read all about you on your Local Google+ Page. From there they decide if they want to call you or come by for a visit. Therefore, you have to make a good first impression! It's super easy for mobile searchers to just click on a phone number and call.*

It's kind of confusing, but you will have a "personal" Google+ Page and a "business" Google+ page. Your business Google+ Page is similar to a Facebook business page and is what the public sees. To manage it all, you will have a Google My Business dashboard. Your Google My Business dashboard is the page where you edit and complete your information; see image below. You have to click on the "My Business" tab on the top left. This is Google's current format; it will probably change tomorrow.

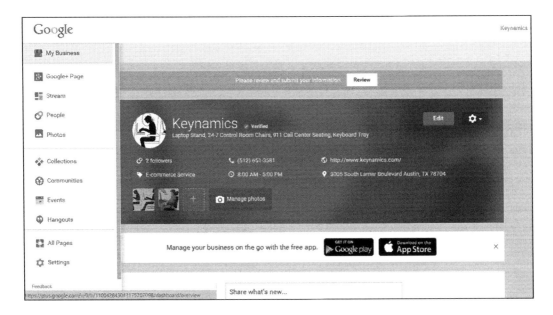

For simplicity, we'll often use the generic terms "Google+ Page," "Google Local Business," "Google My Business," or "Google Maps" to describe this program.

Here is what Google says: "If you previously used Google Places for Business or Google+ Pages Dashboard to manage your business information, your account has been automatically upgraded to Google My Business. Google My Business makes it easier than ever to update business information across Google Search, Maps and Google+." By creating a local page on Google My Business, your business information can show up in Google Search, Google Earth, and other Google properties. In addition, your business gets a Google+ page to connect with your customers.

An account on Google My Business provides an easy way to combine your favorite Google services like Images, YouTube, Social, Search, and other web initiatives into one easy platform, with one easy dashboard. The more completely you fill out your information and the more often you post to Google+, the higher you'll rank in search results.

> *Caution: Be absolutely sure that your name, address, and phone number is consistent across all of these Google platforms. You will see the importance of consistency later in the chapter. For example, don't optimize a different city than your physical address in your YouTube videos!*

Local Search

What we are talking about is *Local Search*, and if you want business from your city or local area, you must participate in this. Let's face it; the printed Yellow Pages are all but dead. Both Verizon and AT&T dumped these divisions for pennies on the dollar years ago.

Standard SEO Efforts are the #1 Factor Affecting Local Search

More proof that the fundamental techniques we teach stand the test of time! Even with all of the latest changes for Google Local, the consensus is that standard optimization practices on our website, optimized for your city, have more power than ever in increasing our success in attracting local visitors.

Yes sir, if folks would have been following Greg's advice from his first book written in 2008, advice about sticking to the fundamentals of website optimization, they would be ranking high in Local Search results today. Standard SEO practices are now considered the number one factor in ranking high for Local Search!

Just remember to add a location parameter to your keyword strategy which should always include "location + keyword" in your keyword phrase.

Online Directories

At the core of your local business are your various listings in online directories. This is how Google started building their list for the map listing in the first place, and it's one way they continue to maintain it. Your local business listing is an online profile that contains just the basics: your business name, address, phone number, and sometimes your website address.

There are many online directories. Some of the larger ones like Google+ Local, Yelp, Bing Places, Internet Yellow Pages, Superpages, and Yahoo Local attempt to list all businesses by category. There are also smaller directories that focus on a niche. Many of these smaller ones are associated with local associations catering to your industry.

If you have been in business for a while, even for a short while, your business will most likely already be included in one of these directories. You should check your listings on all of these directories for correctness. Just Google your business name and see what comes up. If you are brand new, then you will want to register your business with the major ones.

As long as your business name, address and phone number are consistent across all of these directories, and the more visible you are, the more these indexes trust the accuracy of your business data.

Unfortunately most of the directories have incorrect or outdated information, especially if you have moved. This inconsistent data decreases trust and decreases your chances of ranking well in local searches. It's up to you to make sure it's all correct!

Typical Directory Eligibility Test:

- You must have a legal business entity name or DBA
- You need a local phone number that matches your city of location (not a shared phone number, toll-free number, or call tracking number)
- Have a dedicated physical street address (not a shared address, UPS Store, P.O. box, or virtual office)
- Make face-to-face contact with your customers at your address (business is not conducted virtually as in ecommerce)
- Most directories require you to verify each listing you create

   Caution: *There are many low-quality directory sites. These are spammy directories set up only for the purpose of selling local links. When registering your business, be sure they are legit!*

What Does Google Want? Dissecting Google's Own Guidelines for a Local Google+ Page

No matter how many times Google changes the name, or the process, their end game is still the same. They want to provide their users with quality information. We can learn a lot about what Google wants by studying their guidelines. Keeping these guidelines in mind will help us get found for local business, or whatever they decide to call it tomorrow.

What will the Next Version of Google Local Look Like? – It Doesn't Matter!

Rest assured, they will change it again; just keep Google's goals in mind.

Let's dissect what Google has to say about Google My Business. They have some pretty clear guidelines:

"We've come up with a list of guidelines for local businesses to maintain high quality information on Google. Following these guidelines helps avoid common problems, including changes to your information, or, in some cases, removal of your business information from Google."

For best results using Google My Business:

- *Represent your business as it's consistently represented and recognized in the real world across signage, stationery, and other branding.*
- *Make sure your address is accurate and precise.*
- *Choose the fewest number of categories it takes to describe your overall core business."*

1. **"We've come up with a list of guidelines for local businesses to maintain high quality information on Google."** – As usual, Google only wants high quality listings that please their customers, which are also our prospects.

2. **"Following these guidelines helps avoid common problems, including changes to your information, or, in some cases, removal of your business information from Google."** – Pay attention here; you could get removed!

3. **"Represent your business as it's consistently represented and recognized in the real world across signage, stationery, and other branding."** – OK, there is a lot of information to dissect here. First and foremost, DO NOT try and stuff a keyword into your business name. "Joe's Auto Parts" should not be listed as "Joe's Best Auto Parts in Austin". We know that Google uses many sources to verify your business name. Official government sources, local directories, and even the google car that goes around taking pictures for Google Street View. **CONSISTENCY IS THE KEY HERE!** More on Google's verification sources to follow.

4. **"Make sure your address is accurate and precise."** – This is a common problem. Even slight variations can cause you trouble. Accuracy is the key here!

5. **"Choose the fewest number of categories it takes to describe your overall core business."** – Less is better, and as in any keyword strategy, you don't want to water it down. It's easier to win for a few keywords than all of them. Plus, this is your chance to prove you are not spammy to Google.

Google's Main Eligibility Test

"In order to qualify for a local Google+ page, a business must make in-person contact with customers during its stated hours."

Ineligible Businesses on Google

The following businesses aren't eligible for a local page:

- Businesses that are under construction or that have not yet opened to the public.
- Rental or for-sale properties, such as vacation homes, model homes or vacant apartments. Sales or leasing offices, however, are eligible for verification.
- An ongoing service, class, or meeting at a location that you don't own or have the authority to represent. Please coordinate with your host to have your information displayed on the page for their business within their "Introduction" field.

Business Name

Your name should reflect your business's real-world name, as used consistently on your storefront, website, stationery, and as known to customers. NEVER, EVER INSERT A KEYWORD INTO YOUR REAL BUSINESS NAME!

We think Google's naming concept is very similar to the intent of the DBA "Doing Business As" policy of most local governments in the US.

The SBA has a great synopsis of the whole DBA thing:

Register Your Business Name
Naming your business is an important branding exercise, but if you choose to name your business as anything other than your own personal name then you'll need to register it with the appropriate authorities.

This process is known as registering your "Doing Business As" (DBA) name.

What is a "Doing Business As" Name?

A fictitious name (or assumed name, trade name or DBA name) is a business name that is different from your personal name, the names of your partners or the officially registered name of your LLC or corporation.

It's important to note that when you form a business, the legal name of the business defaults to the name of the person or entity that owns the business, unless you choose to rename it and register it as a DBA name.

For example, consider this scenario: John Smith sets up a painting business. Rather than operate under his own name, John instead chooses to name his business: "John Smith Painting". This name is considered an assumed name and John will need to register it with the appropriate local government agency.

The legal name of your business is required on all government forms and applications, including your application for employer tax IDs, licenses and permits.

Do I Need a "Doing Business As" Name?

A DBA is needed in the following scenarios:

Sole Proprietors or Partnerships – If you wish to start a business under anything other than your real name, you'll need to register a DBA so that you can do business as another name.

Existing Corporations or LLCs – If your business is already set up and you want to do business under a name other than your existing corporation or LLC name, you will need to register a DBA.

Note: *Not all states require the registering of fictitious business names or DBAs.*

How to Register your "Doing Business As" Name

Registering your DBA is done either with your county clerk's office or with your state government, depending on where your business is located. There are a few states that do not require the registering of fictitious business names.

Business Address

Use a precise, accurate address to describe your business location. P.O. boxes or mailboxes located at remote locations are not acceptable. Note the exception is for a *Brand Page*. See note on Brand Pages below.

- Make sure that your page is created for your actual, real-world location.
- Use the precise address for the business rather than broad city names or cross-streets. P.O. boxes are not considered accurate physical locations.
- If you need to specify a mailbox or suite number within your physical location, please list your physical address in Address Line 1, and put your mailbox or suite number in Address Line 2.
- If your business rents a temporary, "virtual" office at a different address from your primary business, do not create a page for that location unless it is staffed during your normal business hours.
- Do not include information in address lines that does not pertain to your business's physical location (e.g. URLs or keywords).
- Do not create more than one page for each location of your business, either in a single account or multiple accounts.
- Individual practitioners and departments within businesses, universities, hospitals, and government buildings may have separate pages. See specific guidelines about individual practitioners and departments for more information.

Google+ Page Setup

Again, it does not matter how many times Google changes the name, this process remains relatively the same: **1.** Claim Your Listing; **2.** Get Verified; **3.** Provide accurate information that matches other platforms across the web; **4.** Fill out all that you can: 100% complete on your Google+ Local page; **5.** Be awesome with your content and interactions.

For the latest setup instructions click here:
www.PlayGooglesGame.com/google-local-business-listings

Claim Your Listing

This is the first step in Google's verification process and it starts with you! If you are an established local business, then it's highly likely that Google has already found you. Your job is to go in and claim your business listing as the owner. You do this first by verifying your business listing with Google.

1. If you have not already done so, create a Google account and log on.
2. Set up your Google+ Page—we're talking about your business page here. You will automatically have a Google+ personal page once you register for an account with Google.
3. Select either "Storefront," "Service Area," or "Brand." **A Brand Page is not good for local business.**
4. Search for your business on the map that pops up.
5. Google will give you two choices for verification:
   a. Mail you a postcard with a code.
   b. Text you a code to the business phone number listed.

Note: These steps often change. To see the latest steps visit:
www.PlayGooglesGame.com/google-local-business-listings

Service-area businesses: Service-area businesses—business that serve customers at their locations—should have one page for the central office or location and designate a service area from that point. If you wish to display your complete business address while setting your service area(s), your business location should be staffed and able to receive customers during its stated hours. Google will determine how best to display your business address based on your business information as well as information from other sources. Not all local businesses serve their customers from a brick-and-mortar storefront. For example, some businesses operate from a home address. Others are mobile and have no central location. If your business serves customers at their locations, you should list it as a service area business on Google.

Brand Page: Brands, organizations, artists, and other online-only businesses should create a brand page instead of a local page. Brand pages follow the Google+ page content guidelines. Brands can create Google+ pages to reach out to followers, fans, and customers on Google. Brand, organization, or artist pages don't include address or other physical location information that appears on Google Maps.

Home Based Businesses

Not all local businesses serve their customers from a brick-and-mortar storefront. For example, some businesses operate from a home address. Others are mobile and have no central location. If your business serves customers at THEIR locations, you should list it as a service area business on Google.

Note on UPS Store Mail Boxes

At the time this book went to print and with so many changes on Google local business over the years, we are nervous about using a UPS Store address on Google My Business, even if it's a service area business. There are so many spammers and unscrupulous businesses using private mail box services that it could throw up a red flag for Google's Quality Team to investigate.

Several years ago, Google wiped out all USPS Mail P.O. box listings from their maps! In time, and once Google settles on a definitive platform, hopefully their attitude on this will change.

> *Note: You can legitimately select "Service Area" on your Google My Business settings using a private mail box and it will not show an address. However, if local business is only a small part of your overall business, then, in some cases we think it's better not to list your business on Google My Business at all. You could also consider a Brand page, which does not list an address.*

Following the advice in this book, you can still get high ranking for the search terms of "your city + your keywords"; you just might not show up on the map.

Google's Verification Process

Google knows that the only way they can provide their customers with accurate information is to verify the accuracy of the business listings. Plus, isn't it comforting to know that Google is making an effort to allow the legitimate business owner the chance to verify the accuracy of everything? Wouldn't it be horrible if a dishonest competitor could falsely represent you and place misleading information on your listing? It has happened, so be sure and claim yours as the legitimate business owner!

Google uses many sources to determine your actual name. We'll look at each one below. Just know that consistency and accuracy are paramount. You must review all of these sources to make sure they are correct and match. Many times local directory listings have incorrect and outdated information.

Google Street View Verification

Your name should exactly match whatever you have on your storefront signage. This could be different than your legal business name, as listed on government pages.

Google Street View is a technology featured in Google Maps and Google Earth that provides panoramic views from positions along many streets in the world.

The Google Street view car pictured below has software programs that can determine the name of your business from the photos it takes.

Government Business Listing Verification

There are several common sources that Google uses to verify business names. Your local county government might be responsible for registering your DBA and handling property tax records. Your state government might be responsible for your incorporated, sales taxes, or other legal entity name.

Below is an example of how you can verify your government listings for Travis County in Texas.

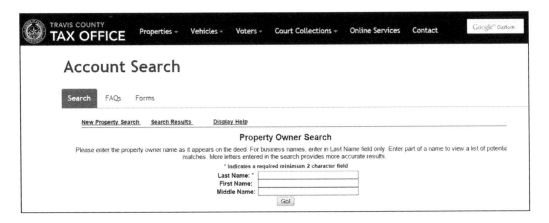

Below is another example of how Greg's Keynamics business is listed on the Texas State Comptroller's Website (sales tax).

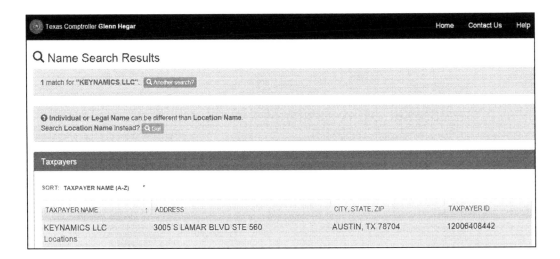

Verifying Through Other Websites' Links and Citations

As we've stated previously, there really is no reason to notify Google about your website. They'll find you. Search engines like Google, Yahoo!, and Bing will find out about your business in two primary ways:

1. When they crawl other websites and notice links that point to your website. They also make note of these and boost your rankings based on the quality and quantity of those linking websites; we discuss more about backlinks in Chapter 5. Just know that for local business, links from high-quality websites within your area, like a chamber of commerce or a city government, are very helpful.

2. They also track citations of your business, and evaluate the value of the websites where these citations appear.

Define: Citations – *Citations are simply mentions or web references of your business name on webpages, accompanied by your address and phone number. These mentions do not have to have a link to your website. One example of a citation is when an online yellow pages directory lists your name, address and phone, but there is no link to your website.*

Popular Directories

Here is a short list of major directories:

- BingPlaces.com
- Smallbusiness.yahoo.com/local-listings
- Dmoz.org
- YellowPages.com
- SuperPages.com
- LinkedIn.com
- MerchantCircle.com
- Yelp.com
- AngiesList.com
- CitySearch.com
- Yellowbot.com
- Whitepages.com
- BBB.org
- Manta.com
- Foursquare.com

Visit www.PlayGooglesGame.com/local-directories for the most up to date list.

Next Steps after Claiming Your Page

After your page claimed, simply follow the tips and progress bar on the dashboard; your goal is to get your listing to 100%. It's kind of paint by number easy!

1. Upload a user image; this shows up in the little circle, and it's what shows up next to your social posts.
2. Upload a cover image.
3. Upload photos of your business—at least 10.
4. Link your page to your YouTube Channel.
5. Only use a local phone number that matches your phone number listed on your website.
6. Enter your hours of operation.
7. Choose no more than three categories that match your About page on your website.
8. Write a great description that also matches your About page on your website; no keyword stuffing!

Tip: Be sure and list a local phone number, using a local area code, directly next to your UPS Store address wherever you place it on your website. Listing only Toll Free 800 numbers is bad for local search!

20 Tips to Get to Ranked at the Top of the Map

Just like any technique that we teach, you are going to need to optimize your website, other websites, and your Local Google+ Page for your keywords; especially your city name.

1. **Be awesome, earn awesome links** – Google tracks how many clicks your page gets from the search results and how long people "stick around" your website and how fast they bounce back to the search results. Therefore, you must grab attention by being awesome.
2. **Citation inconsistency is #1 issue affecting local ranking!** –Consistency among ALL webpages, including your own, is crucial. If your name, address and phone number appear differently across numerous platforms, then search engines like Google will not trust the validity of the information and ding you. Make sure your real address matches the city you are targeting. If you are in an outlying city and you are trying to target the major city, this will be problematic.
3. **Put your city as the first word in the Title Tag of your home page.**
4. **Be social and interactive** – On Facebook, Google+, and Twitter. Be sure to always mention your city and optimize those platforms for your city.
5. **Upload good quality keyword optimized images** – Know that Google is placing your Google+ listing photos by displaying one for each listed business in their main search results, both on Google Images and when they show then blended in with their regular main search results. See Chapter 3 for all the details of Image Search

6. **Place your Google+ badge on your website** – On your Google My Business dashboard go to "Settings" → "For Your Site" and scroll down to copy the embed code.

7. **Make sure you optimize your profiles on other high traffic local sites like Yelp, Foursquare, Citysearch, BBB.org, etc.**

8. **The quantity of inbound local links to your website** – Backlinks from local business organizations like the Chamber of Commerce and BBB are important. We have mixed emotions about BBB accreditation, and we won't go into our opinions here, but when you're evaluating whether or not you want to pay for this service, just know that you get a quality back link out of the deal. It could be very helpful if you are just starting out.

9. **Proper categories limited to three.**

10. **Local area code on My Business page.**

11. **Get reviews; Google is obsessed with reviews** – Get at least 5 reviews; more is always better. Answer all reviews. On negative reviews, always take the high road and present yourself as the good guy, even if they are wrong or insulting.

12. **Study your competition: the high ranked ones** – It's easy to find the citations for your competitors; you do it just like you do for yourself. Search their business name. Make a note for which websites are giving them citations. Submit your name, address, and phone to those sites too.

13. **In very large cities, optimize for an area of town versus the whole city** – It's easier to win in a large city by focusing on an area.

14. **Use your Domain email address to register at Google My Business –**
    Correct: info@keynamics.com
    Incorrect: yourname812@aol.com

15. **Mobile Friendly Website** – Most searches are conducted on a mobile device, and even more searchers searching for local businesses do so from a mobile device. Google tracks how many clicks your page gets from the search results and how long people "stick around" your website and how fast they bounce back to the search results. Therefore, you must have a mobile friendly website. More in Chapter 12.

16. **H1 Headings** – Include your city name.

17. **Content** – Don't forget to include your city in your content; including your Text, Image file names with ALT tags, YouTube video titles—everything we discussed in this book!

18. **Include in your URL structure** – www.PlayGooglesGame.com/houston-seo

19. **Create local content for your blog.**

20. **Direct link to your reviews page** – Make it easy for people to review you. Provide a direct link to your Local Google+ page, print out a postcard with the link and instructions, make a YouTube video showing people how to make a review. The direct link is a very useful and simple process. Simply add **"?hl=en&review=1"** at the end of your Google+ page URL. Your Google+ page URL is currently located on your "About" page. An example of Greg's Keynamics business is:

www.google.com/+Keynamics4u?hl=en&review=1

Please note that Google is likely to change this extension to add to your URL, so click here if that does not work for the latest update:

www.PlayGooglesGame.com/google-review-direct-link

21. **Mis-matched or private WHOIS information** – Don't set your Whois information to private and make sure it matches your address everywhere else.

```
ancient-art-concrete-countertops.com registrar whois          Updated 1 second ago

Domain Name: ANCIENT-ART-CONCRETE-COUNTERTOPS.COM
Registry Domain ID: 612585325_DOMAIN_COM-VRSN
Registrar WHOIS Server: whois.godaddy.com
Registrar URL: http://www.godaddy.com
Update Date: 2014-09-30T12:14:57Z
Creation Date: 2006-09-29T07:18:03Z
Registrar Registration Expiration Date: 2015-09-29T07:18:03Z
Registrar: GoDaddy.com, LLC
Registrar IANA ID: 146
Registrar Abuse Contact Email: abuse@godaddy.com
Registrar Abuse Contact Phone: +1.4806242505
Domain Status: clientTransferProhibited http://www.icann.org/epp#clientTransferProhibited
Domain Status: clientUpdateProhibited http://www.icann.org/epp#clientUpdateProhibited
Domain Status: clientRenewProhibited http://www.icann.org/epp#clientRenewProhibited
Domain Status: clientDeleteProhibited http://www.icann.org/epp#clientDeleteProhibited
Registry Registrant ID:
Registrant Name: Greg Bright
Registrant Organization: Greg Bright
Registrant Street: 3005 S. Lamar Blvd.
Registrant Street: STE D-109-132
Registrant City: Austin
Registrant State/Province: Texas
Registrant Postal Code: 78704
Registrant Country: United States
Registrant Phone: +1.5126513581
Registrant Phone Ext:
Registrant Fax:
Registrant Fax Ext:
Registrant Email: info@keynamics.com
Registry Admin ID:
Admin Name: Greg Bright
Admin Organization: Greg Bright
Admin Street: 3005 S. Lamar Blvd.
Admin Street: STE D-109-132
Admin City: Austin
```

The Whois and Local Business

When you register your domain, we think it's helpful to list your home town as the *Whois* address if you want local business. Upon registration, you always have to give an address for the contact info of the owner of the website. Just be sure it matches exactly what you are giving Google when you verify your business.

It's super easy for Google (or anybody else) to find this. We believe that Google will give a slight ding to a website that is registered by someone in another city or state (or worse yet, a foreign country), and is trying to get local business with that website. Visit www.PlayGooglesGame.com/who-is for instructions to look up the Whois for any website.

> ***Caution:*** *Remember from earlier - Reviews are most valuable when they are honest and unbiased. Google does not want you to review your own business, or if you're an employee don't review your employer. Don't offer or accept money, products, or services to write reviews for a business and don't write negative reviews about a competitor. Don't set up review stations or kiosks at your place of*

business just to ask for reviews written at your place of business.

Black Hat Warning: *Do not list your UPS Store or any P.O. box address on Google My Business as if you could accept customers at that location; it's against Google's policy to do so and also it's misleading to customers. Instead, create a "Service Area Page" or "Brand Page" if you only have a UPS Store address.*

Caution: *Make sure your Name, Address, and Phone Number (NAP) is exactly the same every place you list it, anywhere on the internet, and especially on your website, on Google, and in directory citations. Inconsistent citations and NAP data is by far the most common negative issue facing local businesses.*

Black Hat Warning: *Never, ever place keywords into the official name of your business anywhere on the internet if they are not actually part of your actual business name.*

Best Practices – Action Plan

To review, there are four areas of concern when optimizing for Google Map Listings:

1. **Your On Page SEO** – Review the title tag on every one of your webpages. It should begin with the name of your city.

_____

_____

_____

_____

2. **Your My Business Page** – Set up your Local Google + page 100% complete. Does your Progress Bar show 100%?

_____

_____

_____

_____

3. **Your Off Page SEO** – Factors that you can build which are external to your company including: Local Link Building and Citation building. Do a Google search for your company name (on a separate browser that you are not signed into). Review all of the citations and local directory listings. Contact them if they are incorrect.

_____

_____

_____

_____

4. **Your Social Interactions** – Factors that are dependent on the common public and customers, including reviews and activities on social media. Search for any reviews that you might already have on Google, Yelp, and other local domains. Respond to them—engage with them. Get active on social media; mainly Facebook, Twitter and Google+.

_____

_____

_____

_____

Chapter 10

Facebook... Google is Watching

Google is watching what we do on Social Media - Like a Hawk!

✓ Facebook | Twitter | Google+
✓ Give First
✓ Be Amazing

Love it or hate it, you might as well close up shop if you are not going to embrace Facebook and other social Media—end of story!

That's a bold statement, and it was meant to be. With over 70% of the world's internet users on Facebook, we feel that strongly about it!

Today it's Facebook; who knows what it will be tomorrow. Social media is evolving at a fast pace, but it's here to stay. Plus, it's a fantastic way to grow your business, engage customers, and also to recruit, engage, and motivate employees.

Poll after poll reveals that the majority of Americans say Facebook is their #1 influencer of purchases. Furthermore, almost 100% of customers trust recommendations from their friends and family on social media. What did you do today to influence 70% of your potential customers?

To quote one slightly successful business leader, Sir Richard Branson:

> *"Embracing social media isn't just a bit of fun, it's a vital way to communicate, keep your ear to the ground and improve your business."*

Highlights

Very Important:
- Google's best indication of good content
- Don't ignore 70% of your customers
- Drive traffic to your website
- Facebook Posts and Tweets are showing up in the Google Search Results

Important:
- Give First
- Facebook and Twitter are search engines

Helpful:
- What's up with that hashtag thingy #?

Are You In?

The bottom line is that Facebook brought us to this social media party and everyone's in—are you?

All of the social media platforms have the same basic functionality: posts, pictures, comments, likes, links, shares etc. You might as well learn on Facebook and join the party!

This chapter will be short but important. This is not a book on social media; we're not going to give instructions on how to set up accounts on the various platforms—that would require an entire book itself. Social media, and in particular Facebook, has become such a driving factor in SEO that we decided to give it its own chapter; it's that important!

In this chapter we hope to show you the value of being on social media to build your online community.

Sure you need a personal Facebook account first, in order to set up a business page. And sure it's annoying to look at some of your friends' posts (you can hide those from your view by the way). Just know that Google does not care what you do on your personal Facebook page; they are only watching your business page. Therefore, you could sign up and never be active on your personal page.

Let's imagine… less than 100 years ago, folks were having the same debate over the telephone. I mean why in the heck would you want to talk to someone through a newfangled speaker box, when you can just go down the street and knock on their door and speak to them in person? That's just rude, right?

The fact is that most of your customers love Facebook for its social aspect and they are spending a ton of time on this platform. Because most of us can't just walk down the street and knock on our family member's door, or walk over and visit an old friend, it's really great to be able to keep up with them through pictures, video, and conversation on Facebook. Actually we feel sorry for those who have not embraced it. They are missing out on much happiness and learning. It's funny, those same people will watch hours of mind numbing prime time TV…

Alrighty then, we'll get off our personal Facebook use soap box. However, Facebook for business—use it or get left in the dust!

Facebook – Google's Best Indicator of Good Content

In Google's never ending quest to find the best websites and rank them for their searchers, they watch over the entire internet and are connecting the dots.

211

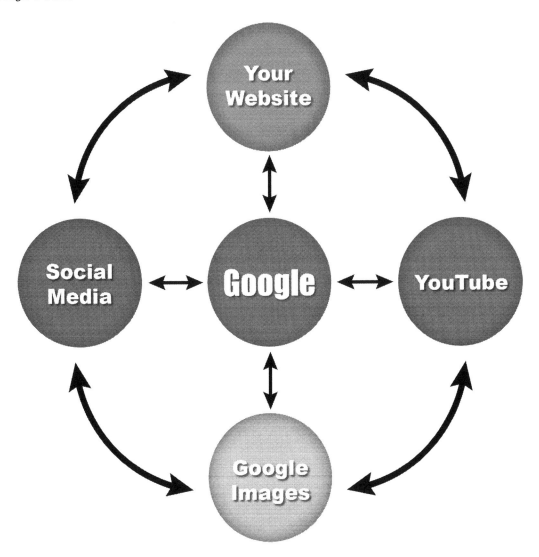

Google Ranks Websites Based on Observing Interactions on Facebook

We know that all Google cares about is content. They have discovered the best way to determine good content by following the likes, comments and interactions of 70% of the internet on one single platform: Facebook!

They are also paying attention to other social media sites like Twitter and of course Google+.

Google is trying to understand what is popular, relevant, authoritative, and original. They track factors such as how many likes your Facebook page has and how many likes each post gets. They also track how many people comment on the post and share it with their friends. They're doing the same thing on Twitter, counting tweets and retweets. They also keep track of the time frame of when the content was shared.

These social media factors are highly weighted when determining how they rank your entire website in the Google search results!

Google Watches All Social Media – Like a Hawk

Activity that we do outside of our website on other internet platforms is called Off Page SEO. Off Page SEO is huge in Google's eyes. They are plugged into every single website in the world, including Facebook, Twitter, Houzz, and LinkedIn, noting everyone's activities.

Social Media Facts

Well, the #1 most important fact is that over 70% of the users of the internet are on Facebook. That's a whole lot of folks you can go after to build your community!

> ***Real World Example:*** *Let us ask you this question. If you had an employee that ignored 70% of your customers, would you fire them?*

According to the Pew Research Center, Facebook is still the king of social media, by a long shot. What we find interesting is that while Facebook's growth is slowing, Facebook users are engaging with it more frequently and becoming very active on it. After all, growth has to start slowing when you're approaching 100% of the entire internet population on the planet.

There are stats to look at for other large social media platforms like Twitter, Instagram, Pinterest, and LinkedIn; however, we'll just focus on Facebook, because it's the 800 pound gorilla.

In fact, people that use more than one social media platform (i.e. Facebook and LinkedIn) are growing sharply. Now more than half the adults who use the internet use two or more social media sites. All major social media platforms are seeing significant growth.

Over half of internet consumers say they stay informed about brands and products through social networking. (Bazaarvoice)

Google is Showing Facebook Business Pages & Tweets in the Search Results

This one fact should be reason enough to set up a Facebook business page today! For a search of brand names, your social media business page profiles are often among the top results in search listings.

If someone is Googling your business name, maybe from a referral or an old customer wanting to look you up again, just know that your Facebook business page will probably show up right under your home page listings in the SERP.

Most users know that they can get a better feel for the personal side of a business by going straight to their social media page versus their website. Often times they just click your Facebook page listing on the SERP when researching a company that they don't know much about. If you have not updated it in a while, that's going to leave a negative impression.

Google Looks for Your Content on Facebook & Twitter

In marketing, we say that it's always best to be where people are looking for you. Google expects you to be on Facebook and Twitter. They know that any business or website that has great content would want to share that great content with the world.

Google also relies on Facebook and Twitter to supply the content that Google searchers are looking for; it's like a free treasure trove of content that Google does not have to pay a dime for—why wouldn't they do it?

Turning Traditional Marketing on Its Ear

Mega stars and big brands alike are bypassing industry's traditional promotional machinery by leveraging social media to amplify their messages for them, while forming communities and direct connections with their customers on social media.

Millennials (Born 1981 – 2000)

- Millennials don't remember life before the internet. This is one of the most tech savvy, digitally wired, mobile groups in history. Most of them came of age when the .com era got rolling and cut their teeth on Google.

- Millennials represent more than one quarter of the nation's population. Their size exceeds that of the 75.4 million baby boomers, according to new U.S. Census Bureau estimates. There are 76 million millennials (born between 1981 and 2000) in the U.S.—27% of the total population.

- Millennials spend $600 billion annually and are expected to spend 1.4 trillion by 2020 according a study done by Accenture. They will surpass the buying power of baby boomers in 2018.

- Millennials are particularly active in learning about brands and products through social networking (66%). (Ipsos Open Thinking Exchange)

- 51% say social opinions influence their purchase decisions, and 46% "count on social media" when buying online. (Bazaarvoice)

- Many Millennials say they have kind of "moved on" from Facebook and are exploring other platforms. Therefore, we need to keep an eye on where they are heading, and be there for them too.

Seniors – Facebook Grew our Market – Thanks!

Yay! Seniors have finally found the internet!

Greg's 77 year old mother joined Facebook kicking and screaming. She figured it was the only way she could keep tabs with her kids and grandkids. Well, it did not take long. Before you knew it she had formed a Facebook group for her 1960 Dental Hygiene graduating class (all 20 of them), and because of that Facebook group they ended up having a 50 year reunion, coming from all over the country. That shows the personal value of Facebook!

It's not just Facebook that seniors are using either. These late bloomers are getting comfortable using the internet, researching on the internet, and shopping on the internet, and we think Facebook has a lot to do with that!

Folks, this is what excites us about Facebook more than just about anything. Not only has Facebook gotten seniors comfortable shopping on the internet, it has encouraged all late bloomers, scaredy-cats, and procrastinators to start shopping on the internet. Yes indeed—thank you Facebook!

Facebook & Twitter are Search Engines

Despite the fact that your Facebook business page is showing up in the Google search results, Facebook is also designed to be a search engine itself.

Ever wonder why that big search box is positioned up top, front and center? Facebook has been vocal that they plan to beat out Google for search, and some predict that Facebook could very well beat Google one day with their vast treasure trove of information and users.

On both Facebook and Twitter, you can search for people as well as products or services. Many of the same keyword strategies we use for high Google ranking apply to our Facebook business pages as well.

Facebook and SEO

There are some experts and business leaders who consider Facebook their #1 influence over SEO and Google ranking.

Of all of their ranking factors, we know that Google values good content the most. Google has figured out a way to observe how the public likes and engages with your content by observing those interactions on Facebook. If people are liking your content on Facebook, it must be good content!

Google is watching things like how many people tweet your content? How many people are sharing your content on Facebook or Google+?

Sure keywords are still important. But it's never the quantity, it's how you use those keywords when you engage with people.

We also know it's important because Google is so closely tied to Facebook. Have you ever noticed that after you Google something (if you're signed into Google Chrome), that you will start getting Facebook ads targeting the same keywords that you searched for.

> ***Tip:*** *Start out your posts and tweets with a question that you know is on the top of your customer's mind. "How Do You...?"*

Social Shares are the New Backlinks

We have previously discussed the value of good quality backlinks—in fact we devoted Chapter 5 to it. A link is a vote; it's like a popularity contest!

Google knows that if someone shares your Facebook posts, or Tweets, that's a genuine vote of confidence. It's hard to manipulate this type of sharing, and for sure it's easy to catch; it's against Facebook's rules to buy likes or shares. Plus that's a very heavy, manual process—a human has to do it.

> *Define: Social Signals* – *Any social media metric that Google uses to factor into their algorithm for ranking you in their index. Likes, Re-Tweets, Shares, Comments, etc. There has been some debate as to whether Google uses social signals to rank your website. That debate is based on a very old video that Matt Cutts (Google's SEO guy) did where he said they did not measure them because the technology was not available to do so. Well, since that comment, they figured out the technology.*

Social Media, Content Marketing, and SEO Work Hand in Hand

Google loves content, and social media sites like Facebook and Houzz engage your customers with your content. It's a perfect marriage—it's that simple!

> *Quick Fact:* *Well, more of an observation. Have you ever noticed that the majority of images listed on Google Image Search for any keywords that have to do with home decor are in either from Houzz or Pinterest?*

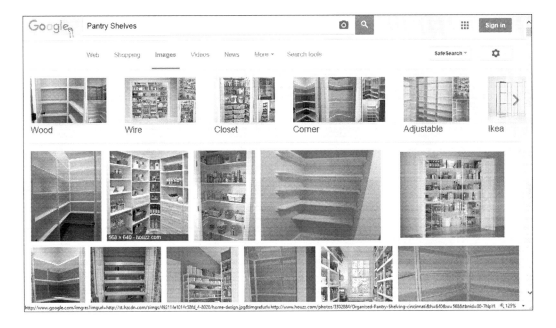

Social Media and Local Search

In the previous chapter we showed you how Google has incorporated local business listings and the Google Map Listings into Google+. We also showed you that Google checks the validity of your local Name, Address, and Phone Number by comparing it to other places on the internet that list that same information. Social media sites weigh heavily in that validation process.

Here's what Google wants to see:

- Facebook users from your local city engaging with you.
- Other Facebook business pages from your local area engaging with you.
- Your Name, Address, Phone Number and Website matching what you gave on your Google My Business map listing.
- Check-ins from mobile devices on Facebook.
- Your engagement with other local businesses.
- Your engagement with local Facebook page users.
- Your city name mentioned by commenters in your posts.
- Other local websites linking directly to your Facebook URL.

***Caution:** If you want local business, when you first setup your Facebook business page, you'll want to give it your real business name exactly as it appears on your Google Maps listing (Google My Business). Facebook calls this your Page Name.*

This is great for Local Search and the Google Map Listings because Google wants your name to match everywhere on the internet. If you try something like this:

Joe's Fine Jewelry & Wedding Rings Wedding Bands Engagement Rings
Google will think you are a spammy website.

Tip: If you are not concerned about local business, consider using a keyword in your business page name. Just don't overdo it, as in the example above.

Making Social Media Work for You

Give First

Anyone can spot self-promotion a mile away. There is a reason that society is leaving traditional media in droves. We all hate being sold to—especially Millennials. Just keep these two words in mind wherever you make a post. "Give First." And don't worry, once you have built a community of loyal followers, they'll buy from you. More importantly, they will amplify your brand for you, for free!

You have to build trust and establish yourself as the authority. Ask yourself, how am I going to help my fans with this post? What information do I have that they will find interesting? Am I being totally genuine with this post? At all costs, steer clear of that hard sell that we are all so wary of.

Tip: Automatically forward your Facebook posts to your Twitter feed. Yes, you can use the Hashtag (#) keyword string in a Facebook post. This is not an ideal use of Twitter, as you will need to keep in mind Twitter's 140 character limit when creating Facebook posts, but for busy business owners, it can be helpful for building a community on Twitter. It will also make your hashtagged keyword searchable in Facebook:
www.PlayGooglesGame.com/feeding-facebook-to-twitter

E-A-T: Expertise / Authoritativeness / Trustworthiness

Also remember these three important words, because they are in Google's *Quality Raters Handbook* which is used by their employees who manually rank your website. E-A-T is Google's acronym for a website's Expertise, Authoritativeness, and Trustworthiness.

As the business leader, you should create authentic resources and authority for your brand within your industry. Google watches the authenticity. Therefore, not only will your customers trust you more, Google will trust you more. Just remember to "Give First," and the more you give, the more trust you'll get back.

Building a Community

Facebook provides a great platform to build a community of loyal customers and advocates. The platform makes it easy for a user to engage with you, no matter what their technical skill level is.

Every day we are hearing success stories of people building their tribe by being in contact with them through Twitter and Facebook. Regular connection is the key. Don't just post your big "Look at me" news and how well your business is doing. Real people can relate better to your setbacks as well as your successes and how you handle both.

Once you get a strong following, your customers will spread your good news for you. The best part is that these are exactly the kind of triggers Google is looking for. Every time someone shares your story Google counts that as a vote of confidence in your content.

How Often Should I Post?

Well, that depends; sometimes less is more. Most businesses start out with one or two posts a week, then monitor the interactions to see what works. Just remember to Give First and make awesome posts. One awesome post a week is better than one mediocre post per day.

Remember, just because you're not posting doesn't mean you can't interact with your customers on a daily basis. Be sure to log on at least once a day to answer questions, like their comments and reply to them. Be sure and *Tag* the commenter that you're replying to; that way for sure they'll get a notice and hopefully come back more often.

Driving Traffic to Your Website with Facebook

OK, this is a big double whammy. Getting Facebook users to click through to your website is a huge benefit of building your Facebook community. Plus, Google tracks this sort of activity.

Below is an example of how Greg uses his profile picture on the Laptop Stand page as a call to action to promote a sale for Facebook fans back on his website. Facebook changes the rules all the time and currently they have strict rules about using too much text or using a call to action on the cover photo, but profile photos are not subject to those same cover photo rules; not today anyway.

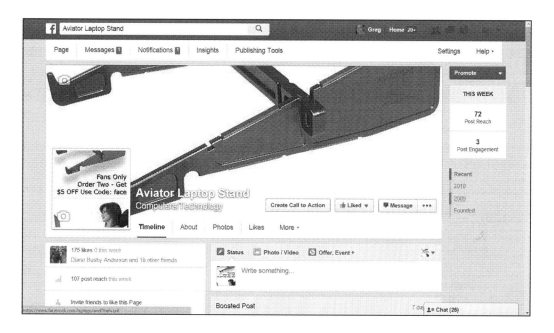

If you are getting tons of click-through to your website from your Facebook posts AND those folks are sticking around and engaging with you on your website, then Google makes a note of it and your rankings will improve on Google Search.

Keep in mind that posts on social media that drive the most traffic back to your website are videos, images, events, and blog posts; the blog post URL link is copied from your blog post on your website.

> *Tip: If you have a really interesting image, entice them back to your website with an offer for a higher resolution version. Facebook reduces the image quality when you upload them to a post. In your text, you might say "Click here for a full size image: www..."*

The good news is that the URL from the blog posts that you make on your website can be copied and pasted into the body of the Facebook post. Not only will the link be live on your Facebook post, it will also pre-populate with an inline preview (frame) of a snapshot from the actual post on your website. The little Facebook preview/snapshot can also pick up an image from the post from your website. This is great for driving traffic back to your website.

221

Of course, Facebook would rather that you take out an ad to drive traffic back to your website, so just keep up with the rules, and leverage them to the best of your ability.

The image below shows both examples. An inline frame of the blog post from Greg's website, with a little preview window "Frame" bringing in an image from his website - remember to always try and include a link back to your website in your Facebook posts.

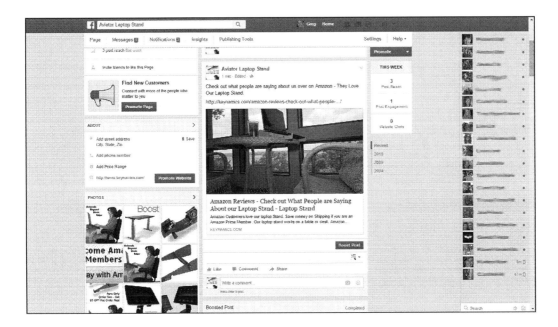

*Tip: **Scheduling Posts on Facebook** – Timing is not always in our favor when creativity strikes and we're ready to make a Facebook post. Remember to keep your audience's schedule in mind. A carefully timed post for when lots of your target market is on Facebook is a wise choice.*
www.PlayGooglesGame.com/scheduling-facebook-posts

What's a Hashtag #?

Yeah we know, it took us a while to get our heads wrapped around this whole hashtag thing too. Hashtags got popular on Twitter; however, you can also use them on other popular social media sites. On Facebook, users can type the hashtag connected to a keyword in the search box, allowing them to search for any similar hashtagged posts by other pages.

__Define Hashtag:__ The # symbol, called a hashtag, is used to identify keywords or topics on most social media platforms. It was initially created by Twitter users as *a way to categorize and search tweets. Hashtags make it easier for users to find posts and tweets with a specific theme or content.*

Hashtags are created by placing the hash character or number sign # in front of a word without a space between them. If there is more than one word, as in a keyword phrase, then there can't be a space between the words either. Everything is all together with no spaces. Note that hashtags on Facebook are actually hyperlinks.

If you spam with hashtags, Google will take note and flag you as a spammy website. Therefore, don't cram a bunch of keyword related hashtags in a single Facebook post or tweet. Use no more than two hashtags per post or tweet.

Only use relevant hashtags relating to the topic of that post or tweet. **"Check out this couple's #honeymoon picture and pretty #weddingring and beautiful #weddingflowers"** would be spammy.

> ***Tip:*** *Facebook posts with images or video embedded are much more likely to be opened and read.*

Popular Social Media Sites

- Facebook
- Google+ (this is not that popular yet, but you must be on here for Google SEO)
- YouTube (YouTube is not only a search engine of videos, it's very social)
- Twitter
- Instagram
- Pinterest
- LinkedIn
- Houzz

> ***Tip:*** *When you first set up your Facebook business page, and after you get a few likes (members) they will allow you to change your Facebook "User Name." This is kind of confusing terminology because what they are actually allowing you to do is change your Facebook Page URL from some random numbers to something more user and keyword friendly. This is not the same as your Page Name – which should always be your exact real business name for local search or your product name with keywords. For example: www.facebook.com/laptopstand*

www.PlayGooglesGame.com/custom-facebook-url

Who Will Take Ownership?

Just like any good business practice, you will need to specify a process (in writing) for your social media program. Depending on how large your staff is, you will want to assign this to someone.

If the business leaders are not interested in being active on social media, then find a responsible employee who enjoys this kind of stuff. Most likely you have someone who just loves to post stuff on Facebook.

Just know that a few minutes a day and the right plan can be great for your brand and your SEO results.

You should make this part of their job responsibility, giving them ample time to engage with your customers during work hours. Check your local labor laws, but you might also consider some kind of compensation during off hours. $1 per post, and $1 per comment, like or share—with a limit of course.

> *Caution: Be very careful allowing an employee access to your social media account on their personal phone or personal computer. There are many stories about employees of prominent companies forgetting that they are logged in as their employer when they make a personal post in poor taste—in very poor taste in some cases. You might have a policy that they can only log in from work computers or a work issued phone.*

> *Tip: Facebook, Google+, and Twitter allow you to put a Badge (button) on your website. You get the embed code from them and place it in your website code. It's pretty simple and your website designer can easily do it for you. Whenever someone clicks on your badge, it takes then directly to your Social Media page.*

Facebook & Employee Recruitment

A huge benefit of being active on social media is that it is a great way to find qualified employees. Sure, LinkedIn is great for recruiting, but we are hearing fantastic success stories from large companies recruiting on Facebook Business pages.

Greg's manufacturing business focuses on metal fabrication, with about 50% of his business coming from Oil and Gas. Manufacturing in general has not done a good job of recruiting employees to replace an aging workforce which is all about to retire.

Oil & Gas in particular is really struggling. A startling statistic that major oil companies are dealing with is that half of the workforce will be retiring by 2020. Smart companies are turning to Facebook to show young folks how interesting the work can be, and dispelling the notion that manufacturing is a dirty, boring job.

On the other hand, we have heard stories of some business leaders in the oil and gas industry that forbid their company to even have a Facebook page. Maybe they did not get the message that 70% of the online world is on it!

> ***Tip:*** *Facebook has exact size recommendations for various images on your Facebook page. There are set sizes for the Cover Photo, Profile Photo, Custom Tab Photo or Logo, Shared Photo. To find out the latest recommended sizes: www.PlayGooglesGame.com/facebook-image-sizes*

Best Practices – Action Plan

1. Establish a process for your Social Media program. Who will run it?

_____

_____

_____

_____

2. How will you promote your Facebook, Google+, and Twitter badges on your website? In your other marketing materials?

_____

_____

_____

_____

3. What creative ways can you think of to drive traffic back to your website?

Play Google's Game

_____

_____

_____

_____

Chapter 11

Google Hates Cheaters

Don't Get Spanked

✓ Black Hat Trickery
✓ The Rules
✓ Google Spam Guy – Matt Cutts

If you're looking for some trickery or quick tips to cheat Google's system, you're in the wrong place. Google hates cheaters and so does everyone else. No one likes spammy websites and we can all smell them a mile away.

We only teach White Hat SEO, the kind of SEO that Google actually asks us to use to help them rank our websites properly for their users (our potential customers). This is exactly the reason that everything that we wrote about in our first book (way back in 2008) still stands true today.

Anyway, the days of cheating Google are long gone. You're going to lose at that game, big time. Google has been hiring the best and brightest PhDs for years. There is no way you, or I, or the spammy website designer claiming to get your website number one on Google, is going to outsmart Google.

> *"Optimizing our websites for the search engines isn't about cheating the system…*
> *it's about building a better website."*

Google has been consistent over the years with their message. "Present good original, content for the enjoyment of your visitors (not simply written for tricking the search engines) and do it often." This "content" can take the form of text, images, and video.

Our techniques are not only effective; they are perfectly acceptable and follow Google's quality guidelines.

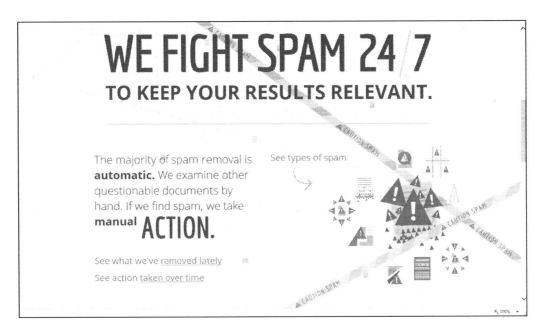

The image above is from a Google tutorial on "How Search Works".

Google's business model has always revolved around one simple mantra: *relevance*. They built their search engine based on the fact that if they could return that perfect website result to a searcher, they would win—and win they did!

We mentioned early on that we only teach *white hat*—Google friendly SEO techniques. Forget about trying to cheat the system; Google is a million miles ahead of you. We'll help you steer clear of the more common mistakes people make, either unknowingly or by *black hat SEO* trickery. Google wants our help in fighting spam. The search engine optimization techniques that we teach will improve the quality and appearance of the content of web sites and serve content useful to users.

Google and all the other search engines are relying on us to be ethical, honest, and fair, providing the information they need to rank us properly for the searchers keywords. Helping searchers find the best web pages for their search queries relates back to their golden rule of relevancy. Google wants searchers to find the highest quality answers, as quickly as possible.

There was a time, before Google, that searches for a local pizza place returned results for companies selling Viagra. We all hated search in those days.

Highlights

Very Important:
- Spend time creating awesome content, not black hat trickery
- If it feels wrong, it probably is.

Important:
- Beware of duplicate content.

Helpful:
- Create content for users, not to trick search engines

Spend Time Building Amazing content – Not Trying to Trick Google

It takes just as much effort to create amazing content as it does to always be chasing the latest trick to cheat the search engines.

Catching Cheaters Helps You

Yes, Sir. Honest internet marketers and business leaders are rejoicing over the fact that Google has finally put all of the cheaters in internet jail! With all the junk cleared out of the way, we can have our legitimate content ranked high.

Beware of the Scammers

You're probably like us; we get several emails a day and a phone call or two with promises to get us on page #1 on Google, which is kind of funny since the callers have not even taken the time to look at our website and realize that we are in the business!

100% of these solicitations are a scam and are from companies that practice *black hat SEO*. Even if these scammers are successful at "temporarily" getting you on page one, they are doing it by cheating. Eventually they will get caught and bring you down with them. (Ask J.C. Penny.)

We hear all the time about an unknowing business owner getting penalized for something their web designer or internet marketer did without their consent. Learn to spot trouble before it gets you penalized or flat out banned.

The techniques we teach in this chapter will enable you to spot these scams. On the other hand, if you manage your own SEO, you will be able to steer clear of these pitfalls. Basically, if it feels like cheating, it probably is.

Google Wants You to Help Them

Google encourages *white hat SEO*. After all, their main goal is to serve up relevant websites that match their searchers' keywords. Relevance is the golden rule with Google; anything done to detract from relevance is either banned already, or will be banned in the near future. Helping Google to serve up your website when someone wants your product or service helps them accomplish their goal of relevance. Imagine if you were searching for pizza and a car dealership showed up in the search results—that would not be relevant, you would not be happy and you would probably never use Google again. Don't worry, that's not going to happen anymore.

The Rules

Google Algorithms Updates

The rules that Google sets out can reward you or penalized you depending on whether or not you follow them.

As an industry, internet marketers and SEO experts expend great efforts to come up with an educated guess as to what Google is currently doing and what they will do next. However, Google isn't giving up their secrets and we have zero control over how they operate their company and the policies that they make. Professional internet marketers abide by the rules, look to see what is working now, and simply repeat the actions to keep in the good graces of Google and stay on top of the rankings.

The rules that rank websites are computer programs called search engine *algorithms*. Google is pretty secretive about the details of their algorithms and holds that information as proprietary. They can change in a second's notice.

Look at Your Website Through Google's Lens

Think about the history of the Google algorithm changes as it relates to how Google tries to identify websites with good content. Put yourself in Google's shoes and start looking at everything through Google's lens.

Here's an interesting comment on the topic by Matt Cutts. It's interesting and revealing what he is saying about trends:

> *"Ultimately, this is why we can't have nice things in the SEO space: a trend starts out as authentic. Then more and more people pile on until only the barest trace of legitimate behavior remains. We've reached the point in the downward spiral where people are hawking…"*

In the beginning, search engines were all about "keywords in the content;" then people started abusing keywords, so they tweaked their algorithm to catch people cheating, using tactics like invisible text, super small fonts, and keyword stuffing.

Then Google came along and started looking at the popularity of "Backlinks to the Content". Google figured it was like a popularity contest. Then people started selling backlinks and Google figured out an algorithm change to catch them.

Of course these things are still important, but now that they have been abused, the Google PhDs have successfully come up with new algorithms to catch the cheaters.

Today it's about how many people are "engaging with our content" on our websites and on other internet platforms. Today it's Facebook, Twitter, LinkedIn, and others; who knows what Google will do tomorrow to measure engagement.

Look at your website through Google's lens:

- Does it have interesting content? Well, let's see, are people talking about it and sharing it (backlinks)?
- Are people talking about it on Social Media?
- Is the business itself talking about it through their blog page?
- Are people clicking on your images from Google Image Search; are they then clicking through onto your website from Google Image Search?
- Are they commenting on your YouTube videos, liking them, sharing them, and clicking through to your website from them?
- And most importantly, do visitors like it so much that they come back often?

Google Webmaster Tools Now Called Google Search Console

Google does offer advice for SEO Experts, Web Designers, Internet Marketers, Webmasters and small business owners managing their own websites. It's been rebranded as *Google Search Console*. This advice can be found here:

www.PlayGooglesGame.com/google-search-console

Something to keep in mind; even though the rules are computer programs, those programs were originally written by human beings. Those human beings happen to be the geeks that work at Google. We always try to "think like a Google geek" when we are deciding, "What would Google do?"

Matt Cutts – The Google Spam Guy

Speaking of humans, Matt Cutts is a software engineer at Google in charge of Google's *Webspam* division. Matt also works with the Search Quality team on search engine optimization issues. Matt's team writes programs which can identify the black hats and their corresponding websites. Think about that for a second. If Matt's job is to identify the black hats and their trickery, then his focus really isn't to give us white hat SEO advice, because that would just tip off the black hats. However, by default, if we know what is bad in Google's eyes, then we can determine what is good.

Through his personal blog and speaking engagements, he gives insight into the company, search engine index updates and SEO issues. Matt is considered the number one liaison between Google and the SEO/Webmaster community. Cutts is also listed as one of the co-inventors on a

Google patent related to search engines and web spam, so he probably knows what he is talking about! Important messages from Matt and a link to his blog can be found here: www.PlayGooglesGame.com/matt-cutts

Matt Talks About the Rules

According to a statement issued by Matt on his blog:

Algorithm update: "Typically yields changes in the search results on the larger end of the spectrum. Algorithms can change at any time, but noticeable changes tend to be less frequent."

Data Refresh: "When data is refreshed within an existing algorithm. Changes are typically toward the less-impactful end of the spectrum, and are often so small that people don't even notice. One of the smallest types of data refreshes is an *Index Update.*"

Index Update: "When new indexing data is pushed out to data centers. From the summer of 2000 to the summer of 2003, index updates tended to happen about once a month. The resulting changes were called the *Google Dance.* The Google Dance occurred over the course of 6-8 days because each data center in turn had to be taken out of rotation and loaded with an entirely new web index, and that took time. In the summer of 2003 (the Google Dance called "Update Fritz"), Google switched to an index that was incrementally updated every day (or faster). Instead of a monolithic monthly event, the Google would refresh some of its index pretty much every day, which generated much smaller day-to-day changes that some people called *everflux.*

Over the years, Google's indexing has been streamlined, to the point where most regular people don't even notice the index updating. As a result, the terms "everflux," "Google Dance," and "index update" are hardly ever used anymore (or they're used incorrectly :). Instead, most SEOs talk about algorithm updates or data updates/refreshes. Most data refreshes are index updates, although occasionally a data refresh will happen outside of the day-to-day index updates. For example, updated backlinks and PageRanks are made visible every 3-4 months."

Google uses extremely complicated mathematical methods of analyzing your content for keywords and how those keywords relate to the "logic" of your wording. One method is called *latent semantic indexing.*

Latent Semantic Indexing

As we noted in Chapter 6. Google employs something called *LSI* or *Latent Semantic Indexing* to catch people who are simply writing content for search engines and not people. LSI identifies patterns in the relationships between the keywords and concepts contained in your textual content. Google is trying to make sure that your text is relevant and that it is logical, based on your keywords.

Google is looking for unnatural relationships between your words. LSI is based on the principle that keywords that are used in the same contexts on other websites tend to have similar meanings. A key feature of LSI is its ability to extract the conceptual content of a body of text by establishing associations between those keywords that occur in similar contexts.

In simple terms it just means that Google is looking for natural content that a human would enjoy reading. They don't look at the number of times a keyword is repeated on a page; they look at how the keyword is associated with the "theme" or context of the page as compared to similarly themed pages throughout the internet.

Google will give more weight to a site's central theme than a particular keyword.

This does not mean that you should not sprinkle your keywords throughout your text. In fact you absolutely should. However, you should do it in a way that looks and reads naturally. Google gives and examples of unnatural text:

> *"There are many <u>wedding rings</u> on the market. If you want to have a <u>wedding</u>, you will have to pick the <u>best wedding ring</u>. You will also need to <u>buy wedding flowers</u> and a <u>wedding dress</u>."*

Writing this way will cause Google to flag your website as a spammy, low quality website and you will never rank high.

As described through this book, as long as you write naturally and for the enjoyment of your readers, you'll be fine. As in the above example, it will be obvious to your readers and to Google when you are simply stuffing as many keywords in as many places that you can.

One Year Domain Registration

Google's Matt Cutts denounces that registering your domain for more than one year helps you. We believe that it can't hurt. Think about it. Fly by night, unrepeatable companies are probably not going to register for more than one year. It does not cost that much money (about $10.00 per year). Go ahead and register your new domain for a three to five year period, and when your domains come up for renewal, renew them for at least three years as well.

The Google Sandbox

Most SEO experts agree that the *sandbox* penalty does not exist anymore. We disagree, to some extent.

The sandbox penalty got its name from the analogy of a toddler playing in a sandbox. Google purposely withholds new websites from showing in the search results for a period of time. Their thinking was that newer websites and businesses might take a while before they were able to offer relevant websites to searchers. They also factored in any fly-by-night companies that they figured would not be around for very long.

As you can imagine, Google probably got a ton of backlash from admitting this. After all, they do make their money selling sponsored links to advertisers, right? Imagine trying to sell a new advertiser and the advertiser knowing they would not be allowed to show up, and the only way to show up would be to pay… that's kind of a conflict of interest.

We still think Google factors this in on a smaller scale. Of course they don't ban new websites from showing up anymore, and it might not be as important as it once was. One thing is for sure; you'll never get Google to admit it. The point is, start early!

Over-Optimization is Spammy

Google has identified websites that are over-optimized. This is based around the infamous Penguin Algorithm update several years ago.

What? After reading this entire book on what to do to be properly optimized and now we tell you this?

Look, we don't worry too much about these trends because they come and go. Most of those rumors are based on what the SEO community has seen happen to overly optimized sites that also practice black hat trickery.

SEO professionals react a lot, because that's all we can do whenever Google changes the rules. Some see these sites penalized and assume that it's because of this or that, when in reality the sites are just plain cheating and Google has figured it out. It's simple, don't cheat, and you won't get penalized. If it feels like cheating, it probably is.

However, with this in mind, we are seeing that Google is getting better every day at culling out relevant websites with awesome content for their searchers and eliminating the black hatters. As mentioned in the keyword section, do not repeat *exact match* keyword phrases too much; it's just plain spammy.

Your links should look natural and authentic, not spammy. Split up your keyword phrases and sprinkle those individual words around your site, and most definitely look for *keyword synonyms* to use in your text content, images, headers, YouTube videos. Sounds like basic English Composition 101, right?

> ***Tip:*** *Use the Google Keyword Planner to find related keywords to give you some variety in your conversations.*

Just remember to stick with your exact match keyword phrases in the most important areas like the title tag of each web page, your internal links, some (but not necessarily all) of your image file names, and in the titles of your YouTube videos.

Content Spam

As far as content goes (the text, images, and video in the main body of your web pages), it has to be logical. If you keep it logical and readable you will stay clear of any penalties and in fact be rewarded with higher ranking. Google really analyzes the content to determine relevance, so you should too.

Just remember, as discussed in Chapter 6, it is imperative that you use the same keywords that you are focusing on in all of the other areas that we have previously discussed within your content too. Google will not reward you if it does not see these same keywords in your content. Google tries to match the words in your content with the keywords in your title (and other meta tags), internal links, image file names, embedded videos, headings, etc.

Spammy Text

The fundamentals never change; even as every new Google algorithm comes out, their message about SEO has been consistent over the years: textual content must be written for the benefit and enjoyment of your visitors. Text should not be written simply to influence the search engines. Google has very sophisticated programs that can sniff out spammy text that is only written to influence search engines. Google will reward you for writing content that your users enjoy, interact with, share with their friends, and come back for more

Keyword Stuffing

Older search engines (pre-Google) simply counted how often a keyword appeared, and used that to determine relevancy and ranking. Google and other search engines today have the ability to analyze a page for keywords, determine if it's logical or if keyword stuffing techniques have been employed, and determine the ranking based off this analysis.

Exact Match Anchor Text

Overdoing *exact match anchor text* got a lot of press because of the Penguin update and we agree. Think about it. If *backlinks* are the number one factor considered by Google, then the black hatters are constantly trying to game the system with this technique. Therefore, Google is constantly looking for ways to spot backlink cheating techniques.

As discussed in Chapter 5, in the real world of receiving back links we talked about how lucky we are whenever someone links to us and that it's a bonus if we can ask them to use anchor text (the visible text that is clickable) containing our keywords in that link. Reality is that most websites that link to us are going to use something generic like "Click Here" as the clickable text.

If someone is cheating, Google has most likely figured this out. Actually, it's pretty easy based on link velocity. Most cheaters are going to have hundreds of exact match links coming in at the same time. Google knows that these are *Unnatural Links*.

Google also expects that a lot of backlinks coming to your site will not be exactly matched to your keywords. They know for sure that 100% of those backlinks are NOT going to have the exact keywords that you are using everywhere on your site. If 100% of all the incoming links are exact match—bingo, Google has identified a black hat! These black hats have bought those links and automatically inserted their best keywords as anchor text.

Exact Match URLs and Hyphens

Exact match URLs and *Exact Match Domain Names* are recommended by us in Chapter 2. Exact match domain names are mainly for folks first launching a new website. Exact match URLs are fantastic for links to your main internal webpages. Remember, if you already have history with your current domain name, don't change it just for the sake of including keywords. We also recommended that you consider separating those keywords with hyphens, noting that this really helps for lower competition keywords.

More rumors went around about the Penguin update that Google might be penalizing for exact match domain names and exact match URLs. Again, some of the SEOs see the effect (penalized sites) and think this is the cause.

In reality, many black hats knew the advantage of keywords and hyphens in the URL years ago, and rushed out to register domains with their exact keywords. It's not the domain name, and it's not the hyphens that are getting them in trouble; it's all the other trickery that they are performing.

Some *SEO research community* websites say it also looks spammy to do this. Their thinking goes, "If it looks spammy, then people will not click on your website address." Maybe so, and that would be a personal preference. We can tell you this: Greg's concrete countertop business is www.ancient-art-concrete-countertops.com and it's been ranked number one for over 11 years. Of course he was smart enough to name his business "Ancient Art Concrete Countertops" in the first place. He gets calls daily (over his competition) from people landing on his site from a Google search. Most of the callers compliment him on his website.

We know for sure that it's a great idea to place your keywords in your internal site links that point to your main pages and blog posts. Just make sure it's natural. We are not advocating creating hundreds of random internal links. We're talking about authentic links to real pages and other important content on your website.

Of course this is not a silver bullet; you have to also be creating amazing content.

Quick Fact: After the dust settled on the notorious Panda and Penguin updates, we found that all 101 tips and techniques in Greg's original book (published in 2008) were still valid. This proves the fundamental and basic nature of the techniques we teach.

Guest Blogging

Advisory: Proceed with Caution! Guest blogging is when you are invited to write an article on someone else's website or blog. Guest blogging is a great way to share your amazing content, and most of us are honored when we're invited to do so.

Guest blogging can be done legitimately, and beneficially, but it's really tricky. Guest blogs throw up a red flag and Google really watches out for them.

Guest blogging was all the rage several years ago. Matt Cutts spoke out on it and caused concern for all of us doing it legitimately.

www.PlayGooglesGame.com/matt-cutts-guest-blogging

"I wanted to give people a heads up mainly because the practice has gotten so spammy. There are certainly reasonable and valid reasons to consider guest posts, but regular site owners should be aware of the risks as well. I was talking to a small business owner recently and she was delighted that someone wanted to write a guest blog post. She thought that her small blog was being validated, when in fact it was being targeted.

Several years ago, I would have said that the default answer when someone proposed doing a guest blog post would 'yes.' However, with the rapid rise of low-quality or spammy sites trying to build tons of links via guest blogging, so I'd say that the default answer now should be 'no.' Of course, if you know the person writing the blog post well, or want to vouch for them, or if the author is happy to nofollow their links, then that changes the calculation–it's much more likely that someone is looking for a new audience instead of a way to get keyword-rich links."

We believe that Google's intent here is to catch those people who are automating hundreds of guest posts or hiring offshore cheap labor to spam a bunch of websites with guest posts, in the guise of coming from the originating business owners. Sometimes this happens without the hosting website's knowledge. These spammers always link the guest post back to their own website.

Outright Trickery

In the early days people were blatant about cheating. Below are some practices that will for sure get you banned form Google.

Google says: "A good rule of thumb is whether you'd feel comfortable explaining what you've done to a Google employee? Another useful test is to ask, 'Does this help my users? Would I do this if search engines didn't exist?'"

Invisible Text

Since keywords in text were the only measure the search engine spiders used before Google, some people added a bunch of repetitive keywords or other commonly searched for text and made it the same color as the background. This text was usually irrelevant to the content of their website.

Therefore, the spiders saw it, but human eyes didn't. From my laptop stand business I could repeat "HP Laptop" a thousand times in the same color text as my background and never have it be seen by human eyes. The spiders would see it and think, "This site must sell a bunch of HP Laptops, so let's give them high ranking on the search term of HP Laptop." Not anymore!

Super Small Hidden Text

Some cheaters make the text so small that human eyes can't read it, but the spiders still can. Or maybe they try to hide it behind an image.

Link Sharing Farms – Link Schemes

As we learned in Chapter 5 and worth repeating here. Link Schemes & Manipulative Linking is cheating. You might be guessing right about know how easy it would be for dishonest people to try and cheat the system. And cheat they did. And caught they got – just ask JC Penney.

Link sharing farms sprang up overnight offering to give you thousands of links. Others found very creative ways to cheat. It worked for a while, then it all came crumbling down. Remember what we said in the beginning. You are not going to outsmart Google, so spend your efforts creating amazing content that people want to link to.

It's Against the Rules

From Google: Any links intended to manipulate PageRank or a site's ranking in Google search results may be considered part of a link scheme and a violation of Google's Webmaster Guidelines. This includes any behavior that manipulates links to your site or outgoing links from your site.

*The following are examples of **Link Schemes** which can negatively impact a site's ranking in search results:*

- *Buying or selling links that pass PageRank. This includes exchanging money for links, or posts that contain links; exchanging goods or services for links; or sending someone a "free" product in exchange for them writing about it and including a link - also known as Link Sharing Farms.*
- *Excessive link exchanges ("Link to me and I'll link to you") or partner pages exclusively for the sake of cross-linking*
- *Large-scale article marketing or guest posting campaigns with keyword-rich anchor text links*
- *Using automated programs or services to create links to your site*

Additionally, creating links that weren't editorially placed or vouched for by the site's owner on a page, otherwise known as unnatural links, can be considered a violation of our guidelines. Here are a few common examples of unnatural links that may violate our guidelines:

- *Text advertisements that pass PageRank*
- *Advertorials or native advertising where payment is received for articles that include links that pass PageRank*
- *Links with optimized anchor text in articles or press releases distributed on other sites. For example:*

"There are many <u>wedding rings</u> on the market. If you want to have a <u>wedding</u>, you will have to pick the <u>best ring</u>. You will also need to <u>buy flowers</u> and a <u>wedding dress</u>."

*(**Note:** The underlined words are hyperlinks in the previous sentence.)*
- *Low-quality directory or bookmark site links.*

(**Note:** *These are spammy directories set up only for the purpose of selling local links. In Chapter 9 we talked about the importance of having listings in local directories – just be sure they are legit!*)

- *Keyword-rich, hidden or low-quality links embedded in widgets that are distributed across various sites, for example:*
- *Widely distributed links in the footers or templates of various sites*

Caution: *Exact Match Anchor Text – Google says: "Links with optimized anchor text in articles or press releases distributed on other sites" <u>can be considered a link scheme</u>. We know that Anchor text is becoming overtly overused and now Google considers this a spammy tactic. While Google thinks it's fine to have a few links that are exact match anchor text, Google also knows that it's unnatural to have hundreds or thousands of text links that exactly match your keywords. Be cautious and don't overdo it. The truth is most outside websites are not going to give you an exact matched anchor text link anyway, and Google knows it. To learn more:*
<u>*www.PlayGooglesGame.com/exact-match-anchor-text-links*</u>

Define: Link Velocity *– Link Velocity refers to how fast links are built to your site in a given period of time. High link velocity could be a bad thing. It's a sure sign that you just bought a bunch of incoming links from a link sharing farm.*

Duplicated Websites – Duplicate Content

This seems to be a little known fact. Google penalizes you if you have duplicated websites. Duplicate sites are two or more different website addresses (URLs) that have the exact same content (graphics and text). Greg learned this the hard way. Soon after launching his laptop stand business, he wanted to have **www.laptop-ergonomics.com** and **www.keynamics.com** be the same exact websites. Unaware that this was an issue, he uploaded everything verbatim to each separate site, resulting in duplicate sites.

Researching SEO one day, he ran across numerous articles on this duplicate content issue. It was only when he started varying both the content (text, image file names, and video) on both sites that they both finally started creeping up in ranking for his keywords.

Also, do not have two separate pages in your website with the same content, as this could be considered a duplicate site and penalized.

Note: Greg has since abandoned the ergonomic target market. Unfortunately, most companies do not allow much budget money for proper ergonomics for their workforce.

Duplicate content can creep in on you from unsuspecting places. For example, if you make a blog post on your website, it could be listed in more than one place on your website, depending on how your website design software organizes them. There are safeguards against this. You should consult your website design software for more information.

Scraper Websites

If all you do is repost or simply copy and paste text from other websites without contributing your own unique content, then you might get penalized as a Scraper website. This scraped content is taken from other, more reputable sites on the assumption that increasing the volume of pages on your website will increase your ranking.

Google gives some examples of scraping:

- Sites that copy and republish content from other sites without adding any original content or value.
- Sites that copy content from other sites, modify it slightly (for example, by substituting synonyms or using automated techniques), and republish it.
- Sites that reproduce content feeds from other sites without providing some type of unique organization or benefit to the user.
- Sites dedicated to embedding content such as video, images, or other media from other sites without substantial added value to the user.

There are many legitimate websites that repost other websites' content. Many news agencies get their stories from Reuters or the Associated Press and republish them. The Huffington Post is another example.

As long as you are bringing value to your users, and not infringing on anyone's copyrights, you're going to be fine. We think Google is smart enough to tell the difference between an automated spammy copying (scraping) and human reposting and paraphrasing for the benefit of re-posters audience.

Review of all Black Hat Warnings

Throughout this book we have noted Black Hat Warning callouts. Let's review them here:

Black Hat Warning: Keyword Stuffing *is an old trick and Google watches this like a hawk. It's super easy for them to detect whenever someone does it and they will flag your entire website as a low quality site, or worse a spammy website, thus knocking you down in the rankings. Never, ever repeat a bunch of keywords ANYWHERE or in any strategy we teach. It will be obvious to you and others when you do this.*

However, Google does encourage us to help them by placing our relevant keywords in the appropriate places. Matt Cutts from Google actually gave a good example of the right and wrong way to place Keywords in Image ALT tags, which could also apply to any place we put our keywords:

Right *- alt="Dalmatian puppy playing fetch"*
Wrong *– alt="puppy dog baby dog pup pups puppies doggies pups litter puppies dog retriever labrador wolfhound setter pointer puppy jack russell terrier puppies dog food cheap dogfood puppy food"*

Mr. Cutts goes on to say "Filling alt attributes with keywords ("keyword stuffing") results in a negative user experience, and may cause your site to be perceived as spam."

Black Hat Warning: *Please don't try and game the system; YouTube will catch you. Google says, "Please do not use these features to game or trick our search algorithms. All metadata should be representative of the content contained in your video. Among other things, metadata added in an attempt to game search algorithms will lead to the removal of your video and a strike against your account."*
www.PlayGooglesGame.com/youtube-black-hat

Black Hat Warning: *We can't offer legal advice. However, almost 100% of all music is copyright protected; the same goes for any images or videos. Google is watching, and they are watching to see if you are uploading videos with copyright protected music violations. They figure if we are cheating here, then we are* *cheating elsewhere and they will penalize, or worse, ban you. It's against Google's and YouTube's terms of service to upload someone else's copyrighted music. Just because you bought a CD of your favorite artist, does not give you the right to upload that music for the rest of the world to hear. Please consult your attorney if you have any questions on this.*

Black Hat Warning: *If all you do is repost or simply copy and paste text from other websites without contributing your own unique content, then you might get penalized as a <u>Scraper</u> website. The Scraper penalty was rolled out with Google's Panda algorithm update. See Chapter 12 for more info on the Panda update. Try to reword the posts in your own language and give them credit and link to them.*

Black Hat Warning: *Do not list your UPS Store or any P.O. box address on Google My Business as if you could accept customers at that location; it's against Google's policy to do so and also it's misleading to customers. Instead, create a "Service Area Page" or "Brand Page" if you only have a UPS Store address.*

Black Hat Warning: *Never, ever place keywords into the official name of your business anywhere on the internet if they are not actually part of your actual business name.*

Learn More: *For the latest quality Guidelines from Google:*
www.PlayGooglesGame.com/google-quality-guidelines

Best Practices – Action Plan

1. You should not have any of these: invisible text – links from link sharing farms – duplicate sites – overuse of keywords – picture links instead of text links – broken links – splash page.

_____

_____

_____

_____

2. Do you have a "Contact Us" link on your home page? Is it a text link?

_____

_____

_____

_____

3. Has your website been indexed? Do you want to submit/register it with the major search engines?

_____

_____

_____

_____

Chapter 12

Engaging Customers & Making Money

Sticky Websites Win

✓ Google Ranks You on Your Engagement
✓ Customers Love You for Your Engagement
✓ Engaged Customers Will Buy From You

Before you can engage a customer, they must be compelled to stick around your website for a while. Internet searchers have very little patience. You have to hit them right away with your best shot.

Once you get a click on your search listing from the Google search results, you have about three seconds to capture and keep a searcher on your website before they hit the dreaded *back button* and return to Google or whatever website they happen to be coming from. Some say that the bounce rate is approaching two seconds.

What a shame it would be to lose a sale after all of your hard work to get high ranking and enticing them to click on your link, then they leave you in less than three seconds—just because your website did not interest them enough to "stick" around.

Worse yet, Google tracks your bounce rate and it's a huge factor in ranking your website in the search results. Google knows that people stick around interesting websites and flee from boring or spammy websites.

Making your website sticky and keeping your potential customers from going back to their previous website is our #1 goal. The art of making websites sticky revolves around four objectives:

1. Getting visitors to stay on your website for as long as possible or until they buy something.
2. Getting them to visit as many of your individual webpages as possible until they buy something.
3. Getting them to come back for more, at later times—to buy something.
4. Getting them to share your content with their friends.

> **Note:** *Google tracks all four of these activities and weighs them all heavily in determining your rankings for the keyword they started their search with.*

When talking about stickiness, we mainly focus on the *Bounce Rate* back to the search engines. However, Google tracks your stickiness equally to any previous website. For example, someone might have clicked to you from your sponsored ad on the previous website, or maybe it was a link from an article written about you.

Furthermore, keep in mind that Facebook, YouTube, and many other popular internet platforms are search engines and you can get traffic from them as well (assuming you have employed our recommendations in this book).

> **Define: Bounce Rate** *– The average number of seconds it takes for a visitor to hit the back button after they have landed on your website from another platform, like google, Facebook, or any other website.*

The bottom line is that you want to get your visitors to hang around your site, and come back for a visit on a regular basis. This is called "Stickiness," and Google rewards for stickiness.

> *Define: Stickiness* – *The longer customers stay on your website and the more often they come back to visit, the more "Sticky" your site is.*

Highlights

Very Important:

- Build Trust & Create Interest in 2 seconds or less!
- Cool graphics and easy reading text.
- Mobile Friendly – Google test.

Important:

- Give them exactly what they expect when they land.

Helpful:

- Sell something!

Building Trust

We mentioned *bounce rate* earlier. Trust is probably the number one factor in keeping your bounce rate low.

Feature Testimonials and Product Reviews

What better way to build trust than from other customers and editorial reviews?

Prominently Feature Your Phone Number

…And contact information, especially on the checkout page. Customers find this very reassuring.

Get a Toll Free Number

This is especially helpful for B2B business, where buyers are calling form a land line. If you conduct business outside of your local area, offer a free way for them to call. They are fairly inexpensive these days. A good one will only charge you a small base rate and then a per minute charge. Just be sure to also list your local number (with area code); it reassures customers and Google that your business is located in the same area they are in.

> *Tip: Some businesses would rather have customers complete the buying process online without having to take the customers' phone calls. We have noticed on our laptop stand business that sometimes online shoppers just want to call to be reassured that we are a reputable business. They are also reassured that they can get in touch with a "Live" person if needed. Once we answer the calls, we encourage the customers to go ahead and complete their purchase online. We do offer to gladly take their order by phone, but we note that it's actually more secure online (because on phone orders we have to write down their credit card information, and our shopping cart's secure server does not store that information). Talking to customers in person is an opportunity to up sell them as well.*

Include a Physical Address

Place it on your contact us page, and in your footer of every page and not just a Post Office Box.

Include an "About Us" Page

Another interesting statistic is that of the folks that do stick around, 80% of them will immediately go to your *About Us* page. Once they feel they can trust you a little bit, they'll want to check you out further. So, you must have an About Us page and it needs do a good job of building trust. Google also looks for an About Us page.

Always Include a "Contact Us" Page

Customers love them and so does Google.

Reassure Them with Your Return Policy

Most of your smarter competitors offer a 30 day return policy. Most credit card merchant accounts require you to offer a 30 day return policy. This is a good business practice and you will want to feature it in a prominent location near the "Add to Cart" button and during the checkout process.

Reassure Them with a Link to Your Privacy Policy on Every Page

Define: Privacy Policy – A statement or promise by the website owner not to share (or in any way give out) the visitors' private information (like email addresses or phone numbers). It's also good business practice to state that you will not use their information to contact them (without their permission), unless it is for shipment or pertinent product information like a recall.

Bright Idea: Some of the policies and ideas mentioned above might seem so obvious to you or your industry that you don't think they merit featuring on your website. You might be thinking, "Everybody knows that." Just remember, if you don't show it, people will assume that you don't offer it.

Tell Them That Your Shopping Cart is on a Secure Server

Even though most every shopping cart is hosted on a secure server, it's reassuring to let them know that once they click "add to cart" and start the checkout process, they will be entering their sensitive information on a secure server.

*Define: Secure Server – You can always tell when you are on a "Secure Server" by the website address. The **http://www.your-name.com** changes to **https://www.your-name.com**. The "s" in the https:// designates a secure server. Secure servers are very restrictive and held to very tight security standards, meaning hackers have a difficult time hacking into them and stealing sensitive information like your customers' credit card information!*

Usability – Sticky Tips

If the average bounce rate is only three seconds, that means you have just a couple of seconds to establish trust. Of course, if you want to make a sale, you must continue to build trust as they scroll and click through your website. You must design your website so it's easy to read, easy to navigate, uncluttered, and uses white space properly. This is where a good website designer can really help you.

Website *Heat Map Studies* originated with observing eye movements (also known as *Eye Tracking* studies) to show were the visitor's eyes land on your webpage immediately after opening it and during those first few crucial seconds of the visit. It's imperative that you establish trust in these physical areas of your website.

Results vary depending on what device they are using, your industry, and your audience, but there is high evidence that the top left area of the webpage gets hit first. You'd better do something in that area to grab and hold attention.

Some studies reveal that their eye movements generally follow a pattern to form an "F". Starting at the top left corner, they read across, forming the top horizontal bar of the "F". Then they skip down and start reading again from the left, but do not go quite as far horizontally, forming the bottom shorter horizontal bar of the "F".

Heat map studies have evolved to study other interactions on a website, including: which areas visitors move their mouse to, which areas are clicked on, and even the users' scroll actions in order to determine where the average *Fold* lies on viewer's screens. The goal of all of these studies is to try to determine which areas of your website people tend to focus on and interact with.

Keep Your Most Important, Attention Grabbing Content Above the Fold

The *Fold* comes from the print newspaper industry and is the basis for a common term in advertising referring to *Above the Fold*. Using an analogy of a newspaper folded in half, lying on a coffee table, the most visible area is going to be the content "above" the fold.

As more and more users access our websites on mobile devices, the fold becomes less and less of a factor because visitors are simply scrolling down with their thumb.

Use a Familiar Website Layout – Don't Make Them Think

People are scanning websites for information fast. If they have to think about it for half a second, they're gone. Don't make them think—it should just flow naturally, just like every other website they see on the internet.

> ***Learn More:*** *Review Chapter 8 for tips on using WordPress templates. Templates are great because they make us conform to industry standards. Without them we tend to get a little too creative!*

Familiarity is good when it comes to fast, easy navigation of your website. For the same reason that you wouldn't change the live link colors from blue to green, you should not change other commonly expected items.

Users expect links to the main pages of your website to be along the top; they also expect a header area on the top, a central body, and one side column.

Keep in mind that over half of searches are done on mobile devices now. That means that standard page layout is turned on its head. You need to think about how your site looks when users are scrolling down with their thumb.

Mobile Friendly?

Google knows that over half of the searches are performed on a mobile device. They have been warning us for years to be mobile friendly. More importantly, we need to accommodate over half of our customers!

In 2015 Google came out and told website owners to get mobile friendly or be penalized. They have never made a statement like this before—so you better pay attention.

This is the first time in history that Google has pre-announced an upcoming algorithm change and they are calling it "significant," which got our attention. Google is even giving a website address where you can check to see if your website is mobile friendly: www.PlayGooglesGame.com/google-mobile-friendly

Google says a mobile friendly website meets the following criteria as detected by Googlebot:

- Avoids software that is not common on mobile devices, like Flash

- Uses text that is readable without zooming
- Sizes content to the screen so users don't have to scroll horizontally or zoom
- Places links far enough apart so that the correct one can be easily tapped

Many mobile friendly websites use a *Responsive Design*, which means the webpage responds, or fits the screen of the device that it is shown on.

Readability

First off, searchers don't like reading a bunch of text, which creates a fine balance because Google likes quality well written text.

Your best bet is to increase the readability of text for improved comprehension and reading speed. It's a fine art and there are many factors that influence ease of readability, including the whitespace surrounding the text, font choices (serif versus sans-serif), font size, line height, background/foreground contrast, as well as spacing. Good readability will enhance the likelihood that a user will continue reading instead of abandoning your website.

> ***Tip:*** *Sans Serif fonts (fonts without serifs) are easier to read on computer monitors. A couple of examples are Arial® and Verdana®. Serifs are non-structural details on the ends of some of the strokes that make up letters and symbols. This tip is a good example of Times New Roman, which is a serif font.*
>
> *Fonts with serifs, while easier to read in print, are harder to read on computer monitors. Use Arial for type points 12 and above, and Verdana® for 10 point and below. Microsoft actually developed the Verdana® font because of the need for a readable font on the early computer monitors. These early monitors had low resolutions, making the text look fuzzy. While today's monitors have higher resolutions and are clearer, the Verdana® font's readability still helps with smaller fonts 10 point and below.* The text in Verdana is purposely spaced a little further apart; therefore, on 12 point and higher, it looks too spaced out—this last sentence is Verdana 12 point.

Never Disable the "Back Button" on Your Website

This is so annoying. You are essentially holding your users "hostage" on the website. When this happens to us we vow never to visit that website nor do business with them again! We bet we're not alone.

You cannot actually disable the Back button on the user's browser. However, with some nasty programming code, you can make it so that the button continues to load the same page. Google penalizes for this.

Don't use a "Splash" Page

Most search engines can't index a splash page. Customers don't like them either.

You might have seen these before. It's like an "introductory" page that a user comes to after clicking the link. This page plays video, Adobe Flash Player, music, or a combination of all three. The page usually has a link that reads "Skip Intro", allowing the user to bypass the video and go to the "real" homepage. At the end of the video it also has an option to enter the "real" website: "Click here to Enter Site."

Always have people land on your real "home" page, or a specific product page, when they link to, or type in your website address. The home page is sometimes called the *Index Page*—for good reason, because Google indexes it!

Splash Pages will hurt your ranking because Google has a hard time crawling them and they are a real pain for users.

Remember, customers want information and they want it fast. Don't place barriers like this between your customer and a purchase decision.

> ***Define: Splash Page*** *– These are pages that usually have some sort of fancy video, music, or Adobe Flash Player animation that visitors must sit through first, before they can "Click to Enter" the main "Real" website.*

People searching want information and they want it fast. They don't want to have to wade through a lot of animations, flashing things, or corny music to get it. The ultimate goal? To convert them into paying customers, supporters, or believers in your worthwhile cause as easily as possible.

Adobe Flash

It is hard for any search engine to crawl and properly index Adobe Flash files. Plus they are not visible on Apple devices!

Furthermore, Google is now warning searchers, right in the search results, who search from an Apple device that a webpage contains Flash and might not work with their device.

Google says that content which cannot be displayed on a mobile device, like Flash, is a "common annoyance" for mobile users, and we know that Google loves its users!

> ***Define: Conversion Rate*** *– The percentage of customers who you actually "convert" to a paying customer versus the total number of visitors, usually calculated over a certain period of time.*

Don't Make People Register Just to Use Your Site

People are in a hurry and you should be respectful of their time. Let them buy the item and get going. After all, you are not Amazon or eBay.

Don't Force People to Fill out a Form Just to Send You an Email

There are usually exceptions to every rule and this is one example. The type of business you are in will come into play here. However, it's usually a good idea to give customers an option to just send you a quick email by putting an email link on your *Contact Us* page.

As good marketers, of course we want to capture as much information as we can about our visitors. A simple *Contact Form* is a fine way to do this.

Therefore, provide customers a contact form where they can fill out details, like email address, name, subject, and comments.

However, don't force customers fill to out a form just to send you an email. Near the contact form place an email link, like info@keynamics.com. Do you really like filling out those forms yourself when you just want to ask a quick question?

Ensure that the "Flow" of the Shopping Cart Checkout is Logical

You don't want customers to get lost or confused, especially when they are trying to give you their money!

Provide High-Quality, Large Images

High speed broadband is so common now, slow loading websites and large images are less and less of an issue than they were before. Furthermore, a good image editing program like Adobe Photoshop can reduce the size of a large picture without reducing the quality.

Put Product Images on Your Shopping Cart Landing Page

An image of the product they are buying reassures customers that they are ordering the right product. This improves their comfort levels before even starting the actual checkout process.

> ***Define: Shopping Cart Landing Page*** *– The page that visitors go to just after clicking the "Add to Cart" button. This page holds all of the items (like a shopping cart) until the shopper is ready to pay or "check out." Customers have the option to pay immediately after adding one single item to the cart, or they can go back to your main website and "continue shopping," hopefully adding many more items to the cart before proceeding to the final checkout and payment.*

Allow the Customer to "Return to Shopping" After They Land on the "Shopping Cart Landing Page"

Most good shopping carts have this feature prominently displayed. It's a great way to increase "Add On" sales.

Display the Shipping Amount/Options on the Checkout Landing Page

Don't make them go halfway through the checkout process just to find out the shipping amount, delivery speed options, or carriers you offer. Most shopping carts can "estimate" this at the checkout landing page for each type of shipping service you offer.

Don't Make the Customer Repeat Typing Entries

Typically your shopping cart will ask for the "billing" address and the "shipping" address. Sometimes the two addresses are different, but if they are the same, allow the customer to just check a box that says it's the same. Use this for email addresses as well, if you ask for it more than once.

Place the "Add to Cart" Button in Obvious Places

Don't make it hard for your customers to instantly click and make a purchase. Put the "Add to Cart" button right by the product image. After all, you will have repeat customers who come back to your website, knowing exactly what they want, and wanting to place the order ASAP.

It's also a good practice to have both the item and the "Add to Cart" button visible on the first or "top" screen. The idea is to be "above the fold" and ***not*** have to scroll down to see this.

Allow People to Easily Go Back to the Previous Page Using the "Back Button" to Correct Mistakes

Some shopping carts lose everything if you hit the back button and the customer has to start all over. Many will just "abandon" the checkout process altogether if this happens.

Put a Search Box on Every Page of your Website

Visitors probably found your site by typing a keyword into a search box. Let them continue the search on your website.

Never Lose Customers When They Click on a Link to Another Website

There is debate on this, as some people say they get offended when another browser tab opens up. We like it though and think that it's a non-issue for most people.

This can be accomplished in your website code, by making sure that outbound links open a "new browser window," thus keeping your website open in the original tab.

Making Money

We saved the best for last! All of the tips and techniques in this book lead to this one goal. Yes, even non-profits and charities need funds to operate. We'll wrap things up with an overview of how to collect the money once you make a sale, and some alternative ways to make money.

Accepting Money

Accepting money online revolves around credit card *Merchant Accounts* and online *Payment Gateways*. Of course the first step is that you'll need a bank account.

A bank account can reside with the traditional brick and mortar banks or an online bank like PayPal. PayPal is similar to your brick and mortar bank in that they also offer merchant services.

We have tried both routes. In our experience PayPal is more user friendly for online merchants, because PayPal was born online!

We also just signed up for Amazon Payments. That's been a big hit with our customers and most are paying this way now. Your visitors can just pay for your goods using their Amazon account.

Selling on Amazon

Well, as they say, if you can't beat 'em, join 'em!

For years Greg fought trying to outrank Amazon on Google. In the early years it was a lot easier to be #1 for the search term "laptop stand" because Greg's laptop stand was the first patented one to hit the market in 2003. Now there are thousands of people selling laptop stands, and he is competing with giants like Walmart, Staples, Best Buy, IKEA, and yes, Amazon.

Greg decided to start selling on Amazon Seller Central and is now using their FBA program. FBA stands for Fulfillment By Amazon, which means they store his laptop stands and iPhone stands in their warehouses and fulfill orders as they come in.

Amazon offers another option for selling, where the only real difference is that Amazon does not store the items; the merchant fulfills orders as they come into Amazon. Greg first started out selling on Amazon this way.

Folks, please note Greg's sales went up 5-fold when he switched to FBA. Here's why:

- As long as your items are inventoried in Amazon's warehouse under the FBA program, then Amazon Prime members get free 2 day shipping!
- Most Amazon Prime members filter their searches so that only products show up with Prime shipping.
- Prime members get no hassle returns by only having to ship the item back to Amazon and not dealing with the merchant.

> ***Learn More:*** *We'll share our latest successes and thoughts on selling on Amazon at www.PlayGooglesGame.com/amazon-selling*

Affiliate Marketing

Basically, as an affiliate, you are being rewarded for the number of clicks you get on your client's ad placed on your website. The client is usually referred to as a retailer or merchant.

Done correctly and sparingly, an affiliate program can add value to your visitors, and money in your pocket. Do it incorrectly and you will come across as a spammy sleaze bag.

When selecting an affiliate program, choose a product category appropriate for your intended audience. The more targeted the affiliate program is to your site's content, the more value it will add and the more likely you will be to rank better in Google search results and make money from the program.

> ***Real World Example:*** *Greg is on the board of the Greater Houston Manufacturers Association. He also manages the website for them. He placed an Indeed widget on the right column and targeted "Houston Manufacturing Jobs" in the Indeed interface. It works very well: visitors often come looking for jobs, and the association gets paid when they click on a job listing in the widget!*

> ***Caution:*** *Google warns that pure, or "thin," affiliate websites do not provide additional value for web users, especially if they are part of a program that distributes its content to several hundred affiliates. These sites generally appear to be cookie-cutter sites or templates with no original content. Because a search results page could return several of these sites, all with the same content, thin affiliates create a frustrating user experience. Learn more at: www.PlayGooglesGame.com/google-thin-affiliate*

Shopping Cart Best Practices for Internet Retailing

A positive user experience can improve your ranking as well. It has the potential to increase your incoming links because people like referring a positive experience to their friends, and Google tracks all of this.

Some of the following tips are a function of the shopping cart service, and are well beyond the scope of most small business owners to incorporate themselves, including us.

However, you should be aware of these practices and make sure that your shopping cart and website design incorporates them. Most shopping cart services are purchased "off the shelf." Therefore, knowing what to look for in the service helps you choose a good one.

> ***Define: Shopping Cart*** *– A shopping cart is a "turnkey" third party service that will provide you with "Web Pages" formatted to take the customer's order and the customer's payment method. Once your customer clicks the "Add to Cart" button, they are actually leaving your website and going to the secure shopping cart website/server without even knowing it.*

The shopping cart service provides the website programming code and a way to relay the customer's credit card (or PayPal) information to your Merchant Account. Your merchant account then transfers the money to your bank account. Usually your merchant account will have certain "approved" shopping carts that it works with. A good shopping cart will allow the pages to have the same look and feel as your main website, so the customers feel like they have never actually "left" your site.

Having a third party handle the shopping cart might help relieve you of tremendous liability; please consult your attorney on this. You don't want to store your customers' credit card information and have to worry about someone hacking into your website and stealing it.

Increase Sales with Related Items on Main Website Pages and Especially on the Checkout Landing Page

"May we suggest fries to go with your burger?"

Be careful with this and any other promotions on your website. You don't want to deter customers from their focus on buying what they intended to buy. For example, a "Pop Up" would be a very bad idea anywhere on your website.

Reduce Abandoned Carts with Reassurance

At every step or required action (like asking for their email addresses), reassure them about your privacy policy, or reassure them with your return policy, warranty, etc.

> *Define: Abandoned Carts – Abandoned carts are unfortunate and very common among internet shoppers. Basically, you've succeeded in getting found from your high ranking, the customer has chosen an item, they start the checkout process in your shopping cart, and then for some reason they just exit your whole website. Some folks are just curious about shipping and getting familiar with your purchase process, possibly to return later to complete the purchase. But most, unfortunately, are lost forever. What a shame, after all of the effort to get them to your site and choose an item, then to lose them.*

Your Contact Information, Privacy Policy and Return Policy Should be HIGHLY Visible on the Checkout Landing Page

The trust factor is never more important than at the checkout landing page.

Best Practices – Action Plan

1. As soon as the customer lands on your webpage, does it convey the message of the keyword they typed into the search box and compel them to look around?

_____

_____

_____

_____

2. Is the landing page cluttered with a bunch of "flashy" stuff?

_____

_____

_____

3. Is your text easy to read?

4. How can I build trust on my website?

ABOUT THE AUTHOR

Greg Bright
The CEO of SEO

Greg Bright is a manufacturer, patent holder, author, and instructor on internet marketing. He is driving phenomenal growth to his businesses by applying the techniques he teaches.

He believes the internet is absolutely our best marketing tool—increasing in importance every day as new generations of buyers and sellers enter the economy. Young buyers don't remember life before the internet and seasoned buyers are changing their habits.

Greg was an early internet adopter, in the 80s and 90s, when he invented and patented a laptop stand. He learned how to bring products to market quickly and efficiently utilizing the free search listings on Google and other search engines.

He went on to write a book on Search Engine Optimization (SEO), developed multiple #1 ranking websites, and became a speaker and adjunct instructor at The University of Texas at Austin, teaching other entrepreneurs how to win at SEO using real world examples from his own businesses.

Today, Greg manufactures his own products and represents other manufacturers in **metal fabrication**, focusing most of his attention on the energy sector. The oil & gas industry is a market that you might think is internet-averse. However, Greg drives 90% of his new business through internet marketing by focusing on SEO and leveraging adjacent tools such as Facebook, YouTube, and Image Search. Greg has been able to drive over 12,000 fans to his Facebook pages by following simple rules of internet marketing.

As opposed to traditional advertising where sellers pursue potential customers, the internet is a place where customers actively search for sellers. It's accessible 24-7 from a device that fits in everyone's pocket. Greg's central question is this: "Will buyers find you or your competitors first?"

This new book features lessons learned from the thousands of businesses Greg has helped online - Greg wants to help you be found.

@TheCEOofSEO
LinkedIn - GregBright
info@PlayGooglesGame.com

Tools & Resources

1. **Matt Cutts – Google SEO & Quality Guy – YouTube Channel**
   www.PlayGooglesGame.com/matt-cutts-youtube-channel
   He also has many, many videos on Google's Channel.

   www.PlayGooglesGame.com/google-youtube-channel

2. **How Google & SEO Works**
   www.PlayGooglesGame.com/how-search-engines-work

3. **Google Search Console Help**
   www.PlayGooglesGame.com/google-search-console-help

4. **Google Search Console "Dashboard"**
   www.PlayGooglesGame.com/google-search-console

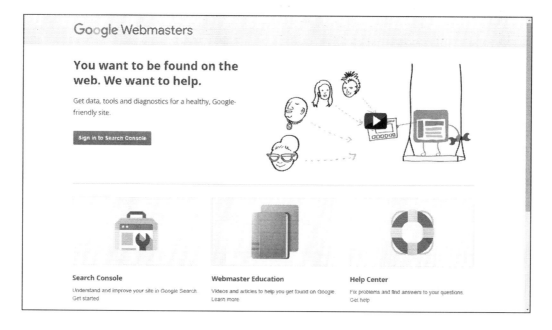

5. **Google's Quality Guidelines**
   www.PlayGooglesGame.com/google-quality-guidelines

6. **Top 5 SEO Tips Working Right Now**
   www.PlayGooglesGame.com/best-seo-tip-today

7. **Official Google SEO Guide:**
   www.PlayGooglesGame.com/official-google-seo-guide

8. **SEO MOZ**
   www.PlayGooglesGame.com/seo-moz

9. **Search Engine Land**
   www.PlayGooglesGame.com/search-engine-land

10. **Get Updates Right From Google**
    www.PlayGooglesGame.com/google-seo-blog

Glossary

***Abandoned Carts* –** Abandoned carts are unfortunate and very common among internet shoppers. Basically, you've succeeded in getting found from your high ranking, the customer has chosen an item, they start the checkout process in your shopping cart, and then for some reason they just exit your whole website. Some folks are just curious about shipping and getting familiar with your purchase process, possibly to return later to complete the purchase. But most, unfortunately, are lost forever. What a shame, after all of the effort to get them to your site and choose an item, then to lose them.

***Algorithms* –** The rules that search engines use to rank webpages.

***Alt Tags* –** Alt tags are the little boxes of text that show up when you hold your cursor over any picture on a website. ALT stands for "alternative text" and helps the visually impaired. Google puts a lot of weight on the keywords that you use in ALT tags.

***Brick and Mortar Business* –** A brick and mortar business is a business in the traditional sense. It has a physical location, versus an internet business, which might only exist on the web.

***Broken Link* –** A link that does not work. You click on it and you get a blank webpage that says something like "Internet Explorer cannot display the webpage."

***Bounce Rate* –** The average number of seconds it takes for a visitor to hit the back button after they have landed on your website from another platform, like google, Facebook, or any other website.

***Citations* –** Citations are simply mentions or web references of your business name on webpages, accompanied by your address and phone number. These mentions do not have to have a link to your website. One example of a citation is when an online yellow pages directory lists your name, address and phone, but there is no link to your website.

***Click Through Rate* –** Google tracks how often a video is clicked on as compared to other videos in the search results for those same keywords. If your video is clicked on more, then you are going to go up in the rankings.

***Clip* –** The whole goal of a video editing program is to lay out and chop up (split) various video (or still image) segments along a timeline into shorter clips that you can manage.

***Compelling* –** The word Google always uses to describe how interesting your website is. They figure the more compelling your website is, the better their users will enjoy it. Google places a very high value on this in their quality ranking factors.

***Compelling Content* –** Consists of the Text, Video, and Images on our websites that arouse interest, attention, or admiration from our visitors in a powerfully irresistible way. "Google's mission is to organize the world's information and make it universally accessible and useful."

***Conversion Rate* –** The percentage of customers who you actually "convert" to a paying customer versus the total number of visitors. Usually calculated over a certain period of time.

***Creator* –** The producer of the video = YOU

***Exporting* –** After all of the editing is done and you are happy with the way the video looks, then you "export" the video from your editor to a folder on your computer in a file format that will easily upload to YouTube. Click here for supported YouTube file formats: www.PlayGooglesGame.com/youtube-exporting-troubleshooter

***Frame* –** Videos are just a bunch of still images (frames) all strung together. Just like old movie reels, when the frames are played at certain speeds, there appears to be motion, but it's really just a bunch of still frames.

***Framing* –** The presentation of visual elements in a video or still image, especially the placement of the subject in relation to other objects. Framing can make an image more aesthetically pleasing and keep the viewer's focus on the framed object. It can also be used to direct attention back into the scene. It can add depth to an image, and can add interest to the picture when the frame is thematically related to the object being framed.

***Google Local* –** Renamed Google My Business – AKA Google Maps – Google Places Google + Local.

***Google Maps* –** A division of Google that has mapped the entire world, including the topography, ocean floors, streets and in some cases the insides of famous buildings. Google's current version of the business listings on the map is called Google My Business.

***Google My Business* –** Google's current version of the business listings on the map. This evolved from Google Local, to Google Places, to Google + Local.

***Google Search Console* –** Google Search Console is a free service offered by Google that helps you monitor and maintain your site's presence in Google Search results. You don't have to sign up for Search Console for your site to be included in Google's search results, but doing so can help you understand how Google views your site and optimize its performance in search results.

Host or Hosting Company – A hosting company actually "hosts" (or stores) your website program files (usually along with other website customers' program files) on a hard drive on their server. Servers allow your website to be accessed by internet users on the world wide web. They usually charge a "rental" fee for this service based on your website size and traffic. This negates the need to have your own server, which would have to be professionally maintained. Some things are wise to rent out.

Hosting Server – The internet is just a bunch of servers connected to each other worldwide. These servers are nothing more than a fancy version of your home personal computer. They are typically stacked on top of one another and the company that ***hosts*** websites might have rows and rows of these "stacks." Your website program will be "hosted" on one of those servers. Most of us rent that space on a "shared" server, meaning that we share the hard drive space (on one of the servers) with many other websites that are hosted on that same server's hard drive.

HTML – (**H**ypertext **M**arkup **L**anguage) The programming language that most websites are written in.

Hyperlink – A hyperlink is any link that opens another page on the internet from your current page, typically indicated by the little arrow on your pointer changing to a hand.

Incoming Links – Incoming links are when any other website has created a clickable hyperlink to your website. These are also referred to as "Backlinks." Hyperlink and Link are used interchangeably.

Index – Indexing is just a fancy word meaning that a particular search engine has included your website within its search results. In other words, they have found you.

Keyword – A keyword is any word (or phrase of multiple words) that a searcher might type into the search box of any search engine.

Keyword Stuffing – Repeating keywords over and over in certain areas of your website – stuffing it full of keywords. This usually penalizes you. For example, you will get penalized if you repeat a bunch of keywords in your keyword meta tag or in the body of your text on any webpage.

Link Velocity – Link Velocity refers to how fast links are built to your site in a given period of time. High link velocity could be a bad thing. It's a sure sign that you just bought a bunch of incoming links from a link sharing farm.

Local Search – The practice of marketing to your local community.

Metadata – In this case YouTube refers to Metadata as any and all additional information provided on a video. This includes the title, description, tags, clickable annotations, and thumbnail image.

Meta Tags – Programming code that works in the background of any website, the most common being HTML (**H**yper**t**ext **M**arkup **L**anguage).

Micro Business – Technically, a small business as defined by the SBA has less than $5 million in sales and less than 500 employees. A Micro Business might have zero employees and can be run by one or two people (typically family members). I tend to view a Micro Business and a "Mom and Pop" business as one in the same.

Natural Search Results – Most search engines return about ten individual website results on the first page after a searcher types a keyword into the search box; this is called the Search Engine Results Page (SERP). The individual ten listings are referred to as the "natural" search results. Do not confuse them with the sponsored (paid advertising) links that are usually listed on the right side of the page, with a few sometimes listed just above the natural results. These "advertisements" are usually indicated as "Paid" or "Sponsored" ads. Natural search results are free.

Privacy Policy – A statement or promise by the website owner not to share (or in any way give out) the visitors' private information (like email addresses or phone numbers). It's also good business practice to state that you will not use their information to contact them (without their permission), unless it is for shipment or pertinent product information like a recall.

Publishing – What you do after the video has been uploaded to YouTube in order to make it live. Note: Only publish after you have optimized your video for search!

Secure Server – You can always tell when you are on a "Secure Server" by the website address. The *HTTP://www.your-name.com* changes to *HTTPS://www.your-name.com*. The "S" in the HTTPS:// designates a secure server. Secure servers are very restrictive and held to very tight security standards, meaning hackers have a difficult time hacking into them and stealing sensitive information like your customers' credit card information!

SEO – SEO stands for "Search Engine Optimization" and involves designing your website to be search engine friendly with the goal of high ranking, so your website can be found on the internet through search engines.

SERP – From Wikipedia – "A search engine results page (SERP) is the listing of results returned by a search engine in response to a keyword query. The results normally include a list of items with titles, a reference to the full version, and a short description showing where the keywords have matched content within the page. A SERP may refer to a single page of links returned, or to the set of all links returned for a search query."

Shopping Cart – A shopping cart is a "turnkey" third party service that will provide you with "Web Pages" formatted to take the customer's order, and the customer's payment method. Once your customer clicks the "Add to Cart" button, they are actually leaving your website and going to the secure shopping cart website/server, without even knowing it.

Shopping Cart Landing Page – The page that visitors go to just after clicking the "Add to Cart" button. This page "holds" all of the items (like a shopping cart) until the shopper is ready to pay or "check out." Customers have the option to pay immediately after adding one single item to the cart, or they can go back to your main website and add many more items to the cart before proceeding to the final checkout and payment.

Site Map – An area on a website that shows all of the links to all of the other pages within the website. For users, just like a regular map, it quickly and easily shows a user how to navigate the entire website. For Google, a sitemap is a file where you can list the web pages of your site to tell Google and other search engines about the organization of your site content. Search engine web crawlers like Googlebot read this file to more intelligently crawl your site.

Social Signals – Any social media metric that Google uses to factor into their algorithm for ranking you in their index. Likes, Re-Tweets, Shares, Comments, etc. There has been some debate as to whether Google uses social signals to rank your website. That debate is based on a very old video that Matt Cutts (Google's SEO guy) did where he said they did not measure them because the technology was not available to do so. Well, since that comment, they figured out the technology.

Spider – Search engines have programs (called Spiders or "Bots") that go out and look at every single website on the internet. They "crawl" every aspect (including file names, text and the actual programming code) of every page of every website on the internet, attempting to rank them by subject matter. They rank both the home page and the individual pages, mostly relating them to keywords that searchers might enter into the search box of the search engine. Again, the page being ranked could be the "Home Page" (the home page is the most important) or any other page within the website.

Splash Page – These are pages that usually have some sort of fancy video, music or Adobe®

Flash® Player animation that visitors must sit through first before they can "Click to Enter" the main "Real" website. If you want to be found, Splash pages are usually bad for users and always bad for search engines.

Stickiness – The longer customers stay on your website and the more often they come back to visit, the more "Sticky" your site is.

Tag – A tag is a small of a piece of programming code (some people call it a "snippet"). You can recognize them by the appearance of the "less than" and "greater than" signs < ABC > in your web design programming code.

Text Link – A link (or hyperlink) is simply a way to jump from one webpage to another, whether it's within the various pages of your site or linking outside to another website. A link is typically indicated by the arrow on your pointer changing to a hand once placed over the link. The link can be a picture (or image) or it can be actual text. If it's text it can be composed of keywords, or it can be the actual web address of the page it's going to. Using "text" links composed of your important keywords is the ***only*** way to go. You can always tell if it's a text link by being able to highlight the actual text (for example if you wanted to copy and paste the text). You can't highlight text from a picture link—because there is not any text there. Also, text links are usually underlined and usually change color when your mouse pointer runs over them.

Transitions – Transitions are a few individual frames that go between video segments. The segments can be videos or still images. The goal is to make the transition smooth, and not jerky or abrupt. This is usually accomplished by fading in and fading out.

Uploading – The step where you are transferring the video file from one of your devices (PC, smart phone, or tablet) to YouTube, via an internet connection.

URL – URL stands for **U**niform **R**esource **L**ocator and is the address that people find you by when pulling up your website on the internet. URL is commonly and informally referred to as a web address or domain name, although the terms are not technically identical. In simplest terms using the example of http://www.example.com/images.html, which indicates a protocol (http), a hostname (www.example.com), and a file name (images.html).

Made in the USA
San Bernardino, CA
04 October 2016